Regime Change in Afghanistan

Regime Change in Afghanistan

Foreign Intervention and the Politics of Legitimacy

Amin Saikal

and William Maley

Westview Press

BOULDER • SAN FRANCISCO • OXFORD

Published in 1991 in the United States of America by Westview
Press, Inc., 5500 Central Avenue, Boulder, Colorado, 80301

Published in 1991 in Australia by Crawford House Press,
PO Box 143, Bathurst, NSW, 2795

Library of Congress Cataloging-in-Publication Data
Saikal, Amin, 1950-
   Regime Change in Afghanistan: foreign intervention and the
   politics of legitimacy / Amin Saikal and William Maley.
      p.   cm.
   Includes bibliographical references and index.
   ISBN 0-8133-1326-0

   1. Afghanistan--Politics and government--1973- 2. Afghanistan
--History--Soviet occupation, 1979-1989. 3. Legitimacy of
governments--Afghanistan. I. Maley, William, 1957- . II. Title.
JQ1765.A1S35   1991
958.104'5--dc20   91-2717
                                               CIP

Printed and bound in Hong Kong

10 9 8 7 6 5 4 3 2 1

Contents

In memory of
Rahima Nikzai Saikal
(1929-1986)

Preface

This book brings together some ideas which we have developed over a considerable period of time, and is based on research which we have at different times published in serial form. Although much of the material appearing in the book has been prepared especially for it, we wish to acknowledge our use of the following works which have been previously published:

Amin Saikal, 'Soviet Policy toward Southwest Asia', *The Annals of the American Academy of Political and Social Science*, no.481, September 1985, pp.104-116.

Amin Saikal, *The Afghanistan Conflict: Gorbachev's Options* (Canberra: Canberra Papers on Strategy and Defence no.42, Strategic and Defence Studies Centre, Research School of Pacific Studies, Australian National University, 1987). This was first published as *The Afghanistan Conflict* (Canberra: Discussion Paper no.4, Legislative Research Service, Department of the Parliamentary Library, 1987-88).

Amin Saikal, 'Afghanistan', in Ramesh Thakur and Carlyle A. Thayer (eds.), *The Soviet Union as an Asian Pacific Power* (Boulder: Westview Press, 1987) pp.153-169.

Amin Saikal, 'Islam: resistance and reassertion', *The World Today*, vol.43, no.11, November 1987, pp.191-194.

Amin Saikal, 'Afghanistan: the end-game', *The World Today*, vol.45, no.3, March 1989, pp.37-39.

Amin Saikal, 'The Regional Politics of the Afghan Crisis', in Amin Saikal and William Maley (eds.), *The Soviet Withdrawal from Afghanistan* (Cambridge: Cambridge University Press, 1989) pp.52-66.

Amin Saikal, 'Russia and Afghanistan: A Turning Point?', *Asian Affairs*, vol.20, Part II, June 1989, pp.165-183.

William Maley, 'Prospects for Afghanistan', *Australian Outlook*, vol.39, no.3, September 1985, pp.157-164.

William Maley, 'Political Legitimation in Contemporary Afghanistan', *Asian Survey*, vol.27, no.6, June 1987, pp.705-725.

William Maley, 'Afghanistan: Society, State, and War', *Current Affairs Bulletin*, vol.65, no.8, January 1989, pp.15-24.

William Maley, 'The Geneva Accords of April 1988', in Amin Saikal and William Maley (eds.), *The Soviet Withdrawal from Afghanistan* (Cambridge: Cambridge University Press, 1989) pp.12-28.

William Maley, 'Afghan Refugees: From Diaspora to Repatriation', in Amin Saikal (ed.), *Refugees in the Modern World* (Canberra: Canberra Studies in World Affairs no.25, Department of International Relations, Research School of Pacific Studies, Australian National University, 1989) pp.17-44.

Fazel Haq Saikal and William Maley, 'Afghanistan: Socialism in One Graveyard', *Quadrant*, vol.33, no.8, August 1989, pp.26-32.

In the course of researching this book, Amin Saikal benefited from the generous assistance of a Rockefeller Foundation Fellowship in International Relations, for which he wishes to register his sincere thanks. He also wishes to record an intellectual debt, stretching for more than two decades, to Dr A.G. Ravan Farhadi. Most of all, he would like to thank his wife Mary-Louise for her wonderfully patient support and forbearance in the face of the pressures which the preparing of this manuscript created. Both authors wish to record their deep appreciation to Professor T.H. Rigby, always a dependable source of wisdom and inspiration. They also wish to express their gratitude to Mr J.L. Richardson and Dr R.J. May for their careful comments on the manuscript. Finally, they would like to thank the Politics Department, University College, The University of New South Wales for the use of its splendid facilities during the preparation of the manuscript.

1

Introduction

This book is a study of regime change in an underdeveloped country marked by a weak state and strong autonomous social organisations. Regime change is in many countries a traumatic and disruptive experience, but few countries have paid as high a cost to retain traditionally accepted relationships of authority as has Afghanistan since the communist coup of April 1978. In this book, we seek to explain the experience of the post-coup period by relating the more salient features of Afghanistan's political and social systems and cultures to broader theoretical propositions about regime maintenance and political legitimation.

The phenomenon of regime change has long intrigued social scientists, and in particular students of comparative politics. The reasons why governments rise and fall are of interest not simply to political and social theorists, but also to political actors intent upon securing a firm base for their exercise of power. The ancient Greek philosophers were especially interested in the way in which one pattern of rule, or constitution, replaced another, and Plato in *The Republic* attempted to link regime change to underlying social factors. 'Constitutions', he argued 'cannot come out of stocks and stones; they must result from the preponderance of certain characters which draw the rest of the community in their wake'.[1]

The focus of the Greeks long influenced the course of debate about the positive analysis of politics. Machiavelli, in *The Prince*, gave specific advice on the techniques which could most effectively secure a ruler's position, and by casting his advice in uncompromisingly realist terms he marked the transition to modern political thought.[2] Nonetheless, it was only in the nineteenth and twentieth centuries, with the advent of systematic social science, that the social foundations of regime change began to receive the rigorous attention which they deserved from mainstream scholars. While Karl Marx focussed largely on advanced industrial societies, and drew on Hegelian dialectics to depict the proletariat as the motor of revolutionary change from capitalism to socialism,[3] the sociologist Max Weber presented a framework for the analysis of politics which offered considerably more to the student of *underdeveloped* societies.[4] His influence on subsequent writings about political development proved to be extremely important, even though it was not always visible on the surface of those writings.[5] From our point of view, the most perspicacious of his analyses related to the bases of *domination*, and he reintroduced a focus on the significance of *legitimation* which had long been insufficiently emphasised in the study of political institutions. It is this aspect of Weber's writings which sheds most light on the dynamics of regime change in Afghanistan and for that reason we make some use of it in the course of this book.

Afghanistan was in many ways neglected as a focus for serious scholarly investigation before it shot to prominence when it was invaded by the Soviet Union in late December 1979. Before the invasion, only a small number of scholars publishing in the West had produced major monographs about the country. These included Vartan Gregorian, Leon B. Poullada, and Hasan Kakar, who published excellent studies of particular periods in Afghan history;[6] Ludwig W. Adamec and Richard S. Newell, who produced significant works on Afghanistan's foreign relations and political system;[7] and Louis Dupree, whose classic *Afghanistan* was avowedly a microcosmic study with 'no single theoretical bias', an 'attempt by an anthropologist to ferret out the patterns, functional and dysfunctional, in the total synchronic-ecological-cultural sense'.[8] Nonetheless, because these books were produced largely by area specialists rather than by scholars specifically interested in examining Afghanistan from a *comparative* perspective, they tended not to address the broader questions about the nature of regime change.

The Soviet invasion produced a surge of interest in Afghan

affairs, and a number of monographs[9] and edited collections,[10] while concentrating on the Soviet invasion and its consequences, inevitably paid some attention to the nature of Afghan social structure and to the process of regime change. However, with the exception of Olivier Roy's *L'Afghanistan: Islam et modernité politique*, none of these works attempted a comprehensive analysis of regime change in Afghanistan within the broader theoretical framework of political legitimation. This is also true of the many scholarly[11] and popular works[12] dealing with the war in Afghanistan, as well as of the analyses of the place of Afghanistan in world politics.[13]

This book attempts to complement the contribution of many of these works, by focussing on the way in which social structure has contributed to the rise, fall, and continuity of Afghan regimes. We point to the role played by what we call *micro-societies* in affecting the position of those who control the instrumentalities of the state. We argue that micro-societies not only have been critical to the legitimation and delegitimation of Afghan regimes in the past, but are likely to play a somewhat similar role in the future—despite the fact that, as a result of a decade of ferocious conflict, the boundaries of micro-societies, and the patterns of loyalty and authority within them, have tended to shift. Nonetheless, the obvious importance of external pressures in shaping regime change in Afghanistan since 1978 has meant that we cannot confine our attention to the dynamics of internal authority relations. For this reason, we have made reference where necessary to the interplay between domestic political forces and foreign influences and manipulations. It goes without saying that the most prominent outside force involved in Afghan politics over the last ten years has been the Soviet Union.

The book is divided into seven substantive chapters. The first sets out a range of theoretical propositions which inform the discussion of Afghan affairs in the subsequent chapters. In particular, we explain what meaning we attach to certain key terms which recur in the discussion which follows. On the basis of these definitions and propositions we provide an account of the historical evolution of the Afghan polity from the middle of the eighteenth century to the communist coup of April 1978, emphasising the way in which the process of state building was affected by the importance of micro-societies to the maintenance of regime legitimacy. We also show how external involvement in Afghan politics placed the stability of Afghan regimes increasingly at risk, especially from the mid-1950s onwards.

The second chapter records the way in which the 1978 coup came about. It details how the actions of the new regime rapidly brought it into conflict with significant micro-societies, forcing it to rely on coercion rather than legitimacy as a principal basis for its survival. It also explains how the endemic factionalism within the 'People's Democratic Party of Afghanistan' (PDPA) prevented it from functioning as an effective agency for the expansion of the regime's influence, and instead encouraged external attempts to boost the position of clients within the party, such as the Soviet leadership undertook in the months preceding its massive invasion of December 1979. Finally, in the light of information which has recently become available, it explores the process by which the Soviet Union reached the decision to intervene with military force, and notes that the Soviet decision was not informed by any deep understanding of the nature of the response to the invasion which was likely from Afghan micro-societies.

Chapter Three concentrates on the development of opposition from Islamic resistance forces (*Mujahideen*) to the Soviet forces and to the new regime headed by Babrak Karmal which they had installed in Kabul. After outlining the strategy pursued by the Soviet leadership, it examines the ways in which Afghans responded to the invasion—ranging from flight from the country to organised, armed resistance. We describe the main resistance organisations, Sunni and Shiite, and examine the different strands of Sunni Islam in Afghanistan which have influenced the character of these organised groups. We also discuss the relationship of these organised groups to the diverse, grassroots resistance generated from within the micro-societies of Afghanistan. The chapter concludes with an account of how a stalemate came to develop in the Afghan War, underlining the inability of Soviet strategy to address and undermine the micro-societal foundations of Afghan resistance.

The fourth chapter deals with the various options before the Soviet leadership to break this stalemate. It shows why the options of massive escalation and unconditional withdrawal were unacceptable, and traces the process by which the policy of *afghanisation* of the war was shaped—and put under the charge of former secret police chief Najibullah, who replaced Karmal in May 1986. It explains why Najibullah's policy of 'national reconciliation' was unable to win his regime the generalised normative support of significant micro-societies, and why the replacement of Karmal failed to produce a united and effective regime. Finally, we outline the way in which the United Nations came to sponsor negotiations in Geneva directed at providing a framework for the withdrawal of Soviet troops from Afghanistan, and the way in which changes within the Soviet leadership, and the rising cost of the war, prompted the USSR at last to make concessions in Geneva which met some of the major demands of the non-communist participants.

Chapter Five focusses on the bargaining which led up to the signing of the Geneva Accords of April 1988, and on the content and implications of the Accords themselves. We set out the major weaknesses of the Accords—most notably their failure to make any provision for free and peaceful self-determination by the Afghan people—and show how they left unresolved the central issue of regime legitimacy which lay at the heart of the Afghan conflict. We also detail the ways in which the Soviet Union was able to turn the content of the Accords to its advantage, and how various developments, such as the death of Pakistani President Zia ul-Haq, left the Afghan resistance in an uncertain position. We conclude that on the eve of the completion of the Soviet troop withdrawal in February 1989, there was no obvious way available to secure a peaceful transition to a legitimate Afghan regime.

The sixth chapter examines events following the completion of the Soviet troop withdrawal, and the reasons why the widely-expected collapse of the communist regime did not come about. It outlines the extent of the Soviet commitment to prop up the regime by supplying it with both military equipment and food for the population of Kabul, as well as advisers to oversee the regime's military and administrative operations. In addition, it details the ways in which the resistance was derailed by both external interferences in the internal politics of the resistance and by lack of coordination in the prosecution of the campaign to oust the regime, as well as the insatiable ambitions of certain resistance figures who were willing to inflict damage on other

Mujahideen groups in order to prevent them from taking the lead in confronting the forces of the regime. The chapter also discusses the gradual dissipation of the relative unity within the regime which the Soviet withdrawal had induced, and looks at the regime crises of July and December 1989, and the attempted coup of March 1990. The chapter concludes with a discussion of the state of affairs in Afghanistan in the wake of all these events.

The seventh chapter investigates the legacy of damage—human, economic, social, and political—left behind by the Soviets. It looks specifically at the way in which changes in the character of Afghan micro-societies have affected the prospects for political order, and shows how the damage inflicted upon Afghanistan almost guarantees a bleak future for the country. It also notes how changes in the international environment made Soviet backing for the regime appear increasingly anomalous, and in this context, it examines possible paths of transition along which the Afghan situation might move.

In conclusion, we address the issue of what kind of conditions might have to be met in order to secure a modicum of stability for a future Afghan regime. We suggest that given the difficulty of building a strong central state capable of restraining the impulses of powerful social groups, a 'consociational' system has the best prospect of providing a degree of order and stability in the long-run. But only an optimist could expect this to come about easily.

Notes

1. Plato, *The Republic of Plato* (London: Oxford University Press, 1941) p.267.

2. Niccolò Machiavelli, *The Prince* (Cambridge: Cambridge University Press, 1988).

3. See Karl Marx, *Critique of Hegel's 'Philosophy of Right'* (Cambridge: Cambridge University Press, 1970) pp.131-142.

4. Weber's views are set out in great detail in Max Weber, *Economy and Society: An Outline of Interpretive Sociology* (Berkeley and Los Angeles: University of California Press, 1978).

5. See Gabriel A. Almond and James S. Coleman (eds.), *The Politics of the Developing Areas* (Princeton: Princeton University Press, 1960); Gabriel A. Almond and G. Bingham Powell, *Comparative Politics: A*

Developmental Approach (Boston: Little, Brown & Co., 1966); and Lucian W. Pye, *Aspects of Political Development* (Boston: Little, Brown & Co., 1966).

6. See Vartan Gregorian, *The Emergence of Modern Afghanistan: Politics of Reform and Modernization 1880-1946* (Stanford: Stanford University Press, 1969); Leon B. Poullada, *Reform and Rebellion in Afghanistan, 1919-1929: King Amanullah's Failure to Modernize a Tribal Society* (Ithaca: Cornell University Press, 1973); Hasan Kawun Kakar, *Government and Society in Afghanistan: The Reign of Amir 'Abd al-Rahman Khan* (Austin: The University of Texas Press, 1979).

7. See Ludwig W. Adamec, *Afghanistan's Foreign Affairs to the Mid-Twentieth Century: Relations With the USSR, Germany, and Britain* (Tucson: The University of Arizona Press, 1974); and Richard S. Newell, *The Politics of Afghanistan* (Ithaca: Cornell University Press, 1972).

8. Louis Dupree, *Afghanistan* (Princeton: Princeton University Press, 1980) p.xxi.

9. Alfred L. Monks, *The Soviet Intervention in Afghanistan* (Washington DC: American Enterprise Institute for Public Policy Research, 1981); Michael Barry, *Le Royaume de L'Insolence: La résistance afghane du Grand Moghol à l'invasion soviétique* (Paris: Flammarion, 1984); Wilhelm Dietl, *Brückenkopf Afghanistan: Machtpolitik im Mittleren Osten* (Munich: Kindler Verlag, 1984); Thomas T. Hammond, *Red Flag Over Afghanistan: The Communist Coup, the Soviet Invasion, and the Consequences* (Boulder: Westview Press, 1984); Anthony Hyman, *Afghanistan under Soviet Domination 1964-83* (London: Macmillan, 1984); Anthony Arnold, *Afghanistan: The Soviet Invasion in Perspective* (Stanford: Hoover Institution Press, 1985); Henry S. Bradsher, *Afghanistan and the Soviet Union* (Durham: Duke University Press, 1985); Olivier Roy, *L'Afghanistan: Islam et modernité politique* (Paris: Éditions du Seuil, 1985); Joseph J. Collins, *The Soviet Invasion of Afghanistan: A Study in the Use of Force in Soviet Foreign Policy* (Lexington: Lexington Books, 1986); André Brigot and Olivier Roy, *The War in Afghanistan* (London: Harvester Wheatsheaf, 1988); and Hafizullah Emadi, *State, Revolution, and Superpowers in Afghanistan* (New York: Praeger, 1990).

10. See Richard Tapper (ed.), *The Conflict of Tribe and State in Iran and Afghanistan* (London: Croom Helm, 1983); M. Nazif Shahrani and Robert L. Canfield (eds.), *Revolutions and Rebellions in Afghanistan: Anthropological Perspectives* (Berkeley: Institute of International Studies, University of California, 1984); Ralph H. Magnus (ed.), *Afghan Alternatives: Issues, Options, and Policies* (New Brunswick: Transaction Books, 1985); Ali Banuazizi and Myron Weiner (eds.), *The State, Religion, and Ethnic Politics: Afghanistan, Iran, and Pakistan* (Syracuse: Syracuse University Press, 1986); Rosanne Klass (ed.), *Afghanistan—The Great Game Revisited* (New York: Freedom House, 1987); Grant M. Farr and

John G. Merriam (eds.), *Afghan Resistance: The Politics of Survival* (Boulder: Westview Press, 1987); Bo Huldt and Erland Jansson (eds.), *The Tragedy of Afghanistan: The Social, Cultural and Political Impact of Soviet Invasion* (London: Croom Helm, 1988); and Milan Hauner and Robert L. Canfield (eds.), *Afghanistan and the Soviet Union: Collision and Transformation* (Boulder: Westview Press, 1989).

11. See Nancy Peabody Newell and Richard S. Newell, *The Struggle for Afghanistan* (Ithaca: Cornell University Press, 1981); Edward Girardet, *Afghanistan: The Soviet War* (London: Croom Helm, 1985); and Mark Urban, *War in Afghanistan* (London: Macmillan, 1990).

12. See Nigel Ryan, *A Hitch or Two in Afghanistan: A Journey behind Russian Lines* (London: Weidenfeld and Nicolson, 1983); Sandy Gall, *Behind Russian Lines: An Afghan Journal* (London: Sidgwick and Jackson, 1983); Patrice Franceschi, *Guerre en Afghanistan* (Paris: La Table Ronde, 1984); Peregrine Hodson, *Under a Sickle Moon: A Journey through Afghanistan* (London: Hutchinson, 1986); Arthur Bonner, *Among the Afghans* (Durham: Duke University Press, 1987); Jan Goodwin, *Caught in the Crossfire* (London: Macdonald, 1987); Sandy Gall, *Afghanistan: Agony of a Nation* (London: The Bodley Head, 1988); and Radek Sikorski, *Dust of the Saints: A Journey to Herat in Time of War* (London: Chatto and Windus, 1989).

13. See Hafeez Malik (ed.), *Soviet-American Relations with Pakistan, Iran and Afghanistan* (London: Macmillan, 1987).

2

State, Societies, and Political Legitimacy

Regime change within a nation-state cannot properly be understood without reference to the fundamental nature of the nation-state's social and political order. A study of such orders immediately immerses one in the discipline of historical sociology. Its broad concern, namely the relationship of rulers and ruled, is a central issue in all political analysis, both positive and normative, and the diversity of social and political structures in historical and contemporary societies explains why it is that the study of a particular society demands close attention to its distinctive attributes. Nonetheless, if comparative insights are to be drawn, it is necessary also to make use of certain concepts which may have application beyond a particular case. For the historical sociologist, perhaps the most important are *state*, *society*, and *legitimacy*.

The *state* is a term used to denote 'a complex set of institutional arrangements for rule' which 'reserves to itself the business of rule over a territorially bounded society'.[1] In practice it takes the form of particular agencies and instrumentalities, and those who control these agencies and instrumentalities are designated either a 'government' or 'regime', largely depending upon whether the predominant basis for generalised acceptance of such control is deemed to be normative or merely prudential. The individuals who make up a regime are strategically placed to exercise power over other residents of the territory, and the way in which such power can be constrained so that it is used for the benefit of the many rather than the few has been a central problem of political theory since Plato addressed it in the dialogues which make up his *Republic*. The fact that the state can function only through human agents means that the sharp distinction which one often finds drawn between 'state' and 'society' is in practice rather more blurred than the usage would suggest. 'Without me', wrote Andrei Platonov '"the people" is incomplete'[2]; and the same applies to 'society', which includes the officers of 'the state', no matter how small in number they may be.

'There are no societies', Jon Elster has written, 'only individuals who interact with each other.'[3] This reminds us that 'society' is at best a useful label and should not be regarded as an organic whole. Nonetheless, we are inclined to emphasise the utility of the term rather than its limitations. In our sense of the term, a *society* is a collection of individual and organisational actors within which key relations between actors are defined by certain shared norms, and the behaviour of actors is to a degree patterned and predictable. Since different norms may be shared to somewhat different extents, a geographical unit may simultaneously embrace both an emerging 'common society' (marked by the increasing acceptance of certain key norms) and many 'micro-societies' (defined by the persistence of norms particular to the 'micro-society' under discussion). This reflects the fact that an individual lives in not one but *many* worlds, and survives most easily when circumstances do not cause the demands of these different worlds to conflict. Identities, as Tapper has argued, are 'essentially changing, flexible, multiple and negotiable'.[4] 'Micro-societies' may act in a concerted fashion, either from self-interest or because a threshhold in the development of a 'common society' has been crossed. Nonetheless, we reiterate that 'societies' are not themselves unified actors. It is the *components* of societies which act, and their being members of societies simply supplies us with some information about the ways in which they may be expected to act.

Societies may be categorised in many different ways, but the exercise of taxonomy does not always do justice to the complexities of the societies which one seeks to analyse. Our main concern is to note the characteristics of what have been called *strong* societies. A strong society is defined by Migdal as one in which 'the overall level of social control is high', and for our purposes the most important species is that which he calls 'web-like societies', where 'social control is spread through various fairly autonomous social organizations'.[5] These are particularly associated with countries in which there is a high degree of ethnic and linguistic fractionalisation, which tends in turn to be associated with distinctive *Weltanschauungen* and norms of behaviour.

Regimes can secure support on a number of different bases. Endowed with sufficient resources, they can exercise considerable *bargaining power. Coercion* is another obvious mechanism by which a regime can perpetuate itself. Its forms are many and varied. On the one hand, it embraces the direct deployment of physical resources to achieve the coercer's aims. On the other hand, it can be embodied in particular institutional structures the mere existence of which deters the voicing of heterodox opinions.[6] However, to base its rule on coercion a regime needs to secure its coercive capacity and it is necessary then to explain how a regime can come to enjoy such capacity in the first place.

Although an external patron can supply a regime with the resources to undertake coercive operations, the most usual basis of a regime's coercive capacity is *legitimacy*. As Rousseau wrote, the 'strongest is never strong enough to be always master, unless he transforms strength into right, and obedience into duty'.[7] Legitimacy, as Rousseau's observation suggests, is not simply support. For a regime to be legitimate, the support which it receives must be both normative, and generalised across the range of issues which it undertakes to resolve. This does not mean that such support must be exhibited by all social groups. Rather, as Agnes Heller has concluded, the 'relative number of those legitimating a system may be irrelevant if the non-legitimating masses are merely dissatisfied'.[8] A recognition of this oft-neglected point underpinned Max Weber's discussion of systems of rule, which focussed on the relationship between a ruler and an executive staff, rather than between a ruler and the wider population.[9] Weber was concerned not simply with legitimacy but with the different forms of organisation by which rule was sustained. In a famous passage, he wrote that 'organized domination requires control of the personal executive staff and the material implements of administration.'[10] The

Carolingian and Mongol empires, the latter a conquest empire *par excellence*,[11] rapidly disintegrated for lack of these means of organised domination.[12]

Where one's interest is regime change, one needs to draw a further distinction: that between the legitimacy of a particular *structure* of rule, and the legitimacy of those who exercise power within it. Pakulski has pointed to the way in which some leaders have rarely based legitimating claims on references to 'the central political institutions and to the most crucial and distinctive aspects of the power structure', and instead have made claims which 'refer to some "peripheral" or unobjectionable issues such as the desirability of certain policies, the moral and intellectual qualifications of the leaders, the interests of the state and the ethical principles of socialism'. Such claims, he argues, 'refer to contingent factors and result in what may be called "quasi-legitimacy"'. They 'cannot generate stable order and systematic compliance because of the absence of the logical connection between the content of the claims and the actual power configuration'.[13] 'In a genuine legitimacy crisis', another scholar has plausibly argued, 'the challenge is to the basic constitutional dimensions of the system and to the most generalized claims of leadership of those in authority'.[14]

The capabilities of the state (in Migdal's words its 'capacities to *penetrate* society, *regulate* social relationships, *extract* resources, and *appropriate* or use resources in determined ways'[15]) depend crucially upon its ability to obtain and maintain an appropriate mix of coercive capacity, bargaining power, and generalised normative support—appropriate, that is, to the nature of the society within which it is functioning. In prosperous liberal democracies, where the role of the state is circumscribed and the rule of law prevails, a high level of normative commitment is usually found. By contrast, where a regime's objectives are out of step with its own capabilities, and in conflict with the key norms of its own society (or of key micro-societies), trouble is to be expected. This was precisely what happened in the months preceding the Soviet invasion of Afghanistan. To understand why, it is necessary to grasp certain characteristics of Afghan society, and of the Afghan state as it had developed by that time.

Afghan Society

Afghanistan has historically been marked by a strong society and weak state. The strength of society has come from its web-like character, in which multiple, largely autonomous, social units, most importantly tribes and their subdivisions, have retained their identity within a political unit in the face of bureaucratic-administrative accretions within their territories. The bases of social fragmentation in Afghanistan have been many and varied, and their effect has been to create a complex array of micro-societies which have interacted in a range of different ways.

Had it not been for the common value system provided by Islam, the grounds for cooperation between these micro-societies may have been so flimsy as to permit much readier penetration of society as a whole by the instrumentalities of the state. Islam has been the central unifier of the Afghan population, even though Afghan Islam has itself by no means been a homogeneous force. While historically the population has been overwhelmingly Muslim, there is a substantial community of adherents to the heterodox Shi'ite sect, which currently accounts for 15-20 per cent of the Muslim population, the remainder constituting the Sunni majority.[16] Furthermore, within these broad categories, a range of different influences have shaped the attitudes of the faithful. In many parts of Afghanistan, Sufism has been an important influence, in particular through the *Qadiriyya* and *Naqshbandiyya* brotherhoods. Amongst the Shia, there have developed schisms between those who see themselves as part of a broader Shi'ite world, with loyalties to the leadership that world throws up, and those who see themselves as first and foremost *Afghan* Shia. Islam is also influenced by regional factors which in certain places give it a shamanistic quality, heavily overlaid with local folklore.[17] We shall return in more detail in Chapter Four to these points of distinction.

Notwithstanding these differences, Islam has provided a common frame of reference on a wide number of important questions: to this extent, Barry's description of Islam as 'the central nerve of Afghan culture' is apposite.[18] This is the very factor which paradoxically has underpinned the development of a loose sense of common identity in Afghanistan, at the same time as it has nourished determined opposition, headed by the *Mujahideen*, to the Soviet Union and its various Afghan surrogates or clients since the PDPA coup. However, as a unifier Islam has had to compete with a number of centripetal influences, of which the following are among the most important.

First, ethnic divisions are a major basis of distinct identity of Afghan micro-societies. Ethnicity is a broad and not particularly satisfactory term, but it captures social homogeneity falling short of the more specific shared norms which may distinguish particular micro-societies. Smith has pointed to a collective name, a common myth of descent, a shared history, a distinctive shared culture, an association with a specific territory, and a sense of solidarity as identifying marks of an ethnic community.[19] Members of the Pushtun ethnic group historically formed possibly the largest single ethnic group in Afghanistan,[20] followed by the Tajiks, Uzbeks, Hazaras, Aimaq, Nuristani, Kirghiz, and a considerable number of smaller groups. For various reasons, ethnicity rarely sparked concerted cooperative activity, but it often made individuals the targets of the activities of others. For example, the Hazaras by virtue of a distinctively East Asian appearance became ready targets for the practice of discriminatory social closure.[21] Furthermore, a crucial aspect of self-identification has often been the language used by a particular group and while ethnic and linguistic groups do not overlap completely, fear of discrimination on the ground of language also has a long history in Afghanistan, and remains today both very much alive and potentially divisive, the major cleavage being between Pushtu speakers and speakers of Dari (a dialect of Persian).

Second, tribal cleavages have been important. The notion of 'tribe' is somewhat elusive,[22] defined by some scholars in quasi-institutional terms[23] and by others in terms which emphasise idioms of organisation and cultural bases of group identity.[24] Nonetheless, carefully defined, the term is capable of being put to effective use. A tribe is a particular type of micro-society, in Gellner's definition a 'local mutual-aid association, whose members jointly help maintain order internally and defend the unit externally'.[25] It is distinctively marked by norms of reciprocity which need not apply within an ethnic group as a whole. In Afghanistan, tribes have been collections of related lineages. Some students of Afghan society have used the word *qawm*, probably best rendered as 'network',[26] to identify such groups, but its elasticity in practice[27] diminishes its analytical utility. The most important tribally-structured *ethnie* has been the Pushtun, which has been divided into two large but historically somewhat hostile categories, the Durrani and the Ghilzai, which are in turn divided into multiple tribes, clans, and families. Since the emergence of the territorial state of Afghanistan, it has been by and large the Durrani Pushtuns who have occupied the main formal offices of power and dominated the upper echelons of the armed forces in Afghanistan, even though it has been from the ranks of the non-tribal Tajiks that the Afghan intelligentsia and bureaucratic staff have largely been drawn.

Third, urban-rural cleavages are important, and even in rural Afghanistan there have been considerable distinctions between rural-dwellers on the basis of social role. The bulk of the Afghan population has engaged in sedentary agricultural activities,[28] with production being both used for subsistence and traded in local markets. To superficial observers rural society may have appeared feudal, with *khans* (lineage leaders) and *maleks* (village leaders) exercising absolute power, either as landed aristocrats or creditors, over landless or debt-ridden peasants. The reality in most areas was far more complex. Authority within micro-societies traditionally was exercised by a *jirgah* or *shura* (assembly), with the influence of the *khan* or *malek* within the assembly determined by a complex range of factors, including the individual's social position, mediating skills, and institutional resources at his disposal. In addition, land holdings in Afghanistan were for the most part small, with some ostensibly large estates being communal lands registered in a single name[29]; frequently there was little expectation on the part of a debtor that he would have to repay, though doubtless many debtors found this to be a grievous miscalculation. The spread of commerce naturally affected the traditional patterns of production in rural Afghanistan, but the roots of commercial society in rural areas were still shallow at the time of the PDPA coup.[30]

Rural society saw many feuds and disputes but these masked an underlying capacity for concerted action which the array of autonomous groups in Afghanistan's web-like society made possible.[31] As Louis Dupree has written, feuds before 1880 'occurred between neighbouring vertical-structured, segmentary groups, but when an *external horizontal force* intruded and threatened indigenous *vertical* structures, regional traditional enemies often united and attempted to throw out the invader.'[32] This could apply at a sectarian level as well. During the 'Hazara War' mounted in 1891-1893 by Amir 'Abd al-Rahman Khan, different Shiite Hazara tribes attempted to unite to defend their heterodox Islamic perspectives in the face of Sunni persecution,[33] yet following the PDPA coup both Sunnis *and* Shia rose spontaneously against the new rulers, who were perceived to pose a fundamental threat to the religion of the Afghan population.

The Development of the Afghan State

These characteristics of Afghan society impacted in many significant ways on the evolution of the Afghan state. The tribal confederation which Ahmad Shah Abdali assembled between 1747 and 1773 reflected the need of Ahmad Shah to draw on the resources of existing micro-societies to create a larger Afghan entity. This contributed greatly to the fragility of his confederation and when his death deprived it of a *charismatic* ruler, its lack of institutional strength—typical of many conquest empires—left it incapable of containing the underlying tensions between the micro-societies which made it up.[34] As the confederation slowly disintegrated it became increasingly open to hegemonial pressures from the Russian Empire in the north and from expanding British colonisation in the Indian sub-continent; these increased still further the difficulties which Afghan central rulers faced. The overall consequence was that Afghanistan slid into a state of disorder and violent internal conflict, fuelled by foreign intervention, which lasted for much of the nineteenth century. This whole period was marked by the inability of any central state instrumentalities or ruler to maintain a stable system of governance through either legitimation or coercion. Only in the face of direct foreign intervention did the micro-societies of Afghanistan unite even temporarily, and the unity was always insufficient to permit sustained state-building.

This situation continued until the advent in 1880 of 'Abd al-Rahman Khan in the aftermath of the Second Anglo-Afghan War.[35] During his rule as Amir (1880-1901) he moved decisively not only to consolidate a central state but also to insulate the state as much as possible from the debilitating Anglo-Russian rivalry, although most of his distaste was reserved for Russia. He was helped by his personal charisma—the designation 'Iron Amir' was well-deserved—and by the fact that his increasing control over the micro-societies of Afghanistan reassured both the British and the Russians that the micro-societies would not be vulnerable to manipulation by either great power to the detriment of the other. A key element in his success was his consolidation of a substantial, disciplined standing army and the effective use of this force to coerce autonomous units into obedience, a tactic he reinforced with the deployment of positive sanctions to divide his opponents. He also moved to secure a steady revenue source for the central state by seeking to extract taxes in cash rather than in kind.

While he made considerable progress in state-building, he ultimately failed, like previous Afghan rulers, to generate an institutionalised political system which could *itself* be a focus of legitimacy. To this extent, politics remained personalised. Similarly, whilst he secured considerable compliance from micro-societies, the latter maintained to a considerable degree their independent existence and capacity for renewal.[36] This capacity remained largely suppressed for the next eighteen years during the rule of his son Amir Habibullah Khan (1901-1919). Although Habibullah was prepared to continue his father's policy of state-building, he proved amenable to more outward-looking policies and had some sympathy with Afghanistan's first major intellectual push for social modernisation, promoted by the journalist Mahmoud Tarzi through the pages of his newspaper *Seraj al-Akhbar*. In particular, Habibullah adopted a more relaxed approach to social and political control and was prepared to view with an open mind the exploitation of Western technological achievements.[37]

Habibullah's son Amanullah (1919-1929) was unable to maintain the subordination of Afghanistan's micro-societies in the face of his aspirations—stronger than any previous Afghan ruler had entertained—to modernise both state and society.[38] In one respect he was successful: he managed to secure independence from Great Britain in international relations, something even the Iron Amir had been unable to regain following its loss in 1879. However, his attempts at domestic modernisation and centralisation enjoyed at best only patchy success, although they did lay the foundation for the subsequent development of a Western-oriented intelligentsia in Kabul. These attempts, together with his failure to develop balanced relations with both Britain and the young Soviet Union, ultimately spawned an alliance against him between a number of micro-societies, and the religious establishment, which proved fatal to his rule. The overthrow of Amanullah in early 1929 by a Tajik bandit, Habibullah, known as *Bacha-i-Saqao* ('Son of the Water Carrier'), was a potent illustration of both the relative strength of society and the relative weakness of the state. Despite Amanullah's best efforts, the legal-rational order which he sought to establish had no appeal to the traditionally important elements in Afghan society and his failure sent out signals which future Afghan rulers could ignore only at their peril.

Habibullah survived only nine months before he was overthrown in a Pushtun backlash led by General Nadir Khan, who assumed the throne.[39] Nadir's Musahiban family, which ruled from 1929 to 1978, in general took great care not to antagonise micro-societies with the capacity to mobilise opposition to its rule. One of the reasons why this dynasty survived so long was its paternalism, and the years of Musahiban rule were notable for relative political stability. Nadir moved rapidly to secure legitimacy for his rule by acquiring the sanction of a Great Assembly (*Loya Jirgah*) which promulgated a constitution the terms of which were patently intended to satisfy the demands of the Islamic establishment.[40] Following Nadir's assassination in November 1933 his son Zahir Shah was content for almost two decades to follow the policy directions shaped by his two prime ministers, his uncles Mohammad Hashem Khan (1929-1946) and Shah Mahmoud Khan (1946-1953). Neither was a radical reformer. Each presided over a tacit compromise between the state and society under which modest economic development and financial reform were conducted at a pace which all parties could accept.

State-Society Tensions in the Post-War Period

The measured pace of this process of reconsolidation was in some ways, however, deceptive. In urban centres in particular, new political forces were coalescing which increasingly developed the potential to influence the operations of state instrumentalities and thereby the policies of the central government. The intelligentsia which had become debilitated following the overthrow of Amanullah began to reconstitute itself as a political force, an early sign being the formation in 1947 of a reformist force, Awakened Youth (*Wikh-i-Zalmaiyan*).[41] Shah Mahmoud's government effectively smashed this organisation in 1952 but its emergence was a potent sign of the changes which were occurring in Afghan urban areas. These changes continued after Shah Mahmoud was replaced as prime minister in 1953 by Zahir Shah's cousin and brother-in-law Mohammad Daoud, and posed increasing problems during the decade between Daoud's entry to office and his resignation in 1963. Nonetheless, it needs to be emphasised that the political forces which were developing in urban areas lacked *rural* counterparts; as a consequence, a widening gulf emerged between the more educated Afghans who were recruited into the various agencies of the state and the large majority who functioned within rurally-based micro-societies.

These tensions were exacerbated by external factors springing from the new geopolitical position of Afghanistan in the postwar period. Two factors above all changed the course of Afghan politics. One was Daoud's personal desire to succeed where Amanullah had failed, by producing a considerable degree of domestic modernisation in certain spheres. The education system was expanded in rural areas, electrification in towns was increased, and steps were taken to improve transport and communications networks.[42] This exercise in state-building presaged the highest degree of centralised administration that Afghanistan had experienced, and its objective was certainly the subordination to the state of robust micro-societies. However, Daoud brought to his office a Pushtun chauvinism which had not so noticeably marked the policies of his predecessors. This sparked off a turbulent border dispute with Pakistan, for within Pakistan's borders were many Pushtuns separated from their

Afghan brethren by the 'Durand Line', the frontier between Afghanistan and British India demarcated in 1893. This ultimately resulted in a series of border skirmishes in the 1950s and to Kabul's backing secessionist movements in Pakistan's Northwest Frontier and Baluchistan provinces, intent on creating from them an independent entity called 'Pushtunistan'.[43] Daoud's energetic prosecution of Afghanistan's case for border revision and modernisation meant that he needed military and development assistance. Although authoritarian and centralist in his politics and approach to nation-building, Daoud had initially requested such aid from Washington because of his and his people's aversion to communism. However, the refusal of the US administration to provide military aid and to play an impartial, active role in resolving the worsening Afghan-Pakistan dispute— on the ground that the land-locked and underdeveloped Afghanistan, with little obvious economic potential, was strategically less important than its American-allied neighbours—made Daoud's government vulnerable to pressure from the Soviet Union.[44]

Consequently, while the post-Stalin Soviet leadership, stressing 'peaceful coexistence' and 'mutual non-interference and respect' among nations,[45] was searching for friends in Third World countries, especially those neighbouring the USSR, Daoud turned to Moscow for all-round assistance. He saw little danger in this in view of his policy of neutrality, Afghanistan's natural unreceptiveness to communism, and his resolve to press on with his efforts to obtain aid from other sources. This crucial factor unfortunately set the scene for increased Soviet penetration of Afghanistan, which took off in 1955 and proceeded apace thereafter. It happened to be the case that the immediate needs of Daoud's regime complemented directly the Soviet desire to discourage wider Western-backed regional cooperation and consequently to counterbalance the American penetration of the region—which had become a concrete problem as Iran, Pakistan and Turkey had drifted into the Western camp. The extent to which Soviet and Afghan objectives complemented each other can be gauged from Penkovskiy's report that by 1961 discussions had even canvassed 'the possibility of sending Soviet troops into Afghanistan for joint operations against Pakistan'.[46]

Thus, in 1955 the USSR commenced a generous programme of

economic and military aid to Afghanistan, amounting to $2.5 billion to 1979.[47] It also openly supported Afghanistan in its dispute with Pakistan, as it did with non-aligned India—another regional state embroiled in serious disputes with Pakistan. Although this prompted Washington to increase its economic aid, America's efforts nonetheless proved to be too little and too late. Its total aid of $532 million during the same period[48] could not hope to match, in terms of either volume or effect, that given by the Soviet Union. Specifically, the Soviet penetration of Afghanistan took three forms. First, the Soviet Union sought with considerable success to make the Afghan economy ever more dependent on the Soviet, by providing low interest loans for purchase of (frequently overpriced) Soviet capital equipment, and by diverting Afghan trade from free world markets.[49] Second, military aid gave the USSR considerable control over the Afghan armed forces, which by the time of the 1978 coup were substantially Soviet-trained and equipped.[50] Third, and perhaps most importantly, Moscow encouraged the covert development of pro-Soviet political groups within the small Kabul-based intelligentsia, which voiced demands for structural political reforms.

The Constitutional Experiment

However, Daoud did not stay in power long enough to face the most serious of these demands. Afghan-Soviet ties expanded far beyond initial expectations, while Afghan-Pakistan relations deteriorated. This resulted in the closure in 1961 of the border between the two sides, with Afghan transit traffic coming to a halt—causing a damaging economic crisis in Afghanistan. The crisis prompted a split between Daoud and the king over the future direction of Afghanistan. Daoud finally found it expedient to resign after ten years' premiership, in the belief that at some time in the future he would be able to resume power through the type of political reforms which the king was by now set to introduce. The king, who for the first time appointed a non-member of the royal family, Dr Muhammad Yusuf, to succeed Daoud, not only sought an immediate improvement of relations with Pakistan, resulting in the prompt opening of the border, but also launched in 1964 a phase of limited 'experiment with democracy'. This enabled different political groups, despite the king's failure ever to ratify a bill legalising political *parties*, to become informally active in the Afghan political scene.[51]

These developments provided the Soviets—otherwise perturbed by Daoud's departure from the scene—with both leverage and opportunities. In the new 'democratic' climate the Soviets, acting through their embassy (the largest foreign mission in Kabul), supported the development in the second half of the 1960s of two pro-Moscow communist groups, the 'Banner' (*Parcham*) and 'Masses' (*Khalq*).[52] They possibly did so not because they envisaged a communist takeover of Afghanistan in the immediate future—for they must have known that prevailing national conditions could in no way have favoured such a takeover—but because they wanted to counterbalance the emergence of other ideological groups and to safeguard themselves against possible adverse eventualities which the Afghan democratic changes might produce. Initially, because of its ideological affinity and the reliability of its leadership, the Soviets preferred the urban-centred *Parcham*, led by Babrak Karmal, to the rural based *Khalq*, which was headed by Nur Mohammad Taraki and Hafizullah Amin. Nonetheless they pushed for the unity of the two within the People's Democratic Party of Afghanistan (PDPA). But to their total dismay, they soon found out that the rivalry between the two groups was intense, due to deep-seated differences along personality and tactical lines and, more importantly, to linguistic division. The *Khalq* was mainly composed of rural Pushtu speakers. The *Parcham* was made up largely of Kabul-based Dari speakers.

In opposition to these groups were four of particular note. One was the 'Islamic Society of Afghanistan' (*Jamiat-i Islam-i Afghanistan*), founded by a group of Islamist instructors of the Faculty of Theology of Kabul University, demanding a radical reorganisation of Afghan society along Islamic lines. Another was 'The Eternal Flame' (*Shuli Javid*), a small but very active Maoist organisation. Although violently opposed to one another, the two tapped a common chord in their opposition to Soviet communism. Third was the ultra-nationalist 'Afghan Nation'(*Afghan Millat*), which among other things called for the return of the Afghan territories that Tsarist Russia had annexed in the late nineteenth century. The fourth was the pro-Western 'Progressive Democracy' group (*Demokrat-i Mutaraqi*), associated with Mohammad Hashem Maiwandwal during both his term as prime minister (1965-1967) and for the remainder of the constitutional period.

The increasing range and diversity of political forces—which social change unleashed and the constitutional experiment brought to light—proved to be the downfall of the experiment as a whole. The Constitution of 1964, although sanctioned by a *Loya Jirgah*, was shot through with unresolved contradictions which were not overcome by informal agreements between political actors. An old political maxim—if you can't run a meeting, wreck it—was applied with ruthless skill by a number of those who secured election to the Lower House (*Wolesi Jirgah*), notably communists such as Babrak Karmal and his *Parcham* associate Dr Anahita Ratebzad (elected in 1965) and Hafizullah Amin (elected in 1969); and a number of individuals sympathetic to Daoud's ambitions to return to public office, notably Gul Pacha Ulfat. These diverse networks were driven together by a shared antagonism to the direction which the politics of the constitutional period was taking. The technical illegality of political parties denied successive constitutional governments the ability to build solid parliamentary bases grounded in party affiliation, and prime ministers appointed by the king were forced to dispense *ad hoc* patronage in order to win crucial votes. This in turn produced an inefficient and insensitive policy-making process, the flaws in which were exposed in devastating fashion when the central government failed adequately to respond to the drought crisis of 1971-72.[53]

The key problem of the Democratic Period was that the legal-rational constitutional system which it embodied had no particular normative appeal to the Afghan population and lacked legitimacy. For Kabuli intellectuals it doubtless was an agreeable form of anarchy, but the fact remained that for the bulk of the population it was the traditional legitimacy of the office of monarch which won the new order such support as it enjoyed. The Democratic experiment did not alter the basic ground-rules which governed the relations between the state and micro-societies. These ground-rules consisted in large part of norms of reciprocity, on the one hand between the Kabul-based Pushtun political and military leadership and Pushtun micro-societies, and on the other between the largely Tajik bureaucratic-administrative elite and the Tajik and to some extent other minority micro-societies. Unfortunately, Zahir Shah was by all accounts a weak figure who made no effective inroads into these ground-rules and furthermore could not personally offset the enfeeblement of the policymaking process which the 1964 Constitution produced. This not only led to a state of inertia within the Afghan government but heightened concern within the Soviet leadership that its political, economic and military investment in Afghanistan might be wasted. This came to a head in 1972 when the king appointed as prime minister Musa Shafiq, one of his younger and more ambitious advisors, who had proved influential in encouraging him to adopt his democratic path. Shafiq was a law graduate of the orthodox Islamic Al-Azhar University (Egypt) and of Columbia University. To strengthen his own position and mute some of the demands of the potentially powerful Islamists, Shafiq immediately sought an Islamic power base for his government. He did so with a resolve not only to strengthen democracy, but also to rationalise Afghanistan's relations with the Soviet Union through seeking more strictly to limit the activities of communists, to enlist foreign aid from sources other than the Soviet Union, and to settle Afghanistan's border and fluvial differences with Pakistan and Iran.[54] This inevitably brought the democratisation and modernisation drive into direct conflict with what the Soviet leadership saw as the ground rules of the country's relationship with the Soviet Union.

Daoud's Republic

In July 1973 Zahir Shah was overthrown by Daoud in an almost bloodless coup. The coup was executed with help from *Parchamis* and *Parcham* sympathisers in the Air Force and Tank Brigade. The coup had a number of distinct causes. The weakness of the constitutional government was certainly a major contributing factor. The inefficient bureaucracy had little to commend it and the armed forces were anything but wholeheartedly committed to the survival of the monarchy.[55] This was partly because they were substantially Soviet-trained and influenced, but also because the prevalence of patronage as the device which governed promotion in the officer corps meant that many young officers who were outside existing patronage networks became disgruntled as their careers ground to a halt irrespective of their talents and dedication.[56] The coup also had a ready leader: Daoud had for years been grinding his teeth with frustration at his exclusion from politics (along with other members of the royal family) by the 1964 Constitution. Thus, the coup was a familiar example of the kicking-in of a rotting door.[57]

The Soviet Union had reasons to be satisfied with the outcome of the coup. Daoud declared Afghanistan a republic and stressed his regime's frienship towards the Soviet Union, which was the first state to recognise the new regime. He expressed 'the hope that the traditional friendly relations so happily existing between the Afghan and Soviet peoples will be further strengthened and fruitful cooperation between our countries in different fields in accordance with the interests of the nations and world peace further expanded'.[58] He also included several closet *Parchamis* in his cabinet, notably Dr Hassan Sharq, Abdul Hamid Mohtat, Nematullah Pazhwak, Faiz Mohammad, and Pacha Gul Wafadar. Daoud's republicanism, his prompt banning of all political groups, and suppression of Islamists and Maoists as well as renewal of hostilities with Pakistan could not but have pleased Moscow. Furthermore, to the Soviet leadership, Daoud was a familiar figure with whom they were experienced in dealing and this may have led those involved in shaping policy towards Afghanistan to overestimate the strength of his commitment to strengthening friendship with the USSR.

However, after consolidating his rule by the mid-1970s, Daoud emerged as untrustworthy from Moscow's perspective. It discovered that Daoud above everything else was a self-seeking nationalist, that his alliance with the *Parchamis* was one of political convenience, and that he desired to balance his relationship with Moscow. Daoud instituted a non-communist one-party system, resolved to rid his administration of communist sympathisers, and invited Western, Japanese and Indian companies rather than the Soviet Union to participate in several major mining, industrial and communications projects, including the first Afghan railway network.[59] He also sought economic aid from alternative sources. He not only reached a *rapprochement* with Pakistan but also sought close ties with the heads of regional oil-rich states, most notably the Shah of Iran and King Khalid of Saudi Arabia, as well as President Sadat of Egypt—all of whom the Soviets regarded as their adversaries. Further, he launched a vigorous campaign to strengthen Afghanistan's position in the Non-Aligned Movement, supporting moves to prevent Cuba from taking over as the Movement's leader.[60]

Daoud did not pick up significant non-communist support to compensate for that which he lost when he parted company with the communist *Parcham* faction. On the contrary, his initial attempts to suppress the more prominent and active Islamists provided the basis for a strong Islamic backlash, which came to a head in a major uprising in the Panjsher Valley in July 1975.[61] One of the leading figures in the uprising was Ahmad Shah Massoud, subsequently renowned as the 'Lion of the Panjsher' (*Sher-i Panjsher*) following the Soviet invasion. Although Daoud succeeded with little difficulty in putting down the uprising, his actions fuelled heightened hostility from a group whose approval might have enabled him to claim a wider base of 'Islamic-ideological' support. Furthermore, the 1974 death in custody of Western-educated former Prime Minister Maiwandwal, who had been arrested and charged with plotting to overthrow Daoud's regime, could hardly have been calculated to win the sympathy of other Western-educated urban Afghans.[62]

Daoud's policies were not *intended* either to offend the Soviets or to cause Afghanistan to drift into the Western camp, but they were devised and executed hastily and in neglect of the fact that the Soviet leadership would perceive them as threatening to its interests. That they *were* so interpreted is quite clear. During an official visit to the USSR in April 1977 Daoud clashed openly with Soviet party leader L.I. Brezhnev when Brezhnev demanded that advisers from NATO countries working on bilateral projects in Afghanistan be expelled.[63] Consequently, as is evident from accounts provided by some prominent *Parchami* figures during their subsequent gaoling by Amin, the Soviet embassy in Kabul directly urged the *Parcham* and *Khalq* in 1977 to forego their past rivalry and reunite within the PDPA in self-defence against Daoud.[64] This led to the bloody coup of April 1978, enabling the

PDPA to seize state power, eliminating Daoud and most of his colleagues who were immediately denounced by the PDPA and Moscow as 'the enemies of the Afghan people'.

The overthrow of Daoud marked the most decisive change of regime in the history of the modern Afghan state. While major political change in the past had sprung from the discontent of leading figures within Afghanistan's micro-societies, the seizure of power in 1978 had no such roots. There was no basis in the country for a mass revolution; those who displaced Daoud's regime merely had at their disposal the forces necessary to mount a coup in Kabul. Yet the ideology and platform of the new rulers committed them to attempt fundamental changes to the prevailing distribution of power between the state and micro-societies. This lay at the heart of the dilemma which the new regime faced.

Notes

1. Gianfranco Poggi, *The Development of the Modern State: A Sociological Introduction* (London: Hutchinson, 1978) p.1.

2. See Evgenii Evtushenko, 'Po moemu mneniiu', *Sovetskaia kul'tura*, 15 April 1986, p.3.

3. Jon Elster, *The Cement of Society: A study of social order* (Cambridge: Cambridge University Press, 1989) p.248.

4. Richard Tapper, 'Ethnic Identities and Social Categories in Iran and Afghanistan', in Elizabeth Tonkin, Maryon McDonald and Malcolm Chapman (eds.), *History and Ethnicity* (London: Routledge, 1989) pp.232-246, at p.233.

5. Joel S. Migdal, *Strong Societies and Weak States: State-Society Relations and State Capabilities in the Third World* (Princeton: Princeton University Press, 1988) pp.34-35.

6. See Rasma Karklins, 'The Dissent/Coercion Nexus in the USSR', *Studies in Comparative Communism*, vol.20, nos.3-4, Autumn-Winter 1987, pp.321-341, at pp.325-326.

7. Jean-Jacques Rousseau, *The Social Contract and Discourses* (London: J.M. Dent, 1973) p.168.

8. Agnes Heller, 'Phases of Legitimation in Soviet-type Societies', in T.H. Rigby and Ferenc Fehér (eds.), *Political Legitimation in Communist States* (London: Macmillan, 1982) pp.45-63, at p.45.

9. See Jan Pakulski, 'Legitimacy and Mass Compliance: Reflections on Max Weber and Soviet-Type Societies, *British Journal of Political Science*, vol.16, Part I, 1986, pp.35-56, at p.36. For further discussion of Weber's

thought, see Rodney Barker, *Political Legitimacy and the State* (Oxford: Oxford University Press, 1990).

10. Max Weber, 'Politics as a Vocation', in H.H. Gerth and C. Wright Mills (eds.), *From Max Weber: Essays in Sociology* (London: Routledge and Kegan Paul, 1948) pp.77-128, at p.80.

11. See John H. Kautsky, *The Politics of Aristocratic Empires* (Chapel Hill: The University of North Carolina Press, 1982) p.68.

12. S.N. Eisenstadt, *The Political Systems of Empires: The Rise and Fall of the Historical Bureaucratic Societies* (New York: The Free Press, 1969) p.29.

13. Pakulski, op.cit., pp.46-47. See also Jan Pakulski, 'Eastern Europe and "Legitimacy Crisis"', *Australian Journal of Political Science*, vol.25, no.2, November 1990, pp.272-288.

14. Lucian W. Pye, 'The Legitimacy Crisis', in Leonard Binder et.al., *Crises and Sequences in Political Development* (Princeton: Princeton University Press, 1971) pp.135-158, at p.136.

15. Migdal, op.cit., p.4.

16. For historical accounts of the Sunni-Shi'ite schism, see Moojan Momen, *An Introduction to Shi'i Islam: The History and Doctrines of Twelver Shi'ism* (New Haven: Yale University Press, 1985) pp.11-22, and Ira M. Lapidus, *A History of Islamic Societies* (Cambridge: Cambridge University Press, 1988) pp.162-167.

17. See Louis Dupree, *Afghanistan* (Princeton: Princeton University Press, 1980) pp.104-107.

18. Michael Barry, *Le Royaume de l'Insolence: La résistance afghane du Grand Moghol à l'invasion soviétique* (Paris: Flammarion, 1984) p.57.

19. Anthony D. Smith, *The Ethnic Origins of Nations* (Oxford: Basil Blackwell, 1986) pp.22-30.

20. For a detailed historical study of this ethnic group, see Sir Olaf Caroe, *The Pathans* (Karachi: Oxford University Press, 1983). The position of Pushtuns in Pakistan has been the subject of numerous useful works, such as Fredrik Barth, *Political Leadership among Swat Pathans* (London: The Athlone Press, 1959), and Akbar S. Ahmad, *Millennium and Charisma among Pathans: A Critical Essay in Social Anthropology* (London: Routledge and Kegan Paul, 1976). Nonetheless, the historical experiences and social networking of the Afghan Pushtuns are distinct from those of their Pakistan-based brethren, and it is perilous to generalise from one context to the other.

21. On the nature of social closure, see Max Weber, *Economy and Society: An Ouline of Interpretive Sociology* (Berkeley and Los Angeles: University of California Press, 1978) p.342.

22. For a useful general discussion of this point, see Patricia Crone, 'The Tribe and the State', in John A. Hall (ed.), *States in History* (Oxford: Basil Blackwell, 1986) pp.48-77.

23. Olivier Roy, *L'Afghanistan: Islam et modernité politique* (Paris:

Éditions du Seuil, 1985) p.23.

24. See Richard Tapper, 'Introduction' in Richard Tapper (ed.), *The Conflict of Tribe and State in Iran and Afghanistan* (London: Croom Helm, 1983) pp.1-82, at p.9.

25. Ernest Gellner, 'The Tribal Society and Its Enemies', in Richard Tapper (ed.), *The Conflict of Tribe and State in Iran and Afghanistan* (London: Croom Helm, 1983) pp.436-448, at p.438.

26. See, for example, Roy, op.cit., p.38, and G. Whitney Azoy, *Buzkashi: Game and Power in Afghanistan* (Philadelphia: University of Pennsylvania Press, 1982) pp.31-32.

27. On this point see Richard Tapper, 'Minorities and the problem of the state', *Third World Quarterly*, vol.10, no.2, April 1988, pp.1027-1041, at pp.1035-1036.

28. Pierre Centlivres and Micheline Centlivres-Demont, *Et si on parlait de l'Afghanistan?* (Paris: Editions de la Maison des science de l'homme, 1988) p.11. For a synoptic study of Afghan agriculture, see Gilbert Étienne, *L'Afghanistan ou Les Aléas de la Coopération* (Paris: Presses Universitaires de France, 1972). Much of interest can also be gleaned from Maxwell J. Fry, *The Afghan Economy: Money, Finance and the Critical Constraints to Economic Development* (Leiden: E.J. Brill, 1974), even though agriculture receives little direct attention.

29. Roy, op.cit., p.117.

30. On the impact of commercial practices in rural areas, see Jon W. Anderson, 'There are no Khans Anymore: Economic Development and Social Change in Tribal Afghanistan', *The Middle East Journal*, vol.32, no.2, Spring 1978, pp.167-183.

31. See Robert L. Canfield, 'Ethnic, Regional, and Sectarian Alignments in Afghanistan', in Ali Banuazizi and Myron Weiner (eds.), *The State, Religion, and Ethnic Politics: Afghanistan, Iran, and Pakistan* (Syracuse: Syracuse University Press, 1986) pp.75-103.

32. Louis Dupree, 'Cultural changes among the Mujahidin and Muhajerin', in Bo Huldt and Erland Jansson (eds.), *The Tragedy of Afghanistan: The Social, Cultural and Political Impact of the Soviet Invasion* (London, Croom Helm, 1988) pp.20-37, at p.28

33. David Busby Edwards, 'The Evolution of Shi'i Political Dissent in Afghanistan', in Juan R.I. Cole and Nikki R. Keddie (eds.), *Shi'ism and Social Protest* (New Haven: Yale University Press, 1986) pp.201-229, at pp.205-206.

34. For different discussions of this period, see M. Nazif Shahrani, 'State Building and Social Fragmentation in Afghanistan: A Historical Perspective', in Ali Banuazizi and Myron Weiner (eds.), *The State, Religion, and Ethnic Politics: Afghanistan, Iran, and Pakistan* (Syracuse: Syracuse University Press, 1986) pp.23-74, at pp.29-36; Ashraf Ghani, 'The Afghan State and its Adaptation to the Environment of Central and Southwest Asia', in Hafeez Malik (ed.), *Soviet-American Relations with*

Pakistan, Iran and Afghanistan (London: Macmillan, 1987) pp.310-332, at p.313; and Barnett R. Rubin, 'Lineages of the State in Afghanistan', *Asian Survey*, vol.28, no.11, November 1988, pp.1188-1209, at pp.1191-1192. For a controversial Afghan study of the evolution of the Afghan state, see Mir Mohammad Ghulam Ghobar, *Afghanistan dar masir-i tarikh* (Kabul: n.p., 1967).

35. On the reign of 'Abd al-Rahman Khan, see Hasan Kawun Kakar, *Government and Society in Afghanistan: The Reign of Amir 'Abd al-Rahman Khan* (Austin: The University of Texas Press, 1979).

36. See Ashraf Ghani, 'Islam and State-Building in a Tribal Society: Afghanistan 1880-1901', *Modern Asian Studies*, vol.12, no.2, 1978, pp.269-284, at p.271.

37. See Vartan Gregorian, *The Emergence of Modern Afghanistan: Politics of Reform and Modernization 1880-1946* (Stanford: Stanford University Press, 1969) pp.181-205.

38. See Leon B. Poullada, *Reform and Rebellion in Afghanistan, 1919-1929: King Amanullah's Failure to Modernize a Tribal Society* (Ithaca: Cornell University Press, 1973).

39. In the general, the rule of Habibullah has been depicted in very negative terms by Afghan historians. For a recent and more positive assessment, see Khalilullah Khalili, *'Ayari az Khorasan: Amir Habibullah, Khadim-i Din-i Rasul Allah* (Peshawar: Tarikh-e Ramadan, 1984).

40. Mohammad Hashim Kamali, *Law in Afghanistan: A Study of the Constitutions, Matrimonial Law and the Judiciary* (Leiden: E.J. Brill, 1985) p.20.

41. See Dupree, *Afghanistan*, pp.496-497.

42. Gilbert Étienne, *Rural Development in Asia: Meetings with Peasants* (New Delhi: Sage Publications, 1985) pp.32-33.

43. For a recent account of the Pushtunistan issue, see S.N. Haqshenas, *Dasayis wa junayat-i Rus dar Afghanistan: Az Amir Dost Mohammad Khan ta Babrak* (Teheran: Komiteh-i Farhangi Daftar-e Markazi Jamiat-i Islami Afghanistan, 1984) pp.366-380.

44. See Leon B. Poullada, 'Afghanistan and the United States: The Crucial Years', *The Middle East Journal*, vol.35, no.2, Spring 1981, pp.178-190, at p.187; Leon B. Poullada, 'The Failure of American Diplomacy in Afghanistan', *World Affairs*, vol.145, no.3, Winter 1982-1983, pp.230-252; and Thomas T. Hammond, *Red Flag Over Afghanistan* (Boulder: Westview Press, 1984) pp.23-28.

45. On the strategy of peaceful coexistence, see Vendulka Kubálková and A.A. Cruickshank, *Marxism-Leninism and theory of international relations* (London: Routledge and Kegan Paul, 1980) pp.206-208. More generally, see Roy Allison, *The Soviet Union and the Strategy of Non-Alignment in the Third World* (Cambridge: Cambridge University Press, 1988).

46. Oleg Penkovskiy, *The Penkovskiy Papers* (New York: Doubleday, 1965) p.87.

47. Henry S. Bradsher, *Afghanistan and the Soviet Union* (Durham: Duke University Press, 1985) pp.24-25.

48. Ibid., p.24.

49. M.S. Noorzoy, 'Soviet Economic Interests in Afghanistan', *Problems of Communism*, vol.36, no.3, May-June 1987, pp.43-54.

50. See Bradsher, op.cit., pp.27-28; and Muhammad R. Azmi, 'Soviet Politico-Military Penetration in Afghanistan, 1955 to 1979', *Armed Forces & Society*, vol.12, no.3, Spring 1986, pp.329-350, at pp.334-335.

51. For details see Dupree, *Afghanistan*, Chapters 23-24.

52. Sabahuddin Kushkaki, *Daha-i Qanun Asasi: Ghaflat Zadagi Afghanha wa Fursat Talabi Rusha* (Peshawar: Shurai-i saqafati Jihad-i Afghanistan, 1986) pp.142-150. For a detailed history of these groups, see Anthony Arnold, *Afghanistan's Two-Party Communism: Parcham and Khalq* (Stanford: Hoover Institution Press, 1983). Two other works, Beverley Male, *Revolutionary Afghanistan* (New York: St Martin's Press, 1982), and Raja Anwar, *The Tragedy of Afghanistan: A First-hand Account* (London: Verso, 1988) address the history of the communist movement in Afghanistan. However, both are strongly ideological in tone, and suspect on key points of fact. They should therefore be treated with considerable caution.

53. See Michael Barry, *Afghanistan* (Paris: Éditions du Seuil, 1974) pp.175-183.

54. Kushkaki, op.cit., pp.80-97. The dispute with Iran stemmed largely from disagreements over the distribution of the waters of the Helmand River in the Sistan area. It was amicably settled by an agreement in March 1973. See Amin Saikal, *The Rise and Fall of the Shah* (Princeton: Princeton University Press, 1980) p.172.

55. See Hasan Kakar, 'The Fall of the Afghan Monarchy in 1973', *International Journal of Middle East Studies*, vol.9, 1978, pp.195-214.

56. Ralph H. Magnus, 'The Military and Politics in Afghanistan: Before and After the Revolution', in Edward A. Olsen and Stephen Jurika, Jnr. (eds.), *The Armed Forces in Contemporary Asian Societies* (Boulder: Westview Press, 1986) pp.325-344, at p.335.

57. For further discussion of the coup, see Christine F. Ridout, 'Authority Patterns and the Afghan Coup of 1973', *The Middle East Journal*, vol.29, no.2, Spring 1975, pp.165-178; and Shaheen F. Dil, 'The Cabal in Kabul: Great-Power Interaction in Afghanistan', *American Political Science Review*, vol.71, no.2, June 1977, pp.468-476.

58. See 'President Daoud Replies Friendly Congratulatory Messages', in Abdul Aziz Danishyar, *The Afghanistan Republic Annual* (Kabul: Government Press, 1974) pp.30-32, at p.30.

59. See Saikal, *The Rise and Fall of the Shah*, p.200.

60. Bradsher, op.cit., p.66.

61. For a detailed account of how this backlash developed, see the interesting memoirs of Mohammad Es'haq, 'Evolution of the Islamic movement in Afghanistan', *AFGHANews*, vol.5, nos.1-4, January-February 1989.

62. See Etienne Gille, 'La mort de Maywandwâl', *Les Nouvelles d'Afghanistan*, no.44, October 1989, p.20.

63. Abdul Samad Ghaus, *The Fall of Afghanistan: An Insider's Account* (McLean: Pergamon-Brassey's, 1988) pp.178-179.

64. Private sources: the most notable such informant was Suleiman Laeq, who returned to prominence following the Soviet invasion of Afghanistan.

3

The New Regime

The PDPA came to power under remarkable circumstances. There was little in its history which would have led one to the conclusion that it was ready to take power and command generalised normative support. Had it not been for its infiltration of the military, it would have remained a marginalised cluster of frustrated political activists and opportunists. The 1977 reconstitution of the PDPA had done virtually nothing to eliminate the longstanding tensions between *Khalq* and *Parcham* leaders and there was little to suggest that the party leaders were capable of winning control of the instrumentalities of the state.

All this changed on the evening of 17 April 1978, when Mir Akbar Khyber, a journalist and member of the *Parcham* faction, was shot dead by two callers at his house in Kabul.[1] The consequences of this homicide were momentous. His funeral provided an opportunity for a wide range of Afghans, by no means all communists, to demonstrate their dissatisfaction with the autocratic rule of Daoud, whose secret police was rumoured to have had a hand in the killing. Between ten and fifteen thousand people accompanied Khyber's body to its resting place near the Bala Hissar fortress in Kabul. This manifestation understandably alarmed Daoud, who responded a week later by placing a large number of prominent Afghan communists under arrest. However, by the time the first wave of arrests had been completed, leaders of the PDPA had been able to secure the backing of the Soviet Embassy for a coup attempt and when elements in the armed forces loyal to Hafizullah Amin commenced their moves against Daoud they received decisive support from aircraft which it has been suggested were piloted by members of the Soviet Air Force.[2] Eyewitness testimony points to active participation by Soviet advisers in the direction and execution of the coup,[3] as has the recent admission by Soviet Lieutenant-General A.D. Sidorov that Soviet servicemen were engaged in 'military actions' in Afghanistan from 22 April 1978— five days *before* the coup.[4] Within a matter of days, the old political order in Afghanistan was gone forever.

The PDPA's seizure of state power was reasonably well planned, but politically premature. The coup, spearheaded largely by Kabul-based groups of Soviet-trained airforce and tank brigade officers under Colonel Abdul Qadir and Major Aslam Watanjar, was executed with exceptional accuracy and sophistication, but the PDPA as a *political* force was in no way equipped to rule effectively. It lacked cohesion, administrative experience, and popular support in a country whose population could neither accept a ruling force which arose from outside the established traditional norms of authority nor approve its alien ideology, least of all 'Godless communism'. Neither faction of the PDPA had ever managed to attract more than a few hundred committed members in a country with a population variously estimated at 12-15.5 million[5] (with 13.05 million perhaps the best estimate[6]). This critical manpower shortage was ultimately to have a devastating effect on the regime. It was clear from the start to both the PDPA leadership (which now included Taraki as president and prime minister, Karmal as first deputy prime minister, Amin as foreign minister and deputy prime minister, and Colonels Qadir and Watanjar as Defence and Communications ministers respectively) and the Kremlin that the PDPA's rule of the renamed 'Democratic Republic of Afghanistan' (DRA) could not survive for very long without Soviet political, economic and military support. This obliged the PDPA leadership to express its full loyalty to Moscow and plead for all-round assistance, and it led the Kremlin to commit itself deeply to the survival of the PDPA. The Soviets immediately recognised the new regime, and began to pour massive economic and military aid into the country, as well as advisers to assist in the running of the Kabul bureaucracy, and improve the operational capacity of the armed forces. From a pre-1978 level of around 1,000 the number of advisers leaped by late 1979 to between 5,000 and 7,500.[7] Amin did not hesitate to describe the April 'revolution' as a 'true continuation of the Great October revolution' of 1917.[8]

In one respect, the takeover even improved on the Bolshevik coup. In Russia, the use of terror against political opponents was somewhat delayed, erupting following an attempt on Lenin's life in August 1918.[9] In Afghanistan, on the other hand, the new regime moved immediately against urban notables whom the regime feared might be a source of opposition and a focus for other discontented elements. As well as Daoud's associates, the initial sweep picked up a wide range of individuals who had been involved not with his regime but with earlier governments from the period of the Constitutional experiment. Those arrested included former prime ministers Nur Ahmad Etemadi and Musa Shafiq; other prominent figures such as former UN General Assembly president Abdul Rahman Pazhwak, and other figures from previous governments, notably Dr Abdul Samad Hamed, Sabahuddin Kushkaki, Abdul Tawab Assifi, and Dr Ravan Farhadi.[10] In addition, members of *Shuli Javid* and *Afghan Millat* were seized in large numbers.

Within two months the purge hit the ranks of the party itself. This was hardly surprising. Even when the party had been a marginal force in the mid-1960s, the animosities between *Khalqis* and *Parchamis* had proved uncontainable. With so much more at stake after the coup, it was even less likely that they could be managed. In this particular power struggle, the *Khalq* under the leadership of Taraki and Amin proved victorious. The purge moved in two stages. In the first stage, in late June and early July 1978, prominent *Parcham* members of the PDPA Central Committee were despatched abroad as ambassadors; these included Babrak Karmal (to Prague), Dr Anahita Ratebzad (to Belgrade), Abdul Wakil (to London), and Dr Najibullah (to Teheran). The second stage came with claims of a wide-ranging *Parcham* conspiracy to seize state power. At this point, Defence Minister Abdul Qadir, Army Chief of Staff Shapur Khan Ahmadzai, and Planning Minister Sultan Ali Kishtmand were arrested, and the more prominent *Parcham* ambassadors wisely decamped from their positions and obtained protection within the Soviet bloc. The net effects of these episodes were to increase the dominance of the *Khalq* within the PDPA and to put its radical policy proposals on top of the regime's agenda. Amin in particular was a beneficiary of these developments, as his longstanding rival Karmal was undoubtedly the figure most likely to pose an obstacle to him. Given the intimate relations which Karmal had enjoyed with Moscow, the Soviets seem to have been worried at this turn of events,[11] although it did not of course prompt any change in the USSR's commitment to the survival of the PDPA regime.

In the Countryside

It needs to be emphasised at this point that the coup in Kabul had little if any immediate effect in rural areas. Military bases around the country acquiesced in the developments in Kabul, as the deaths of Daoud and all his close associates left no obvious immediate alternative to the new rulers. Furthermore, in rural areas the administrative agencies of the central government were designed more to strike *compromises* with micro-societies than to produce substantial *change* in the ways in which those micro-societies functioned. This had not been a problem under either Zahir Shah or Daoud; it became a serious problem for the PDPA, because unlike its predecessors it was committed to bringing about change in the very spheres in which it was administratively and militarily the weakest.[12]

The world views of the more prominent *Parchamis* and *Khalqis* owed little to serious sociological study and more to what Bradsher has called 'teahouse political talk'.[13] Their approach involved a crude application to Afghan circumstances of certain vulgarised notions drawn from various Marxist-Leninist tracts. The party platform, initially published in the mid-1960s in the newspaper *Khalq*, gives a good indication of the standard of analysis of which the PDPA leaders were capable. Clearly echoing *The Communist Manifesto*, it proclaimed that class struggle was the 'most outstanding subject of contemporary history'. It went on to blame Afghanistan's material poverty on 'feudalists', 'big businessmen' and 'imperialistic monopolizing companies'. The 'backwardness of past centuries' was to be eliminated 'within the lifespan of one generation'. The aim of the party was 'to realize a complete society which can be accomplished through socialism'.[14]

These simplistic precepts were to a considerable extent reflected in the concrete policies which the regime proclaimed, and attempted to implement. The most provocative of these related to land and debt, and to the position of women. The first topics were addressed in Decrees 6 and 8 of the Revolutionary Council, issued respectively on 12 July 1978 and 28 November 1978. The former dealt with 'usury' and moved to abolish debts secured by realty owed by a wide range of rural dwellers. But as Louis Dupree pointed out, legal abolition of usury 'did not eliminate the small farmer's need for extra capital, and no viable alternatives had been established by the DRA before the Decree was promulgated'.[15] Thus, to the extent that it was given effect by local administrators, the Decree disrupted the stable pattern of commercial lending in rural areas. The Decree on land reform was even more ill-considered and seemed almost calculated to offend as wide a range of groups as possible.[16] In restricting ownership of prime lands to amounts totally inadequate for animal pasture, the regime showed a particular disregard for the needs of the two million pastoral nomads in Afghanistan.[17] Furthermore, the regime's moves did not address the problems of rural water and seed supply, and thus did little but outrage those whose holdings were adversely affected by the initial decree.[18]

Most controversial of all was the Decree dealing with the position of women. Here it is important to recognise that major differences had begun to develop between the lifestyles and social roles of well-placed urban women, mostly in Kabul, and rural women. In urban areas, the position of women had attracted attention even during King Amanullah's reign. The practice of veiling in the *chador* had been informally abandoned within official circles when Zahir Shah's wife and a number of other prominent women appeared at the 1959 Independence Day parade without veils. By the 1960s, it was possible—although on a limited scale—for urban women to attend Kabul University and secure election to the *Wolesi Jirga*; indeed, a distinguished woman graduate, Kubra Nurzai, served as Health minister from 1966 to 1969. By 1978, these changes had of course benefited only a minority of women even in urban areas, but they were an important demonstration that it was not impossible *per se* for women in urban areas to play an active and visible role in a number of social spheres.[19] In rural areas, the situation was quite different. Women performed distinct tasks within a household economy and the institution of marriage was traditionally part of an exchange contract in which cash or goods were conveyed from the groom to the family of the bride. Although this doubtless often functioned as no more than an accretion to the wealth of the bride's father, in principle it was not intended to be a price but rather a fund to provide security for the bride in the event that the marriage failed. Such payments were the direct target of Decree 7, issued on 17 October 1978, which *inter alia* fixed a ceiling of 300 Afghanis on the amount which could be paid.[20] This sparked off ferocious opposition, particularly from within religious circles for whom the payment was an integral part of the Islamic marriage ceremony. It also was seen by fathers—not all motivated entirely by fear of financial disappointment—as an insulting devaluation of their daughters.

These reforms actually had little *direct* effect upon Afghan rural society. There were two reasons for this. First, as the above remarks suggest, the proposals were riddled with contradictions and simply did not come to terms with Afghanistan's complex sociological realities. Second, the regime in any case lacked the body of experienced cadrés which would have been required to implement the proposals.

At the same time as these concrete policies were surfacing, the regime took a number of initiatives deeply offensive to Afghans in both rural and urban areas. These were symbolic rather than practical, but a regime with no strong basis for claiming legitimacy can hardly afford to alienate important circles with steps that stand little chance of winning it support. The most striking examples of these initiatives were a change in the colour of Afghanistan's flag—from the traditional green, red and black to a communist red—and the replacement of an important Islamic symbol, the Pulpit (*mumbar*), with a *Khalqi* symbol. Other examples were the introduction of blatantly political and ideological elements into the (coeducationally-administered) 'literacy campaign' and the dissemination of communist literature and symbols, notably pictures of V.I. Lenin, in places where predictably they would be met with scorn.

The PDPA's Weaknesses

The backlash created by these substantive and symbolic policies might have swamped *any* regime which thus confronted a wide range of Afghanistan's micro-societies. But the inherent weakness of the PDPA meant that trouble was almost unavoidable. We have already noted the PDPA's lack of manpower. This problem was greatly aggravated by the organisational inefficiency of the party. Its limited supply of cadres were rapidly thrust into roles for which nothing had prepared them. On the one hand, they were being asked to perform bureaucratic tasks which they found unfamiliar. On the other, they were forced to function in a social *milieu* which they could not comprehend. Detribalised leftists from Kabul were in no position to penetrate what Dupree once called the 'mud curtain' surrounding the rural village power structure.[21] They all too frequently proved utterly insensitive to the symbolic interpretation which their individual actions would attract.[22] Many of the party's cadres came, in Marxist terms, from the *Lumpenproletariat*. In normal circumstances, few would have been qualified by their education and culture for more than the most menial positions. It proved easy for the hard-core PDPA leadership to indoctrinate, secularise and manipulate such individuals. Suddenly catapulted into what were in their eyes relatively powerful positions, they proceeded to prove the wisdom of the old Afghan proverb that one should beware of the beggar who becomes king. A desire to exercise power for its own sake was only one symptom of the problem. More damaging were indicators of what in Afghan society appeared to be gross moral turpitude, notably a rather blatant taste for wine and women.

This kind of conduct struck at a number of key codes of behaviour valued within important micro-societies. It offended against both religious and traditional mores. Furthermore, it compounded the suspicion spawned by the regime's substantial and symbolic policies that the new rulers were at heart *atheists*. As one observer has argued, atheism 'to the Afghan moral conscience implies filthiness, gluttony, drunkenness and sexual promiscuity'.[23] Ordinary Afghans witnessing such conduct naturally inferred that atheism lay behind it. It cannot be overemphasised that this is an extremely damaging suspicion in Afghan society and that rumours, once in circulation, can be enormously difficult to control.[24] King Amanullah was grievously damaged by rumours that he was an idolator and that he had gone mad after eating pork during his trip to Europe in 1928; even stronger rumours about the PDPA leadership, not all of them ill-founded, were circulating widely within a few months of the coup. Many rumours spread about the drinking and womanising of the new leaders; one particularly ubiquitous rumour linked Babrak Karmal and Dr Anahita Ratebzad in an adulterous relationship.

These caused outrage in both rural and urban areas and confronted the regime with a growing crisis of legitimacy. While urban centres became increasingly restless, active opposition broke out more or less simultaneously in a number of different rural localities. The first major uprising which seriously challenged the authority of the regime occurred in Nuristan in the last quarter of 1978.[25] This was followed by larger uprisings in the Bala Hissar military fortress in Kabul and in March 1979 in Herat. The latter revolt was particularly serious as it involved large numbers, including air force units, and Soviet advisers and their families were among the casualties. The suppression of this uprising cost 3,000-5,000 Afghan lives,[26] and left no doubt about the urgency of the situation by which the regime was confronted. The dubious loyalty of Afghan military units became apparent at this time (underlining the importance of Weber's emphasis on the loyalty of the administrative staff as an important determinant of legitimacy). The obligations of the conscript soldiers within the army to the micro-societies which were the primary foci of their loyalties were in many cases much more powerful than their commitments either to the regime or to the armed forces as an institution. As a result, defection from the services—a most unusual phenomenon before 1978—began to be a major problem. This reduced the strength of the armed forces—which numbered 80,000-100,000 before the PDPA coup—to between 50,000 and 70,000 by late 1979.[27] Thus, a major instrument for the maintenance of regime control had begun to lose its effectiveness within one year of the overthrow of Daoud.

The Ascendency of Amin

It was in this context that Hafizullah Amin assumed the office of prime minister in March 1979, replacing Taraki. Amin's assumption of the prime ministership had to be handled with considerable care because of the way in which a cult of personality had been constructed around Taraki. This cult was designed to compensate for the weakness of the party structure, and to legitimise the PDPA's rule by synthetic charisma, imputing to the new president amazing qualities which set him apart from ordinary mortals.[28] Amin did not see Taraki in quite this light. For many years they had enjoyed a fairly tense relationship with each other. Amin had described it as akin to the relationship of fingernail to flesh, but this belied the complexity of the situation. While Taraki was a good deal older than Amin, and was able to exploit this to boost his relative position, he was neither as shrewd nor as ruthless as his junior. When Amin attributed to Taraki the remark that 'those who plot against us in the dark will vanish in the dark',[29] he was probably reflecting his own views rather than those of his amiable but less competent superior. His conduct on assuming the prime ministership is certainly consistent with this interpretation. The strategy which he opted to pursue in dealing with the opposition magnified rather than reduced the regime's problems.

While in no sense a popular figure, Amin survived as the 'strongman' of the regime in part because of the efficiency of a secret police force which he was instrumental in creating and on the loyalty of which he could largely rely. It was called the Afghan Interests Protection Service or AGSA (*Da Afghanistan da Gato da Satalo Adara*), and was headed by an especially sadistic *Khalqi*, Asadullah Sarwari.[30] This secret police proved to be particularly ruthless and practised not simply the strategic detention of regime opponents but wholesale terror against large components of the civilian population in urban areas. Kabul in 1979 became a city swathed in fear, and the reprisals carried out against those who stepped out of line were grim indeed. A particularly gruesome illustration came on 23 June 1979 when there was a serious disturbance in the Hazara quarter of Kabul. Troops fired on the demonstrators and a reprisal followed: three hundred Hazaras were trucked to a field outside Kabul where half were buried alive with a bulldozer and the other half drenched with gasoline and set on fire.[31] Nonetheless, Amin's control of AGSA was not complete, something demonstrated when, in connection with larger events in September 1979, Sarwari quit his post to seek refuge in the Soviet Embassy.

The events of September 1979 were a culmination of intensifying Soviet concern about the directions which regime policies in Afghanistan were taking. As we have already noted, the USSR was perturbed by the 1978 purge of *Parchamis*, which displaced those Afghan communists who had been most closely linked with agencies of the Soviet government. It was obliged to exert pressure on the *Khalq* regime in order to protect those *Parchamis* who remained in the regime's prisons, a somewhat distasteful task for any patron power to perform.[32] Yet the Soviets also had more direct interests of their own to protect and this led them in December 1978 to sign a bilateral Treaty of Friendship with the Afghan regime.[33] The treaty committed the parties to 'take by agreement appropriate measures to ensure the security, independence, and territorial integrity of the two countries'.[34] This paved the way for a future Soviet military intervention if circumstances made it seem necessary. Nonetheless, a Soviet military intervention was hardly a step to be taken lightly, and faced with the growing intransigence of Amin the USSR's first step was to attempt his replacement with another more amenable political figure. The choice of figures who could take his place was by mid-1979 *extremely* limited. The Amin-Taraki leadership had systematically eliminated, under the very eyes of Soviet advisers, most alternative political forces apart from *Parchamis* and some Islamic intellectuals who either sought refuge in Pakistan or survived in prison through family connections. This left Babrak Karmal as virtually the only figure who could be promoted as an alternative to Amin. Given the difficulty of removing Amin through formal institutional processes, the Soviets hatched a plot with Taraki—by now well aware of the threat which Amin's ambitions posed for him. However, their attempt to eliminate Amin miscarried disastrously: Amin survived an attempt on his life and removed Taraki, whose death was reported by the *Kabul Times* in a terse backpage report in early October. Sarwari and his collaborators

Aslam Watanjar, Sayid Mohammad Gulabzoi and Sher Jan Mazdooryar, made their way to the Soviet Embassy and the political police was retitled the Workers' Intelligence Institute or KAM (*Kargari Astekhbarati Muassessa*), and was headed first by Aziz Ahmad Akbari and then by Hafizullah Amin's nephew Asadullah Amin.[35]

Amin attempted to distance himself from Taraki in a number of different ways. First, Taraki's cult of personality disappeared overnight. He was denied the immortality offered by a public mausoleum, certainly because it would have offended Islamic teachings on burial and possibly because the signs of asphyxiation would have been too obvious. A new cult of personality was created with Amin at its centre—his photograph replaced Taraki's in public places and he figured prominently in all of the media—but on the whole it did not reach the absurd heights to which the cult surrounding Taraki had soared. Second, Amin placed great rhetorical stress on the slogan 'Security, Legality and Justice', by which he implied that whatever 'excesses' had thitherto occurred were the responsibility of his predecessor. In this connection, a lengthy list was displayed in the Interior Ministry containing the names of some 12,000 individuals who had disappeared in custody,[36] although the release of information was discontinued in the face of public protests in the vicinity of the ministry building. Third, he promised to establish a constitution and set up a constitutional commission to embark on the task of drafting one.

All this was fiercely ironical, for the reality of life under Amin was anything but legal and constitutional. Random arrests took place on a massive scale; those arrested were executed in large numbers in Pul-i Charkhi prison outside Kabul without even the remotest semblance of a fair trial; and Amin sought to secure his position not by the establishment of a legal-rational constitutional system but through the promotion to positions of power of members of his own family. Apart from placing Asadullah Amin in charge of KAM, he appointed his brother Abdullah Amin as chief of security in a 'Northern Zone' embracing Kunduz, Takhar, Baghlan and Samangan, and his son Adurrahman Amin as deputy president of the Khalqi Organisation of Afghan Youth.

Neither the murder of Taraki nor Amin's ascendency held the

slightest joy for the Soviet leadership. Amin was in no doubt whatever that the USSR was behind the move to depose him. In June 1979 Vasilii Safronchuk had been appointed as deputy to Soviet ambassador Aleksandr Puzanov with the specific mandate of restructuring the regime, something which the East German ambassador admitted to an American diplomat,[37] and Puzanov had given Amin a pledge of safety to lure him into the failed trap (much as Iurii Andropov had trapped Hungarian leader Imre Nagy with a similar guarantee in 1956).[38] Amin's immediate reaction was to demand that Puzanov be recalled. This was a humiliation which Moscow had no option but to accept; nonetheless, it was not something to be forgiven. Puzanov was no negligible figure. He had been a member of the Central Committee of the Soviet Communist Party, chairman of the Council of Ministers of the Russian Republic, and had served as ambassador in Afghanistan since the time of Zahir Shah.

Having lost the confidence of the Soviet leadership, Amin began to look in other directions for support, which could only have made him look even worse in Soviet eyes. His chances, of course, were never very good. He had a meeting with the US chargé, J. Bruce Amstutz, but this came to nothing, largely because relations with the US had become glacial following the death in Kabul early in 1979 of kidnapped US Ambassador Adolph ('Spike') Dubs in a bungled rescue attempt for which the US administration held Amin to blame.[39] Potentially more rewarding were dealings which he undertook with the Pakistan regime of General Zia ul-Haq. Pakistan was in an entirely different geopolitical position from the USA. While events in Afghanistan mattered little to remote bureaucrats in Washington, they weighed heavily in the calculations of Pakistani decisionmakers. Pakistan had already been subjected to a burdensome flow of Afghan refugees into the North West Frontier Province and Baluchistan, and a number of groups committed to overthrowing the Kabul regime had headquarters established on Pakistani soil. Amin sought a meeting with Zia—which Zia understandably refused—and a meeting which was scheduled with Zia's representative Agha Shahi was prevented by logistical problems from taking place.[40]

No matter what rhetoric of 'reform' Amin produced, or what external support he solicited, the rule of the *Khalq* was doomed.

By the time Amin displaced Taraki the regime had by its policies and actions lost whatever chance it had of winning legitimacy. The micro-societies of rural Afghanistan had found a common cause, namely the need to defend their honour, Islamic values and traditional ways of life—all with deep cultural roots—and mounted armed and unarmed resistance to the intrusion of the state into rural areas. In urban centres, the regime's suppression of pre-communist social organisations and networks proved equally offensive. Even where the PDPA's cadrés were not physically liquidated, the split between *Khalq* and *Parcham*, as well as the further schism in the *Khalq* following the murder of Taraki, proved insuperably debilitating. Furthermore, it was impossible to compensate for the regime's lack of legitimacy by further application of coercion. The application of coercion simply provoked even more intense popular opposition, requiring the application of coercive resources at a higher level.[41] For Amin, this was hardly an option. Only the USSR could provide such resources, and the Soviet leaders were the last people to whom Amin could safely turn. His dilemma was complete.

The Soviet Invasion

Having exhausted its political options with Taraki and Amin, the Kremlin elected to take military action. The Soviet invasion of Afghanistan aimed to achieve the very political objectives which the Soviets had failed to secure through the PDPA-*Khalqi* rule. The public statements of the Soviet leadership after the invasion did not suggest that it reached its invasion decision in a vacuum and in neglect of its possible consequences. Brezhnev subsequently stated that '... the moment had come when we could no longer fail to respond to the request to us from the government of friendly Afghanistan. To act otherwise would mean abandoning Afghanistan to the lacerations of imperialism' and 'looking on passively while on our southern border there arose a seat of serious danger to the security of the Soviet Union'.[42] The Soviet leadership had nearly four months from Amin's takeover of the PDPA leadership to examine the costs and benefits of all options open to it. It had already sent two major investigative missions to Afghanistan. One was under the head of the Central Political Directorate of the Soviet Armed Forces, General Aleksei Epishev, and the other was directed by the commander of Soviet ground forces, General Ivan Pavlovskii, who had headed the invasion force in Czechoslovakia in 1968. It appears that these missions, and especially that headed by Pavlovskii, had two main purposes: to assess very closely the situation on the ground in Afghanistan; and to activate all the necessary infrastructural and logistic mechanisms of support the Soviets had secured before and after the PDPA's assumption of power. The Soviets carried out these missions on the pretence that they were there to help the Amin regime.

The general assumption at the time was that these missions recommended in favour of an invasion. However, recent reports in the Soviet press have cast doubts on this assumption. Pavlovskii has stated that he reported to Defence Minister D.F. Ustinov that 'there was no need to send troops into Afghanistan'.[43] The KGB representative in Kabul, it is now maintained, argued in favour of invasion, but the military did *not*.[44] Some specialists who might have preached caution went unconsulted. Academician Bogomolov of the Institute for the Study of the World Socialist System pointed this out in a sharp letter to the press in March 1988.[45] Furthermore, subsequent public statements by prominent Soviet citizens have also raised questions about whether the decision to intervene was taken in as formalised a manner as Brezhnev's remarks suggested: Boris El'tsin claimed in March 1989 that the decision was taken by Brezhnev, Ustinov, Central Committee secretary M.A. Suslov, and foreign minister Gromyko.[46] It has been on reasoning such as this that the present Soviet leadership has relied in order to shift the blame for the invasion conveniently onto individuals who are no longer around to defend themselves.

These recent revelations may well bring us closer to a complete understanding of what bureaucratic forces participated in the making of the decision. However, as such statements can obviously serve the ulterior purpose of exculpating members of the present Soviet leadership from the sin of having driven the Soviet Union into a quagmire, they should perhaps not be taken at face value. As Major-General Kim Tsagolov remarked in

January 1990, 'the impression is being formed that in every aspect attempts are being made to put the blame on those who have already died in order to protect the living—those people who prepared an analysis of the situation in Afghanistan prior to the entry of the troops'.[47] To conclude that the Soviets blundered into Afghanistan without careful thought is to ignore the possibility that the top echelon of the leadership studied the situation carefully and was prepared to accept costs which to a subsequent Soviet leadership were simply unacceptable.

Whatever the complexities of the Soviet decision-making process in this particular case, signs that the USSR *might* intervene in Afghanistan were apparent to a number of well informed outside observers. The most important among these was Dr Zbigniew Brzezinski, National Security Adviser to US President Carter, who had expressed his concern as early as March 1979 over 'the Soviets' creeping intervention in Afghanistan'. On 19 September he informed the president that 'a direct Soviet invasion of Afghanistan was becoming more probable'.[48] However, as the Soviets could have safely assumed, Washington found itself helpless. This was partly due to a conflict between Brzezinski and Secretary of State Cyrus Vance[49], who refused either to quarrel too much with the Soviets for fear that this would encourage the Congress not to ratify the SALT II Treaty or to take action which might have deterred the Soviet invasion, and partly due to the preoccupation of the US administration from 4 November onwards with the seizure of its Teheran Embassy by Islamic militants.

Appropriately enough, the Soviets chose the holiday period between Christmas and New Year, when the state machineries in the Western world were largely inactive, to airlift to Afghanistan some 50,000 heavily equipped motorised troops, occupying Kabul and certain other strategic places in the country. As has recently been admitted by Soviet historian Iurii Gankovskii, a sub-unit of Soviet troops helped kill Amin and his entourage;[50] the USSR accused Amin of being a 'CIA agent' and put its trusted ally Babrak Karmal in his place. Brezhnev congratulated Karmal on being 'elected' leader of the PDPA. Soviet sources also contended that the Soviet Union had dispatched only a 'limited contingent' of its troops to allow the PDPA to rectify Amin's mistakes, put Afghanistan's 'national democratic revolution' on its right path, and defend the country against the 'imperialist-backed internal reaction and foreign aggression'.[51] The Soviets attempted to legitimise their invasion by claiming that their forces were invited to Afghanistan under the December 1978 Treaty; but they never produced any document containing such an invitation. Nor did they explain on what basis Karmal and his top colleagues, expelled from the party in 1978 and excluded from any public office, had standing to issue so momentous a request.[52]

The Soviet invasion sparked off a great deal of debate, especially in the West, about possible wider Soviet motives. A number of writers, some but by no means all of them notorious as Soviet sympathisers, labelled it a 'defensive' act, designed for the limited objective of protecting desirable Soviet security and political interests, and signifying no wider Soviet ambitions. Such figures generally accepted the Soviet action as a 'limited intervention' and cautioned the West against overreacting.[53] On the other hand, many branded it the most flagrant Soviet aggression ever outside the Warsaw Pact countries. They saw it as a first step towards fulfilment of a Soviet historical and ideological ambition to achieve regional domination, and called for an immediate Soviet troop withdrawal and for effective regional and Western reponses, including material assistance to the Afghan resistance and a strengthening of the defences of the receptive frontline states, most notably Pakistan. Washington and Beijing, on the whole, sided with this interpretation.[54]

Yet there were many others, including a number of serious scholars of Afghan politics and society, who found acceptable neither the passivity underlying the 'defensive' interpretation nor the extremity inherent in the 'offensive' posture. They attributed the Soviet action to a variety of factors, ranging from Soviet concern for its international prestige, which could not allow it to let an ideologically-allied protégé regime fall in favour of a possibly hostile Islamic one, to a Soviet misperception and miscalculation of the likely costs which would result from its involvement in Afghanistan. At any rate, under the impulse of their support for the right of nations to free self-determination and their opposition to the use of force by the superpowers as a means to settle conflicts and impose their will on other countries, they condemned the Soviet action and demanded international support for the legitimate cause of the Afghan people against foreign imposition. Whatever the Soviets' and their supporters' justification, they contended that since the Soviet troops had crossed the internationally recognised borders of a poor and weak small state, their action constituted a military invasion which could not and ought not to be condoned in the international community. This argument found acceptance with a great majority of states, which routinely approved resolutions in the United Nations General Assembly calling for the unconditional withdrawal of all foreign troops from Afghan soil.[55]

Whatever the individual merits of the above arguments, in retrospect and in the context of subsequent Soviet actions one vital aspect of the invasion needs to be reiterated: that it followed a long and complex period of growing Soviet involvement in Afghanistan. In shaping this background, unforeseeable political developments in Afghanistan, and the frequently naive and shortsighted actions of successive Afghan rulers, played as much a part as did Soviet actions. However, changing regional and international circumstances, which reflected a marked impotence on the part of the United States, gave rise to opportunities for the Soviet Union. All this created a crisis in Afghanistan that led the Kremlin leaders to deem an invasion to be necessary to protect their perceived interests. Nonetheless, there is no evidence to suggest that the Soviet leadership, when it decided to invade, had any solid grasp of the magnitude of resistance from Afghan micro-societies that it was likely to encounter or of the way in which Islam could function as an ideology of resistance—let alone a considered strategy for coping with such difficulties. Yet concerted resistance was exactly what emerged, and it turned the Soviet occupation of Afghanistan into a nightmare.

Notes

1. Anthony Arnold, *Afghanistan's Two Party Communism: Parcham and Khalq* (Stanford: Hoover Institution Press, 1983) p.57.

2. Zalmay Khalilzad, *The Security of Southwest Asia* (New York: St. Martin's Press, 1984) p.17.

3. Abdul Samad Ghaus, *The Fall of Afghanistan: An Insider's Account* (McLean: Pergamon-Brassey's, 1988) pp.197-198.

4. 'Dlia tekh, kto voeval', *Krasnaia zvezda*, 12 October 1989, p.2.

5. See Marek Sliwinski, 'Afghanistan: The Decimation of a People', *Orbis*, vol.33, no.1, Winter 1989, pp.39-56.

6. Noor Ahmad Khalidi, *Demographic Profile of Afghanistan* (Research Note no.106, International Population Dynamics Program, Department of Demography, Research School of Social Sciences, The Australian National University, 14 December 1989) p.5.

7. See J. Bruce Amstutz, *Afghanistan: The First Five Years of Soviet Occupation* (Washington D.C.: National Defense University Press, 1986) p.38.

8. Quoted in Zalmay Khalilzad, 'Intervention in Afghanistan: Implications for the Security of Southwest Asia', in William L. Dowdy and Russell B. Trood (eds.), *The Indian Ocean: Perspectives on a Strategic Arena* (Durham: Duke University Press, 1985) pp.338-351, at p.339.

9. See S.P. Mel'gunov, *'Krasnyi terror' v Rossii* (Berlin: n.p., 1924).

10. Amnesty International, *Violations of Human Rights and Fundamental Freedoms in the Democratic Republic of Afghanistan* (London: ASA 11/04/79, September 1979) pp.B(i)-B(vi).

11. See Arnold, op.cit., pp.67-73.

12. Thomas J. Barfield, 'Weak Links on a Rusty Chain: Structural Weaknesses in Afghanistan's Provincial Government Administration', in M. Nazif Shahrani and Robert L. Canfield (eds.), *Revolutions & Rebellions in Afghanistan: Anthropological Perspectives* (Berkeley: Institute of International Studies, University of California, 1984) pp.170-183, at pp.179-182.

13. Henry S. Bradsher, 'Communism in Afghanistan', in Hafeez Malik (ed.), *Soviet-American Relations with Pakistan, Iran and Afghanistan* (London: Macmillan, 1987) pp.333-354, at p.339.

14. For a text of the platform, see Arnold, op.cit., pp.137-148.

15. Louis Dupree, *Red Flag Over the Hindu Kush: Part III: Rhetoric and Reforms, or Promises! Promises!* (American Universities Field Staff Reports: No. 23-Asia, 1980) p.6

16. For a very detailed discussion of the land reform package, see Latif Tabibi, 'Die afghanische Landreform von 1979: Ihre Vorgeschichte und Konsequenzen', unpublished doctoral dissertation, Freie Universität Berlin, 1981.

17. Bahram Tavakolian, 'Women and Socioeconomic Change among Sheikhanzai Nomads of Western Afghanistan', *The Middle East Journal*, vol.38 no.3, Summer 1984, pp.433-453, at p.452.

18. See Olivier Roy, 'What is Afghanistan Really Like?', *Dissent*, vol.28, no.1, Winter 1981, pp.47-54.

19. On the position of Afghan women, see Erika Knabe, 'Afghan Women: Does Their Role Change?', in Louis Dupree and Linette Albert (eds.), *Afghanistan in the 1970s* (New York: Praeger, 1974) pp.144-166; Isabelle Delloye, *Des Femmes d'Afghanistan* (Paris: Éditions Des Femmes, 1980); Fahima Rahimi, *Women in Afghanistan* (Liestal: Stiftung

Bibliotheca Afghanica, 1986); and Bernard Dupaigne (ed.), *Femmes en Afghanistan* (Paris: Amitié Franco-Afghane, 1986).

20. See Nancy Hatch Dupree, 'Revolutionary Rhetoric and Afghan Women', in M. Nazif Shahrani and Robert L. Canfield (eds.), *Revolutions & Rebellions in Afghanistan: Anthropological Perspectives* (Berkeley: Institute of International Studies, University of California, 1984) pp.306-340.

21. See Louis Dupree, 'Afghanistan: Problems of a Peasant-Tribal Society', in Louis Dupree and Linette Albert (eds.), *Afghanistan in the 1970s* (New York: Praeger, 1974) pp.1-12, at p.8.

22. David Busby Edwards, 'Origins of the Anti-Soviet Jihad', in Grant M. Farr and John G. Merriam (eds.), *Afghan Resistance: The Politics of Survival* (Boulder; Westview Press, 1987) pp.21-50, at pp.40-41.

23. Robert L. Canfield, 'Western Stakes in the Afghanistan War', *Central Asian Survey*, vol.4, no.1, 1985, pp.121-135, at p.128.

24. On the political potency of rumours, see Colin Seymour-Ure, 'Rumour and Politics', *Politics*, vol.17, no.2, November 1982, pp.1-9.

25. Richard F. Strand, 'The Evolution of Anti-Communist Resistance in Eastern Nuristan' in M. Nazif Shahrani and Robert L. Canfield (eds.), *Revolutions & Rebellions in Afghanistan: Anthropological Perspectives* (Berkeley: Institute of International Studies, University of California, 1984) pp.77-93.

26. Amstutz, op.cit., p.41. For recent works discussing the Herat uprising, see Olivier Roy, 'Naissance de la Résistance hérati', in Etienne Gille (ed.), *Herat ou l'art meurti* (Paris: Amitié Franco-Afghane, 1989) p.31, and Radek Sikorski, *Dust of the Saints: A Journey to Herat in Time of War* (London: Chatto & Windus, 1989).

27. Amstutz, op.cit., p.180.

28. On the functions of personality cults, see Graeme Gill, 'Personality Cult, Political Culture and Party Structure', *Studies in Comparative Communism*, vol.17, no.2, Summer 1984, pp.111-121.

29. See 'Our Revolution is Secure', *Asiaweek*, vol.4, no.45, 17 November 1978, p.40.

30. Amstutz, op.cit. , p.264.

31. Michael Barry, 'Répressions et guerre soviétiques', *Les Temps Modernes*, no.408-409, July-August 1980, pp. 171-234, at p.204.

32. See Amin Saikal, 'Soviet Policy toward Southwest Asia', *The Annals of the American Academy of Political and Social Science*, no.481, September 1985, pp.104-116, at p.109, and Anthony Hyman, 'Afghan intelligentsia 1978-81', *Index on Censorship*, no.2, 1982, pp.8-10, 13.

33. For a detailed discussion of the treaty, see Henry S. Bradsher, *Afghanistan and the Soviet Union* (Durham: Duke University Press, 1985) pp.97-98.

34. Ibid., p.97.

35. Amstutz, op.cit., p.265.

36. The posting of this list is reported by Bradsher, *Afghanistan and the Soviet Union*, p.120. Amin made evasive statements about the list to a Spanish correspondent (BBC *Summary of World Broadcasts*, Second Series, FE/6286/C1/1, 1 December 1979) and to an Indian journalist (BBC *Summary of World Broadcasts*, Second Series, FE/6297/C1/1, 14 December 1979 and Second Series FE/6301/C1/1, 19 December 1979).

37. Raymond L. Garthoff, *Détente and Confrontation: American-Soviet Relations from Nixon to Reagan* (Washington D.C.: The Brookings Institution, 1985) p.904.

38. Ibid., p.906. On the Nagy pledge, see Noel Barber, *Seven Days of Freedom: The Hungarian Uprising 1956* (London: Macmillan, 1974) pp.224-226.

39. For details, see Thomas T. Hammond, *Red Flag Over Afghanistan: The Communist Coup, the Soviet Invasion, and the Consequences* (Boulder: Westview Press, 1984) pp.86-88.

40. See Bradsher, *Afghanistan and the Soviet Union*, pp.122-123, 179.

41. This point is elaborated in William Maley, 'Social Dynamics and the Disutility of Terror: Afghanistan 1978-1989', in V. Shlapentokh, C. Vanderpool, T. Bushnell and J. Sundram (eds.), *State Organized Terror: The Case of Violent Internal Repression* (Boulder: Westview Press, forthcoming).

42. L.I. Brezhnev, *Izbrannye proizvedeniia* (Moscow: Politizdat, 1981) Vol.III, p.443.

43. Igor' Beliaev and Anatolii Gromyko, 'Tak my voshli v Afganistan', *Literaturnaia gazeta*, 20 September 1989, p.14.

44. See 'Kak prinimalos' reshenie', *Krasnaia zvezda*, 18 November 1989, pp.3-4. For a discussion of this and other recent sources, see Cynthia Roberts, *'Glasnost'* in Soviet Foreign Policy: Setting the Record Straight?', *Report on the USSR*, vol.1, no.50, 15 December 1989, pp.4-12, at pp.4-8.

45. Oleg Bogomolov, 'Kto zhe oshibalsia?', *Literaturnaia gazeta*, 16 March 1988.

46. See Sergei Belitsky, 'Authors of USSR's Afghan War Policy', *Report on the USSR*, vol.1, no.17, 28 April 1989, pp.11-12.

47. BBC *Summary of World Broadcasts*, SU/0674/A3/2, 29 January 1990.

48. Zbigniew Brzezinski, *Power and Principle: Memoirs of the National Security Adviser 1977-1981* (New York: Farrar, Strauss & Giroux, 1983) pp.426-428.

49. See Hammond, op.cit., chapter 12.

50. BBC *Summary of World Broadcasts*, SU/0453/A3/10, 8 May 1989.

51. See Hyman, *Afghanistan Under Soviet Domination, 1964-83*, pp.176-177.

52. For a recent discussion, see Etienne Gille, 'L'"appel"', *Les Nouvelles d'Afghanistan*, no.45, December 1989-January 1990, pp.22-24.

53. The most influential proponent of this interpretation was

undoubtedly George F. Kennan, author of the policy of 'containment' in the postwar period. See George F. Kennan, *The Nuclear Delusion: Soviet-American Relations in the Atomic Age* (London: Hamish Hamilton, 1984) pp.161-167.

54. See President Carter's remarks in *Keeping Faith: Memoirs of a President* (London: Collins, 1982) pp.471-472.

55. United Nations General Assembly, *Resolutions* 36/34, 18 November 1981; 37/37, 29 November 1982; 38/29, 23 November 1983; 39/13, 15 November 1984; 40/12, 13 November 1985; 41/33, 5 November 1986; 42/15, 10 November 1987.

4

The Opposition

The Soviet invasion of Afghanistan produced a prompt reaction from Afghan micro-societies. This reaction manifested itself in three distinct ways. First, some groups chose to go into exile. Second, other groups, directly and immediately vulnerable to the coercive forces which the USSR had introduced, found it necessary to reach some accommodation with the regime. Third, a large number of groups took up arms against the Karmal regime and its Soviet backers. In order to explain why different collections of individuals reacted in different ways it is necessary to give a brief outline of the strategy which the Soviets adopted to consolidate the position of their surrogates.

The Soviet Union's first move following the invasion was to reshuffle the PDPA leadership. The *Parchamis* who had been disgraced in 1978 were promptly restored to public office and a purge of *Khalqis* was carried out. The extent of this purge was limited by the need to protect communist networks, nurtured over a period of years by the *Khalqis*, in the armed forces; but it nonetheless removed from the scene a number of prominent figures who had been associated with Amin. Some of these people, most notably Amin's brother and nephew, were subsequently reported to have been tried and executed; a large number of others were imprisoned at Pul-i Charkhi.[1] Surviving members of Amin's family were also put in Pul-i Charkhi, allegedly for their own protection.[2] As for the survival of the regime, the Soviets adopted a long-term, low-cost strategy and hoped that within a short space of time they would be able to overcome the opposition forces which had brought the regimes of Amin and Taraki to such a debilitated condition.

Soviet strategy had two dimensions. The first consisted of a series of swift and sharp military operations against what were taken to be centres of political power.[3] These were designed to achieve two major goals. One was to assert Soviet control as quickly as possible over a number of critical spheres: (1) the PDPA leadership; (2) the disintegrating PDPA power structure and administrative and military apparatuses; (3) Afghanistan's major cities, particularly Kabul; (4) major military bases, especially the Bagram and Shindand bases near Kabul and Herat respectively, which were already to a large extent in the hands of Soviet advisers; and (5) key communications points and lines. The Soviets plainly considered this necessary to establish a structure for their nationwide command of Afghanistan, and well within the capability of their intended limited troop deployment.

The other goal was to stop the *Khalqis* and the *Parchamis* from continuing their disastrous factional fighting and therefore to bring about urgently-needed party unity within the PDPA under Karmal. The Soviets moved forcefully to reconstruct the administrative and security structures of both state and party. For this purpose they brought in thousands more civilian advisers, many of them Soviet Tajiks (who share a common language and physical appearance with many Dari speakers of Afghanistan) to man the PDPA administrative and security apparatuses. They renamed the secret police the *Khadamati-i ittila'at-i dawlati* (Government Information Service, known by its acronym KHAD) and charged it with the task of serving as a central instrument of the PDPA-Soviet rule under the charge of the *Parchami* Dr Najibullah. Commanded and assisted directly by several KGB operatives, Najibullah embarked upon the transforming of KHAD into a ubiquitous secret police. Where AGSA and its successor KAM had relied primarily on the application of direct coercion, KHAD was to be deployed not only to penetrate the society wherever and in whatever way possible, but also to watch party members and activists at all levels.

The Soviets were for the most part content to leave most of the smaller towns and countryside either in the hands of, or wide open to, opposition forces and to concentrate on pressing the claim that the PDPA was the only legitimate party in Afghanistan. Nonetheless, a number of substantial operations *were* carried out in rural areas in the months following the invasion,[4] and these pointed to the second dimension of Soviet strategy. Soviet forces were deployed in such a way that Soviet personnel, backed impressively with heavy weaponry (including T62 tanks, heavy field guns, MIG 21 and 23 and Sukhoi fighter/bombers and the MI-8 HIP and MI-24 HIND helicopter gunships), could make their operational presence felt extensively within both urban and rural areas, and could adopt an offensive posture for limited operations whenever necessary. The apparent Soviet expectation was that careful use of the USSR's rather limited military power could deter the urban population from rising in opposition, dissuade rural opponents from attacking Soviet-dominated urban centres and strategic military and communication points and lines, and hinder outside support for opposition elements, particularly that from and through Pakistan and Iran.

This strategy was linked to an intensive campaign of agitation and propaganda, the objectives of which were to market Karmal's rule, and their own invasion, to the Afghan people and to counter mounting regional and global criticisms of their Afghan adventure. Karmal and Soviet spokesmen pledged their deep respect for the Afghan people's long-held traditions and Islamic faith and promised the muting of many of the policies introduced by Taraki and Amin, including the land reform proposals. They committed themselves to beginning a new 'stage of the April 1978 revolution', directed towards the achievement of 'national freedom and prosperity'. They thus sought to present themselves as forces of liberation and defenders of the Afghan people.[5]

In this campaign the Soviet Union enjoyed the support of only one democracy—India. Its public position was clearly outlined in a speech by the Indian representative, Brajesh Mishra, at the Emergency Session of the United Nations General Assembly on 11 January 1980. The Indian spokesman, in a carefully worded declaration, stated that 'the Soviet Government has assured our Government that its troops went to Afghanistan at the request of the Afghan Government, a request that was first made by President Amin on 26 December 1979 and repeated by his successor on 28 December 1979, and we have been further assured that the Soviet troops will be withdrawn when requested to do so by the Afghan Government. We have no reason to doubt such assurances, particularly from a friendly country like the Soviet Union, with which we have many close ties.'[6] The Indian representative even criticised the General Assembly's discussing the Soviet invasion, and abstained from supporting the resolution condemning the Soviet action which was overwhelmingly adopted on the votes of other member states. While Indian spokesmen subsequently backed away from the candour of this declaration, the thrust of India's policy remained one of support for the PDPA regime and hostility towards the Afghan resistance.[7]

The Soviet leadership may have hoped that once helped to its feet by these manoeuvres the PDPA regime would possess sufficient administrative and military capabilities of its own to carry out most of the responsibilities of effectively governing Afghanistan. This would have allowed the Soviets rapidly to streamline their forces into a supporting role for the PDPA and to withdraw most of them once any opposition forces were exhausted and the stability and continuity of PDPA rule was ensured. In such circumstances, Soviet civilians, and military and security advisers would be able to guide and control the PDPA's rule from behind the scenes without the presence of substantial combat forces in Afghanistan—a position similar to that in a number of Warsaw Pact countries. Thus, the success of the Soviet military campaign and the consequent Soviet ability to achieve its basic political objective were linked to and conditioned upon one another.

Popular reactions

The Soviet strategy was flawed from the outset because it did not properly take into account the precise character of the opposition to communist rule which had emerged in Afghanistan following the April 1978 coup and which grew in dramatic ways in the wake of the invasion itself. The Soviet diagnosis reflected a simplistic perception of the distribution of social and political power in the countryside and a crucial misunderstanding of the nature of state-society relations in the country as a whole. In particular, the Soviet strategy appeared to attach little weight to the binding force which Islam could provide for the various

Islamic micro-societies, for whom it could function as an effective ideological focus for anti-Soviet and anti-communist resistance.

To the outside world, the most palpable way in which Afghans reacted to the Soviet invasion was by quitting the country. In December 1979 there were 402,100 registered Afghan refugees in Pakistan. By July 1980 this figure had risen to over a million and by January 1982 to over 2.5 million.[8] For the most part, these were rural Pushtuns from areas reasonably close to the border with Pakistan, who could leave at relatively low cost. However, there were also urban dwellers of diverse backgrounds who had left in the face of political persecution.[9] Iran, too, received a large number of refugees, many of them adherents of Afghanistan's Shiite minority. These external refugee populations, especially that in Pakistan, entrenched the internationalisation of the Afghanistan conflict. Public international agencies such as the Office of the United Nations High Commissioner for Refugees, the World Health Organisation and the World Food Program all became involved in the supply of sustenance to the refugees. Furthermore, the refugee camps provided a basis for a sustained resistance movement, as rural opponents deposited their families in Pakistan before returning to Afghanistan to combat the regime.[10]

In urban areas the invasion met with mixed reaction. There were a number of notable demonstrations in Kabul protesting the presence of Soviet forces, most dramatically on 21-22 February and 28-29 April 1980, when school and university students took to the streets.[11] However, these were suppressed with great ferocity and did not escalate into a mass popular movement of the kind which contributed to the downfall of figures such as the Shah of Iran. Soviet forces were not in the least inhibited by ties of kinship or identity from using against civilians the full force of the arsenal at their disposal and this successfully deterred a large number of urban-dwellers from active involvement in attempts to overthrow the regime. Nonetheless, once resistance in the streets had been stamped out pockets of resistance continued to harrass the regime and its officials. Such groups were behind the assassinations in July 1980 of Wali Yusufi, deputy minister of Higher Education, and in April 1981 of Brigadier Ghulam Sakhi, deputy head of KHAD, and Sharafuddin Sharaf, commander of the Revolutionary Defence Militia. As time went by, these urban cells increasingly developed links with other organised resistance groups.

The reaction to the Soviet invasion which in the long run was to thwart the USSR's objectives was *organised, armed opposition*. In the previous chapter, we noted that before the end of 1978 resistance to the PDPA regime had already broken out. This was not in any sense an *organised* resistance; rather, in various parts of the country outraged individuals and local groups reacted similarly to similar provocations. They resembled what Almond and Powell have called *anomic* or *nonassociational* interest groups, marked by 'the intermittent pattern of articulation, the absence of an organized procedure for establishing the nature and means of articulation, and the lack of continuity in internal structure.'[12] Nonetheless, even before the invasion, various more structured opposition groups had begun to take shape, although their activities were initially of limited military impact as they had not succeeded in establishing coherent military organisations or effective links with groups coalescing within Afghanistan. These groups came to be known as *Mujahideen* ('Warriors in the Way of Islam') and were sustained by distinctive attributes of Islam in Afghanistan.

The following parties[13] in time came to be the most important. The *Hezb-i Islami Afghanistan* (Islamic Party of Afghanistan) was a well-organised Pushtun group, with a rigidly disciplined internal structure. It came into existence before the Soviet invasion, but after initial splits within its leadership ranks it fell under the control of a young, dogmatic, radical Islamic activist, Gulbuddin Hekmatyar. It upheld a puritanical Islamic approach to its military operations and political ambitions. Its goal was to establish an 'Islamic government', although the lines on which it would be structured were unclear. Hekmatyar was a controversial figure. He had been a student activist at Kabul University from the mid-1960s but failed to complete a degree when he was imprisoned after being accused of involvement in the death of a student, Saidal Sokhandan, associated with the Maoist organisation *Shuli Javid*.[14] Fighting units associated with the group were largely concentrated in Afghanistan's Ghilzai Pushtun-dominated eastern and southeastern provinces, although small *Hezb* enclaves survived in the north. The significance of Hekmatyar stemmed rather from his integral relationship with Pakistan's military establishment, with which he had been in contact since at least 1974.[15] The party's extreme dogmatism was publicly denounced by the Soviets, but also viewed with great caution by other *Mujahideen* groups.

A second party, also called the *Hezb-i Islami Afghanistan*, came into existence as a breakaway faction from the above. While similar in ideological and political outlook, as well as ethnic composition, to Hekmatyar's *Hezb-i Islami*, it was led by an elderly traditional theologian, Mawlawi Mohammad Younis Khalis. It drew support from traditionalist clergy and although organisationally much looser than Hekmatyar's party it proved militarily much more successful, largely because of the skill of its two main field commanders, Abdul Haq (in and around Kabul) and Jalaluddin Haqqani (in Paktia province). Abdul Haq paid successful visits to certain Western countries, particularly Britain where he was received by Prime Minister Margaret Thatcher.

The *Jamiat-i Islam-i Afghanistan* (Islamic Society of Afghanistan) shared basic Islamic goals with the above two, but differed from them not only in its ethnic composition but also to some extent in its political orientation. Its followers were predominantly Dari speakers, including many intellectuals, and it was quite moderate in its political behaviour. It was led by one of the original founders of the Islamist movement of the late 1960s, Burhanuddin Rabbani, a former professor in the Faculty of Theology of Kabul University. While well organised both politically and militarily, it was particularly strong in northern and western provinces of Afghanistan. Ahmad Shah Massoud (in the Panjsher Valley north of Kabul) and Ismael Khan (in Herat Province) emerged as its most able field commanders.

The *Ittihad-i Islami Afghanistan* (Islamic Unity of Afghanistan) was a minute Pushtun-dominated group, which derived its influence primarily from its leader, Abdul Rasul Sayyaf. A relative of Hafizullah Amin, he had obtained a graduate degree from Al-Azhar University in Cairo before being appointed as an associate professor (*pohanmal*) in the Faculty of Theology at Kabul University. Imprisoned under Daoud and throughout the period of rule by Taraki and Amin, he moved to Pakistan in early 1980. He was the recipient of lavish funds from several conservative Arab states, particularly Saudi Arabia, and was reputed to be a promoter of the puritanical theological school of

Sheikh al-Wahhab, although this particular school historically had no following within Afghanistan.

The *Mahaz-i Milli Islami Afghanistan* (National Islamic Front of Afghanistan) was led by Sayid Ahmad Gailani, *pir* of the *Qadiriyya* Sufi brotherhood. It drew support from adherents in different parts of the country, although most importantly in the south and southwest. Gailani had been *pir* since 1947 and enjoyed the loyalty of a number of influential tribal leaders. The *Mahaz* also proved to be the chosen party of many supporters of the old royal family and Gailani maintained close links with Zahir Shah.

The leaders of two other parties were also close to Zahir Shah. The *Harakat-i Enqilaab-i Islami Afghanistan* (Islamic Revolutionary Movement of Afghanistan) was particularly strong in central and northeast Afghanistan, with its main base of support being in the Ghazni province, southeast of Kabul. It was led by an Islamic traditionalist, Mawlawi Mohammad Nabi Mohammadi, and secured substantial support from the supporters of traditional Islam. Mohammadi had been a member of the *Wolesi Jirga* during the constitutional period and had been involved in at least one widely publicised clash with Babrak Karmal.

The *Jabha-i Milli-i Nijati Afghanistan* (Afghan National Liberation Front) revolved around a traditionally influential Islamic family under the leadership of Professor Sibghatullah Mojadiddi. It had followers among both Pushtu and Dari speakers, who operated in different parts of southern and eastern Afghanistan. The Mojadiddi family, which had played an important role in the overthrow of King Amanullah, had been targetted for attack even before the Soviet invasion: on 18 January 1979 Mohammad Ibrahim Mojadiddi, a prominent Sufi known by the title *Hazrat-i Shor Bazaar*, had been arrested with twenty male relatives ranging in age from 19 to 65, and only one was ever seen again. Professor Mojadiddi was a theologian of some distinction who had headed the Islamic Centre of Copenhagen after a colourful early career which included a term of imprisonment during Daoud's first premiership following a charge that he had plotted to assassinate N.S. Khrushchev.[16]

The Shia resistance in Afghanistan, largely but not exclusively located in the Hazarajat region, formed a special case. The first resistance organisation to emerge was the *Shura-i Ettefaq*

(Council of Unity), established in September 1979. Headed by Sayid Ali Beheshti, it gave voice to the traditional concerns of the Hazaras. Their history was an unhappy one of being all too frequently victims of marginalisation and discrimination, a result in part of their distinctive physical appearances and rituals. The *Shura* in its functioning resembled not a political party but rather a local indigenous administration.

A second Shi'ite group was the *Harakat-i Islami* (Movement of Islam), headed by Sheikh Assef Mohseni. It contained both Hazaras and non-Hazaras and was initially sympathetic to the young Iranian revolution, deriving inspiration from Iran's new Islamic regime under Ayatollah Ruhollah Khomeini in much the same way as many Hazaras had been inclined to do even before the revolution, during the rule of the Shah. However, its sympathies wilted over time, especially as the Iranian regime threw its weight behind two radical groups which willingly accepted direct instructions from Tehran. The first of these was the *Sazman-i Nasr* (Organisation of Victory); the second was the *Sepah-i Pasdaran* (Protective Guards). These gradually were augmented by other groups under Iranian sway.[17] Iran's approach to the Afghan resistance proved utterly sectarian; only Shi'ite groups were accorded logistical support from Iranian territory, something which proved immensely inconvenient for Sunni groups such as the *Jamiat* with strong support in western Afghanistan.

The Question of 'Islamic Fundamentalism'

Western analyses of these parties all too frequently categorised them simply as either 'fundamentalist' (the groups led by Hekmatyar, Khalis, Rabbani, and Sayyaf) or 'moderate' (the groups led by Mohammadi, Gailani, and Mojadiddi). This crude approach oversimplified the bases of division between the different groups. It is true that the *Mujahideen* were by no means ideologically homogeneous. But homogeneity was hardly to be expected, for a number of reasons. First, the fundamental schism within Islam, between Sunnis and Shia, was reflected in the composition of the Afghan population, as noted in Chapter Two. Second, even within the dominant Sunni Muslim population of

Afghanistan, numerous schools of thought have flourished at different times. Many of these schools originated from within the larger Sunni domain and only some of them from within Afghanistan itself. But in most cases the interaction of these strands of thought with local culture and traditions produced distinctive patterns of thought and practice, similar but not identical to thought and practice elsewhere in the Islamic World.[18]

This interaction has led to the emergence of three broad strands of Sunni Islam in Afghanistan. These one might label *intellectual* Islam, *Sufi* Islam, and *village* Islam. Of course, within these categories too there have been important distinctions.

Intellectual Islam reflects a desire to justify Islam in *historical* and *intellectual* terms. It has had a place in the territory of modern Afghanistan since the first arrival of Islam in the eighth century. But for many centuries it remained the preserve of the courts of various rulers whose writ held sway. In these circles it lay at the heart of an immensely rich culture, marked by elaborate schools of theology, cosmogony, and eschatology. The pronouncements of Muslim intellectuals frequently served to legitimate the rule of particular dominant individuals or families. The ruler was seen as God's principal vicegerent on earth, and thereby as worthy of obedience from his subject population. It has only been since the late nineteenth century that intellectual Islam has provided a basis for criticism of the state and the demand for reform rather than the rationalisation of the *status quo*. A decisive figure in the modern emergence of this critical dimension of intellectual Islam was the reformer Sayyid Jamaluddin al-Afghani (1838-1897), who thought it necessary to reform the Muslim world by ridding it of foreign domination while enabling it to adapt to conditions of modernity. To this end, he made first use of the notion of 'Islamic socialism', seeing it as entailed by Islam itself.[19]

Echoes of this kind of thought were to be found in the Islamic reformism of Mahmoud Tarzi and his 'Young Afghan' followers. However, its contemporary manifestations owe less to al-Afghani and Tarzi than to radical thinkers who came to prominence in the Middle East after the First World War, and whose elaboration of a theology which challenged the fundamental character of the secularist state found willing listeners amongst Afghan Muslim intellectuals in the 1950s and 1960s. These radical thinkers included the Egyptian essayists Hassan al-Bana and Sayyid Qutb, and the Indian-Pakistani writer Sayyid Abdul Ala Maududi. Their Afghan followers—a number of whom had studied at the Islamic al-Azhar University in Cairo—included Dr Ghulam Mohammad Niazi and Burhanuddin Rabbani.[20] These people laid the foundations for an intellectual Islamic movement, partly embodied in an organisation called the *Jamiat-i Islami*, to serve as a counterweight to communist ideas to which Afghanistan had become increasingly vulnerable through its growing ties with the Soviet Union after 1955. If these individuals are to be given a label, it should be that of Islamist.[21]

It is misleading to characterise the Islamists as 'fundamentalists'. First, while firmly believing in the eternity and totality of the central principles of Islam and of Prophet Mohammad's traditions (*sunna*), which formed the bases for the original ideal Islamic society (*ummah*) that Mohammad set up in compliance with the Qur'an, they do not hold the Islamic principles and *sunna* as frozen in time in their historical applicability.[22] Second, the label 'fundamentalist' is not an illuminating one, either in general[23] or in the Afghan context.[24] It obscures much more than it clarifies. As Roy has pointed out, in a country like Afghanistan, 'where daily life revolves around the practice of Islam and customary law in the non-tribal zones is impregnated by the *shari'at*, fundamentalism does not mark a great departure from traditionalism'.[25]

Sufi Islam, which is viewed in certain Western circles as a species of mysticism,[26] contrasts sharply with intellectual Islam in both the extent of its intellectual foundations and its methodology. Sufism is a highly venerable tradition, rich in culture and highly organised, and its doctrines and practices have not changed markedly since the different Sufi brotherhoods took shape. Sufism emphasises esoteric or intuitive revelation, sought by an individual under the instruction of a spiritual mentor or *pir*, who can thereby acquire a considerable following.[27] To the Sufi, the very attempt to justify Islam in intellectual terms is misconceived; revelation to the Sufi must be esoteric or intuitive rather than a consequence of the rational application of the mind. In practice, Sufism is a spiritual rather than social doctrine, concerned above all with the relationship between the individual and God, rather than with the implementation of a particular model of social organisation. For this reason, Sufis have frequently been anathematised by religious radicals who see Sufism as an unconstructive retreat from the tasks which the Qur'an sets for a good Muslim. Nonetheless, Sufi brotherhoods have not historically proved to be passive in the face of assault from instrumentalities of power, whether indigenously Afghan or external; on the contrary, they have often provided the basis for relentless opposition to any encroachments upon their style of religious practice. In this sense, at least, they have had much in common with the Islamists.

Village Islam justifies Islam in traditional terms. It is by far the most ubiquitous form of Islam in Afghanistan and is reflected in the rituals of the local prayer-leader (*mullah*), who is not a member of any organised hierarchy and often can claim only the remotest intellectual acquaintance with any elaborate schools of Islamic theology. Sufism is influential at the village level in some areas, but so are pre-Islamic beliefs such as the fear of the Evil Eye. Village Islam has historically been vulnerable not only to manipulation by the state but also to manipulation by forces either opposed to the state or simply pursuing their own interests. Apostasy is defined in terms of departure from *ritual*,[28] and it was to a considerable extent the indifference of PDPA cadres to the rituals of village Islam which sowed the seeds of their problems.

Using these broad categories to identify certain influences or tendencies within the leaderships of the Sunni resistance parties, one can say that Rabbani and Sayyaf reflect most markedly the influence of intellectual Islam, followed by Mojadiddi. Hekmatyar has also been influenced by the radical dimension of intellectual Islam, although he has given it an authoritarian interpretation which contrasts with the more moderate approach of Rabbani and the *Jamiat*, and has exploited it to provide an ideological justification for his pursuit of personal ambition. On the other hand, Gailani more than the others derives his authority from Sufism, while Khalis and Mohammadi have many followers from amongst the practitioners of village Islam.

The Broader Resistance

While all these groups—Sunni and Shiite—comprised the organised components of the Afghan resistance, the resistance itself reached far deeper into the micro-societies of Afghanistan than could organisations of this type.[29] The resistance was a diverse, grassroots phenomenon with many different components: the exile and internal parties we have already mentioned; commanders associated with resistance parties; local commanders; local committees, and agents within the communist regime. With the Soviet invasion it tended to shed the anomic, nonassociational characteristics which marked the earliest outbreaks of resistance, but the potential even for resistance of this kind remained as a firm reinforcement of other forms of resistance.

Some commanders were satisfied to remain entirely independent of outside organisations. A number of these were simply opportunists who adopted either hostility to the regime or alliance with it as their interests dictated. Esmatullah Muslim was the most famous commander in this category.[30] However, many commanders within Afghanistan developed ties with one (or more) of the exile parties. In some cases this was a product of identification with the goals of the party; thus, most Sunni parties enjoyed at least some presence in most Sunni-populated areas, even if in many cases the presence was hardly more than nominal. In other cases it resulted from ethnic or tribal attachments. For example, the *Jamiat*, led by an ethnic Tajik, proved particularly popular in the north of Afghanistan where the proportion of Tajiks in the population was relatively high. Similarly, the *Hezb-i Islami* of Khalis became well entrenched in certain Ghilzai Pushtun tribes in the south and southeast.

In still other cases, affiliations were predominantly or entirely prudential, a product of the need for commanders to obtain access to externally-supplied military equipment, the distribution of which within Afghanistan was in the hands of the leaderships of the exile parties. Those commanders who were most heavily motivated by this kind of consideration often proved adept at shifting between parties to maximise their takings, creating the impression that commanders were substantially beyond the control of the Peshawar-based leaderships. There was undoubtedly a considerable amount of truth in this impression, not the least because problems of communication meant that day-to-day decisions inevitably fell to commanders to take. Commanders, furthermore, were isolated from the hothouse atmosphere of *emigré* politics upon which personal animosities and antagonisms notoriously thrive. Nonetheless, it is interesting to note that those commanders who developed the greatest reputations for military prowess were as a rule those who maintained a consistent affiliation with a single party—such as Ahmad Shah Massoud and Ismael Khan of the *Jamiat*, and Abdul Haq and Mawlawi Jalaluddin Haqqani of the *Hezb-i Islami* of Khalis.

The resistance commanders differed in significant ways from traditional leaderships in rural Afghanistan; hence they were not susceptible to techniques of manipulation by a central regime which might have proved effective in other circumstances. Even before the Soviet invasion, the regime of Taraki and then Amin had embarked on what Bennigsen and Lemercier-Quelquejay have called 'the slaughter of the tribal aristocracy'.[31] This left a vacuum which was filled by younger, more highly educated Afghans, who were much better equipped to mount effective campaigns of resistance against a central regime. The massacres of 1978-79 also gave rise to obligations under various customary codes to effect revenge, obligations which could not honourably be subordinated to mere concerns of interest.

Soviet Strategy Embattled

These resistance forces proved equal to the task of thwarting the USSR's strategy, which soon ran into trouble. This rapidly became evident, not so much because anything went drastically wrong with the Soviet military campaign, but because the Soviet military commitment (and Soviet strategy for its use) proved inadequate to achieve the Soviet leadership's basic *political* objective. This in turn placed the Soviet forces under increasing strain. The Soviets could not enlist the support of a large number of the *Khalqis*, who could not credit that Amin had invited the Soviet invasion and who felt betrayed and humiliated by the Soviets' killing of their leader and wresting power from them in favour of the *Parchamis.* The Soviets' action intensely inflamed the already deep-seated *Khalqi-Parchami* feud, which according to the cultural code of the Pushtuns could be resolved only by bloodshed and the elimination of one side. This resulted in hundreds of relatively experienced *Khalqi* administrators and field officers either taking up arms against the regime or working from inside the PDPA administration to undermine the *Parchamis* and the Soviets, and in many more leaving for exile abroad. Prompted by their common Islamic religion and patriotic feelings, Afghan people in both urban centres and rural areas viewed Karmal as worse than Amin, and in collaboration with the resistance began to mount formidable ideological and physical opposition.

It is instructive in this respect to contrast the failure of Soviet tactics in Afghanistan with the success of those which were used by the Soviet Army in the 1920s and early 1930s against the *Basmachi* movement in Central Asia. This movement was not organisationally unified and at its peak, in 1921-1922, appeared to have commanded the support of no more than 10,000 combatants.[32] Islam, while undoubtedly a key factor in the *Basmachi* movement, was defused by a strategy of elite cooptation, which constituted a psychological blow from which the *Basmachis* never recovered.[33] Nonetheless, many refugees fled to Afghanistan from Turkestan and Kazakhstan as resistance in Central Asia was suppressed, and these and their descendants were, at the time of the Soviet invasion, among the most anti-Soviet elements of the Afghan population. In Afghanistan, the Soviet Union had no success in coopting significant elites and confronted a range of micro-societies which were united by detestation of communism and backed by important outside forces—backing of a kind that the *Basmachi* movement never managed to attract.

The Afghan *Mujahideen* massively outnumbered the *Basmachi* and showed much greater skill both in waging effective *valley-mountain guerilla warfare* and in harassing Soviet forces in cities and other strategic places. In this form of guerilla warfare the *Mujahideen* often exploited Afghanistan's rugged terrain to attack Soviet forces and convoys passing through valleys or mountain passes. Perhaps no *Mujahideen* commander exemplified this as well as Ahmad Shah Massoud. He largely succeeded in turning the Panjsher Valley—located strategically 95 kilometres north of Kabul between northern and southern Afghanistan and on the main Soviet supply lines through the famous Salang Pass—into one of the *Mujahideen*'s strongholds, virtually a state within a state. He also largely succeeded in using his Panjsher powerbase to develop a unified command in most of the northern provinces bordering the Soviet Union. He was ultimately able to establish a 'Supervisory Council of the North' (*Shura-i Nazar*), which brought together individual commanders from the northern provinces within a well-defined political and military structure. From 1980, the Soviet-PDPA forces launched numerous massive operations against Panjsher, but with little success.[34] In 1983 they found themselves in so desperate a position that the Soviets had to negotiate a six-month ceasefire directly with Massoud—a ceasefire which Massoud skilfully exploited to coordinate bigger operations afterwards.

The Kremlin was not entirely successful in weathering either regional or global criticisms, although it managed largely to override the limited and ineffectual political and economic sanctions levelled over its invasion.[35] The ability of commanders such as Massoud to maintain their operations was enhanced by the supply of military hardware from various outside sources. *Mujahideen* access to such supplies limited still further Soviet performances inside Afghanistan. The martial law regime of General Zia ul-Haq of Pakistan felt acutely intimidated by the Soviet invasion of Afghanistan and was prepared to provide haven for *Mujahideen* leaders and to permit the transit through its territory of supplies for resistance commanders—although it naturally moved to ensure that its closest associates amongst the *Mujahideen* leaders, notably Hekmatyar, received the lion's share.[36] Pakistan was able to exploit its position as a 'frontline state' to secure a six-year economic and military aid package of approximately $3 billion.[37] Apart from Pakistan, the major external supporters of the resistance were the USA, China, and certain Middle Eastern states. Virtually for the first time in the history of US-Soviet relations, Washington found itself in a position to help cause the Soviets humiliation in a Third World country. While President Carter shaped the USA's initial response to the Soviet invasion, it was his successor President Reagan who was best placed to devise a workable aid

programme for the Afghan resistance. His administration moved
to coordinate (via the US Central Intelligence Agency) a delivery
of arms from the international market to the *Mujahideen*,
estimated by various sources to range in value in different years
from $30 million to $80 million up to 1985.[38] The Chinese
leadership, fearing 'Soviet encirclement',[39] saw a parallel
between the Soviet invasion of Afghanistan and Soviet support
for Vietnam in its occupation of Kampuchea. China also had poor
relations with Soviet-leaning India, with which it had earlier
fought a brief border war. It drew on this complex of factors to
harden its position against the USSR, increasing its support for
India's regional   opponent Pakistan and maintaining and
strengthening its rapprochement with the US.[40] Finally, a number
of anti-communist but oil-rich Muslim Arab states, led by Saudi
Arabia, moved to give generous financial help.

The overall result was that despite the fact that the
Afghanistan crisis lost much of its initial urgency in world politics,
the Afghan people's resistance in general increased in magnitude
and effectiveness, and continued to prevent the Soviets from
achieving even their basic political objective. The Soviets'
fundamental problem appeared to be their inability to secure in
Kabul a workable PDPA government with an effective
administrative-military machine. Karmal and his top colleagues
did not trust one another and the PDPA remained bloodily
factionalised. The colourful career of Abdul Qadir, one of the
most prominent figures involved in the 1978 coup, illustrated this
rather clearly. Rescued from disgrace by the Soviet invasion, he
was wounded by a *Khalqi* gunman on 14 June 1980.[41] He
recovered to become Defence minister in September 1982 but in
May 1983 had to be hospitalised after being bashed by his deputy,
Major-General Khalilullah, former commander of the Kabul City
Garrison.[42] In July 1984 the word spread that Qadir had shot
Major Aslam Watanjar, then the Communications minister,[43] and
on 3 December 1984 it was announced that Qadir had been
replaced by the army chief of staff, Brigadier Nazer
Mohammad.[44] A 1985 source reported Qadir under arrest.[45] In
addition to the stresses imposed by continuing *Khalq-Parcham*
rivalry, the regime's frail governmental structures were riddled
with inefficiency and corruption, and to an extent were
penetrated by the agents of the *Mujahideen*.

The Soviet failure in the political realm was reflected in the Soviets' military position. It forced them increasingly to take over not only administrative duties but also military operations. The Soviet strategists appeared to realise that neither the Soviet forces' initial defensive posture of holding onto their original gains and fighting only when attacked, nor their extensive use of heavily equipped motorised troops in the face of the *Mujahideen*'s successful guerilla warfare, could take the Soviets very far. They consequently engaged in a step-by-step process of changing their mainly defensive campaign of pacification into a predominantly offensive one. While replacing some of their regular troops with special counter-insurgency units, which from 1983 came to include the élite *Spetznaz* commando units, the Soviet forces precipitately resorted to 'seek-and-destroy' missions against the opposition wherever possible. They maximised their firepower and applied extreme coercion, ranging from violently and brutally confiscating property and rounding up people for military service and interrogation under torture, to burning crop fields and blanket bombing of towns and villages. Atrocities and human rights violations became routine, and were documented not only by academic specialists[46] and Amnesty International,[47] but by Professor Felix Ermacora, appointed as Special Rapporteur on Human Rights in Afghanistan by the UN Human Rights Commission.[48] This process was intensified from early 1984, with an unprecedented escalation of Soviet firepower. The prime objectives were not only to force urban dwellers into acquiescence but also to terrorise, starve out[49] and depopulate the actual and suspected opposition-held towns and valleys in order to deprive the *Mujahideen* of their popular sanctuaries and means of livelihood, and to block their supply and infiltration routes.

However, the Soviet offensive operations, which intensified over time, proved to be as unsuccessful and counterproductive as the earlier Soviet efforts. Although the operations impressively projected Soviet fire-power and ability to cause mounting civilian casualties and property destruction, they were unable to break the back of the resistance and subdue popular opposition in general. They were necessarily in proportion to the Soviet troop-strength and therefore of limited value in stamping out the resistance. As Moscow deemed it politically and militarily expedient (presumably in relation to Soviet resources and priorities, and regional-global circumstances) to keep its troops at a steady level of about 120,000, the Soviet forces were unable to cope with the types of operations for which they were not originally deployed.

With the war engulfing all of the 29 provinces of Afghanistan, which the Soviets in 1980 divided into seven military zones, the Soviet forces had to deal with the *Mujahideen*'s frequent attacks from different strongholds in the mountains, valleys and cities throughout the country, forcing them to spread out too thinly. They proved incapable of undertaking sustained operations and holding territories for a reasonably long time in order to force the *Mujahideen* out of their sanctuaries and prevent their returning to them permanently. For example, in early 1986 the Soviets destroyed two important *Mujahideen* bases on the border with Pakistan. One was in Barikot and the other in Zhawar. The latter was a model base, on which the *Mujahideen* prided themselves. However, within a few months the *Mujahideen* were able to return to these bases and rebuild them.[50]

Meanwhile, the Soviets' and PDPA's killing of many thousands of civilians and destruction of their property had a dual effect. On the one hand, these tactics were very damaging to the structure of a significant number of micro-societies. Families were the social unit most dramatically affected, but in many areas the effects cut much deeper, breaking up traditional communities and authority patterns upon which the stability of various micro-societies had been based. On the other hand, the behaviour of the Soviet forces and their regime associates provided a common foe against which discrete surviving groups could unite, or at least cooperate. The immense hatred for the Soviets and their surrogates among the Afghans contributed markedly to the functioning of the resistance. Many individual Afghans were sustained by the belief that they did not have much more to lose and had to defend their religion, honour, land and way of life as a means of upholding their historical pride and gaining Islamic martyrdom in the world hereafter. They became increasingly ferocious and revengeful, to the extent even of mercilessly stoning Russians and their collaborators and mining their bodies.[51]

The material costs of the war for the Soviets rose sharply

towards the end of 1986 to an average of more than \$15 million a day,[52] with some sources asserting the loss of one plane of some kind or another almost daily.[53] This was so partly because of the improved anti-aircraft defence system of the *Mujahideen*, with the delivery to them of American Stinger missiles at the rate of 20 a month from mid-1986 and 100 a month from April 1987, and a number of British Blowpipe missiles.[54] The *Mujahideen's* successful integration of these shoulder-fired missiles into an air-defence system made up of missiles, machine guns and light cannon dramatically reduced their vulnerability to the intensified air-power on which the Soviet-PDPA forces heavily relied for their wide range of operations. There were also frequent reports of a steady drop in the morale and discipline of the Soviet troops. Cases reported among them ranged from drug addiction and stealing, looting and selling weapons to the *Mujahideen* for the purpose of buying drugs and other commodities, to indiscriminate beating and shooting of civilians in broad daylight—all reflections of boredom and frustration.

Moreover, with the costs of the war mounting, the Soviet involvement grew to be unpopular with the Soviet public, despite Moscow's massive propaganda that its troops in Afghanistan had been fighting heroically to defend the Afghan people against 'external, imperialist aggression'. Although it was extremely difficult to tap the extent of the Soviet public's displeasure, numerous eyewitness accounts and occasional Soviet media and press reports indicated it to have been quite considerable. An unofficial poll conducted by human rights activists in Moscow in 1984 found that 62 per cent of respondents did not support the war and, more significantly, that 41 per cent of Communist Party members did not either.[55] An opinion survey published in mid-1985 suggested that only one quarter of the Soviet adult urban population approved of Soviet policy in Afghanistan or expressed 'confidence in the eventual success of official policy'.[56] And in 1987 a poll in Moscow carried out jointly by the Sociological Research Institute of the USSR Academy of Sciences and the French polling organisation IPSOS found that 53 per cent of respondents favoured a total withdrawal of Soviet troops from Afghanistan.[57] These findings were reinforced in a number of other studies, which emphasised the particular intensity of opposition in the Central Asian and Baltic republics of the

USSR.[58]

There is no doubt that the leaderships of the seven main Sunni groups suffered from personal rivalries and ideological, ethnic and linguistic differences. But this did not necessarily affect the fighting capacity and operational unity of the combat *Mujahideen* inside Afghanistan. A number of important factors accounted for this. First, it is certainly true that diversity, not unity, and Islamic spiritual strength and moral cohesion, not technological sophistication, have historically underpinned much of the Afghan people's resistance to outside imposition. However, after years of fighting a world power, the *Mujahideen* at all levels found it necessary to cooperate considerably in their struggle, for the sake of survival and continuation of the resistance. Second, whatever the nature and extent of squabbles among the leaders of the *Mujahideen* groups in Pakistan, the *Mujahideen* field commanders and their unit guerillas throughout the period of Soviet occupation became experienced and skilled not only in the art of combat and maintenance of social support but also in the ability to adjust to changing enemy tactics. They were not as politicised as their Pakistan-based leaders and were geographically remote from them. For the *Mujahideen* within Afghanistan, fighting became a way of life; they had little else to do—a fact which may be a source of major problems for Afghanistan in the future whatever the political status of the *Mujahideen*. Third, the shift in the Soviet-PDPA strategy to forward fighting without an increase in manpower did not help the Soviets much either. It forced their troops to spread themselves further and further. They were at no stage able to conduct successful sustained operations for a necessary length of time, or to cut the *Mujahideen*'s infiltration/supply routes for more than a short period. Fourth, although the Soviets' depopulation of many areas caused severe food shortages for the *Mujahideen*, the latter's traditional existence on a limited diet and ability to transport food from other areas compensated for such shortages. As usual it was the civilian population that suffered most. Fifth, contrary to public opinion, the degree of polycentrism which characterised the *Mujahideen* proved quite beneficial under the prevailing circumstances. Had the *Mujahideen* been united under a single leadership, they would have been vulnerable to the Soviets' and their surrogates' attempts either to co-opt or buy off such a leadership.

None of these factors meant that the *Mujahideen* were able to achieve a position of superiority over the professionally trained, better-equipped and better-provided Soviet troops. The *Mujahideen* could not achieve the capacity to win a decisive military victory against the Soviets and thus force them to leave Afghanistan unconditionally. Rather, the *Mujahideen* were able to *maintain* their resistance, depriving the Soviets of the opportunity to consolidate even their initial gains. By the PDPA's own admission, the *Mujahideen* in 1985 still controlled two thirds of Afghanistan,[59] with wide operational access to major cities, more importantly Kabul.

In sum, the political and military approaches of the Soviet Union, whether based on coercion, exchange, or the attempted manufacture of regime legitimacy, ultimately proved ineffectual. The Soviets and the regime failed to consolidate their initial hold on Kabul and other major cities. Life in the capital was not secure for anyone, including the Soviets. Even their embassy and residential compounds were periodically attacked by the *Mujahideen* and Kabul was often cut off from the rest of the country. Parts of Afghanistan's second and third largest cities, Kandahar and Herat, frequently changed hands between the PDPA-Soviet forces and the *Mujahideen* and were virtually ruined, like many more cities and numerous towns. The *Mujahideen*, on the other hand, successfully set up several liberated zones and increased their activities especially in the northern provinces bordering the USSR. Meanwhile, the PDPA and Soviets were unable to build an effective Afghan army. Despite the extensive application of coercive means to draft people into military service in the limited areas under the regime's control, the army's strength in 1986 did not exceed 30,000-40,000 and even so more than two thirds of these troops could not be trusted and were prone to defection.[60]

The overall result was a situation of stalemate. As this stalemate dragged on, so did its human, material and political costs for the Soviets. The prospects of a Vietnam-type syndrome, together with a generational leadership change in the Soviet Union from the ultimately conservative elements to younger and more reform-minded individuals, prompted the Kremlin to look for alternative options to that of military pacification in order to escape from this costly dilemma.

Notes

1. Afghan Information Centre *Monthly Bulletin,* no.60, March 1986, pp.13-14; *Monthly Bulletin* no.68, November 1986, p.14; *Bulletin du CEREDAF,* no.23, June 1986, p.2.

2. See Raja Anwar, *The Tragedy of Afghanistan* (London: Verso, 1988) p.187.

3. For details of these initial operations, see Henry S. Bradsher, *Afghanistan and the Soviet Union* (Durham: Duke University Press, 1985) pp.205-239, and Mark Urban, *War in Afghanistan* (London: Macmillan, 1990) pp.51-74.

4. For details, see Urban, op.cit., pp.60-61, 62-63.

5. See Zalmay Khalilzad, 'Soviet-Occupied Afghanistan', *Problems of Communism,* vol.29, no.6, November-December 1980, pp.23-40.

6. For the full text of Mishra's statement see United Nations General Assembly, Sixth Emergency Special Session, *Provisional Verbatim Record of the Third Meeting,* Document (A/ES-6/PV.3, General Assembly, United Nations, 11 January 1980).

7. For details, see Amin Saikal, 'The Regional Politics of the Afghan Crisis', in Amin Saikal and William Maley (eds.), *The Soviet Withdrawal from Afghanistan* (Cambridge: Cambridge University Press, 1989) pp.52-66.

8. For a discussion of problems of enumeration, see Nancy Hatch Dupree, 'The Demography of Afghan Refugees in Pakistan', in Hafeez Malik (ed.), *Soviet-American Relations with Pakistan, Iran, and Afghanistan* (London: Macmillan, 1987) pp.366-395, and Nancy Hatch Dupree, 'Demographic Reporting on Afghan Refugees in Pakistan', *Modern Asian Studies,* vol.22, no.4, October 1988, pp.845-865.

9. For a memoir recounting one such flight, see Ayesha Tarzi, *Red Death* (Cambridge: The Islamic Texts Society, 1985).

10. See Fazel Haq Saikal and William Maley, *Afghan Refugee Relief in Pakistan: Political Context and Practical Problems* (Canberra: Department of Politics, University College, The University of New South Wales, 1986); Pierre Centlivres and Micheline Centlivres-Demont, 'The Afghan Refugees in Pakistan: A Nation in Exile', *Current Sociology,* vol.36, no.2, Summer 1988, pp.71-92; and William Maley, 'Afghan Refugees: From Diaspora to Repatriation', in Amin Saikal (ed.), *Refugees in the Modern World* (Canberra: Canberra Studies in World Affairs no.25, Department of International Relations, Research School of Pacific Studies, Australian National University, 1989) pp.17-44.

11. See Etienne Gille, 'Avec les manifestants d'avril à Kaboul', *Les Nouvelles d'Afghanistan*, no.2, November 1980, pp.18-19.

12. Gabriel A. Almond and G. Bingham Powell, *Comparative Politics: A Developmental Approach* (Boston: Little, Brown & Co., 1966) pp.76-77.

13. We would emphasise that in the following discussion we use the words 'party' and 'parties' simply as convenient shorthand labels for the groups which we discuss. We do not intend to suggest that these 'parties' are markedly similar to political parties in Western liberal democracies.

14. See Edward R. Girardet, *Afghanistan: The Soviet War* (London: Croom Helm, 1985) p.169.

15. John Fullerton, *The Soviet Occupation of Afghanistan* (Hong Kong: South China Morning Post, 1983) p.69.

16. See *Brief Biography of Professor Sibghatullah al-Mojaddedi* (Peshawar: Afghan National Liberation Front, n.d.) p.6.

17. For a recent categorisation and description of Shiite resistance groups, see Robert L. Canfield, 'Afghanistan: The Trajectory of Internal Alignments', *The Middle East Journal*, vol.43, no.4, Autumn 1989, pp.635-648, at p.643.

18. See Louis Dupree, *Afghanistan* (Princeton: Princeton University Press, 1980) pp.95-111; and Eden Naby, 'The Changing Role of Islam as a Unifying Force in Afghanistan', in Ali Banuazizi and Myron Weiner (eds.), *The State, Religion, and Ethnic Politics: Afghanistan, Iran, and Pakistan* (Syracuse: Syracuse University Press, 1986) pp.124-154.

19. See Amin Saikal, 'The Conceptual Origins and Interpretations of Islamic Socialism', *Australian Outlook*, vol.40, no.1, April 1986, pp.39-47, at p.39.

20. See Olivier Roy, *L'Afghanistan: Islam et modernité politique* (Paris: Éditions du Seuil, 1985) p.95.

21. See ibid., passim.

22. Amin Saikal, 'Islam: resistance and reassertion', *The World Today*, vol.43, no.11, November 1987, pp.191-194, at p.191.

23. Bernard Lewis, *The Political Language of Islam* (Chicago: The University of Chicago Press, 1988) pp.117-118.

24. Eden Naby, 'Islam within the Afghan Resistance', *Third World Quarterly*, vol.10, no.2, April 1988, pp.787-805, at p.794.

25. Roy, op.cit., p.12.

26. See Julian Baldick, *Mystical Islam: An Introduction to Sufism* (London: I.B. Tauris, 1989).

27. Roy, op.cit., pp.55-62.

28. For an illuminating discussion of the potency of ritual, see David I. Kertzer, *Ritual, Politics and Power* (New Haven: Yale University Press, 1988).

29. On this, see Olivier Roy, 'Nature de la Guerre en Afghanistan', *Les Temps Modernes*, no.503, June 1988, pp.1-37.

30. See Arthur Bonner, *Among the Afghans* (Durham: Duke

University Press, 1987) pp.257-258.

31. Chantal Lemercier-Quelquejay and Alexandre Bennigsen, 'Soviet Experience of Muslim Guerilla Warfare and the War in Afghanistan', in Yaacov Ro'i (ed.), *The USSR and the Muslim World* (London: George Allen & Unwin, 1984) pp.206-214, at p.209.

32. Chantal Lemercier-Quelquejay, 'Muslim National Minorities in Revolution and Civil War', in S. Enders Wimbush (ed.), *Soviet Nationalities in Strategic Perspective* (London: Croom Helm, 1985) pp.36-60, at p.53.

33. On the Basmachi movement, see Martha Brill Olcott, 'The Basmachi or Freemen's Revolt in Turkestan 1918-24', *Soviet Studies*, vol.33, no.3, July 1981, pp.352-369; and Eden Naby, 'The Concept of Jihad in Opposition to Communist Rule: Turkestan and Afghanistan', *Studies in Comparative Communism*, vol.19, nos.3-4, Autumn-Winter 1986, pp.287-300.

34. See Urban, op.cit., passim.

35. See Margaret Doxey, 'Sanctions Against the Soviet Union: The Afghan Experience', *The Year Book of World Affairs 1983* (London: Stevens & Sons, 1983) pp.63-80, and Kim Richard Nossal, 'Knowing when to fold: Western sanctions against the USSR 1980-1983', *International Journal*, vol.44, no.3, Summer 1989, pp.698-724.

36. Amin Saikal, 'The Pakistan Disturbances and the Afghanistan Problem', *The World Today*, vol.40, no.3, March 1984, p.105.

37. See Shirin Tahir-Kheli, *The United States and Pakistan: The Evolution of an Influence Relationship* (New York: Praeger, 1982) pp.104-106. This aid was renewed in 1987 for a further six years at a cost of $4 billion: *Keesing's Record of World Events*, vol.33, no.3, March 1987, p.34995.

38. For details of outside arms aid to the resistance, see J. Bruce Amstutz, *Afghanistan: The First Five Years of Soviet Occupation* (Washington D.C.: National Defense University Press, 1986) pp.202-214; and Selig S. Harrison, 'The Afghan arms alliance', *South*, no.53, March 1985, pp.16-21.

39. For interpretations of China's reactions, see Gerald Segal, 'China and Afghanistan', *Asian Survey*, vol.21, no.11, November 1981, pp.1159-1174; and Yaacov Y.I. Vertzberger, *China's Southwestern Strategy: Encirclement and Counterencirclement* (New York: Praeger, 1985).

40. See R.K.I. Quested, *Sino-Russian Relations* (London: George Allen & Unwin, 1984) pp.154-156.

41. See *Afghanistan: Chronology of Events Since April 1978* (London: Foreign and Commonwealth Office, September 1980) p.10.

42. See *Afghanistan Chronology: January-May 1983* (London: Foreign and Commonwealth Office, August 1983) p.6.

43. See Amin Saikal, 'The Afghanistan crisis: a negotiated settlement?', *The World Today*, vol.40, no.11, November 1984, pp.481-489. at p.484.

44. BBC *Summary of World Broadcasts*, FE/7818/C/1, 5 December 1984.

45. See *Les Nouvelles d'Afghanistan*, no.23, June 1985, p.4.

46. See Michael Barry 'Répressions et guerre soviétiques', *Les Temps Modernes*, nos.408-409, July-August 1980, pp.171-234; Bernard Dupaigne (ed.), *Les droits de l'homme en Afghanistan* (Paris: Amitié Franco-Afghane, 1985); Michael Barry, Johan Lagerfelt and Marie-Odile Terrenoire, 'International Humanitarian Enquiry Commission on Displaced Persons in Afghanistan', *Central Asian Survey*, vol.5, no.1, 1986, pp.65-99; and outstandingly, Jeri Laber and Barnett R. Rubin, *"A Nation is Dying": Afghanistan under the Soviets 1979-87* (Evanston: Northwestern University Press, 1988).

47. See Amnesty International, *Democratic Republic of Afghanistan: Background Briefing on Amnesty International's Concerns* (London: ASA/11/13/83, October 1983); Amnesty International, *Afghanistan: Torture of Political Prisoners* (London: ASA/11/04/86, November 1986); and Amnesty International, *Afghanistan—Unlawful Killings and Torture* (London: ASA/11/02/88, May 1988).

48. See *Rapport sur la situation des droits de l'homme en Afghanistan* (E/CN.4/1985/21, Human Rights Commission, Economic and Social Council, United Nations, 19 February 1985); *Situation of Human Rights in Afghanistan* (A/40/843, General Assembly, United Nations, 5 November 1985); *Report on the Situation of Human Rights in Afghanistan* (E/CN.4/1986/24, Human Rights Commission, Economic and Social Council, United Nations, 17 February 1986); *Situation of Human Rights in Afghanistan* (A/41/778, General Assembly, United Nations, 9 January 1987); *Report on the Situation of Human Rights in Afghanistan* (A/42/667, General Assembly, United Nations, 23 October 1987); *Report on the Situation of Human Rights in Afghanistan* (E/CN.4/1988/25, Human Rights Commission, Economic and Social Council, United Nations, 26 February 1988); *Situation of Human Rights in Afghanistan* (A/43/742, General Assembly, United Nations, 24 October 1988); *Report on the Situation of Human Rights in Afghanistan* (E/CN.4/1989/24, Human Rights Commission, Economic and Social Council, United Nations, 16 February 1989); and *Situation of Human Rights in Afghanistan* (A/44/669, General Assembly, United Nations, 30 October 1989).

49. See Frances D'Souza, *The Threat of Famine in Afghanistan* (London: AfghanAid, 1984).

50. See *Strategic Survey 1986-1987* (London: International Institute for Strategic Studies, 1987).

51. For a general discussion, see Laber and Rubin, op.cit., pp.69-76.

52. For an American figure of $15-18 million, see *The Friday Review of Defense Literature*, no.9, March 1987, p.5; for a discussion of various estimates of war costs before 1986, see Bradsher, op.cit., pp.270-271.

53. See Bernard E. Trainor, 'Afghan Air War: U.S. Missiles Score', *The*

New York Times, 7 July 1987, p.6.

54. Ibid.

55. See 'USSR: Unofficial Poll on Popular Opposition to Afghan War', *Current Analyses* (Washington D.C.: Bureau of Intelligence and Research, Department of State, Report 1107-CA, 18 June 1985).

56. *The Soviet Public and the War in Afghanistan: Perceptions, Prognoses, Information Sources* (Munich: Radio Free Europe/Radio Liberty, Soviet Area Audience and Opinion Research, AR 4-85, June 1985) p.1.

57. See Christopher Walker, 'Poll reveals most Russians want Afghanistan pull-out', *The Times*, 2 November 1987, p.9.

58. See Alexandre Bennigsen, 'The Impact of the Afghan War on Soviet Central Asia', in Rosanne Klass (ed.), *Afghanistan—The Great Game Revisited* (New York: Freedom House, 1987) pp.287-299; Taras Kuzio, 'Opposition in the USSR to the Occupation of Afghanistan', *Central Asian Survey*, vol.6, no.1, 1987, pp.99-117; and Maya Latynski and S. Enders Wimbush, 'The Mujahideen and the Russian Empire', *The National Interest*, no.11, Spring 1988, pp.30-42.

59. See Najibullah's remarks to an Indian journalist, quoted in 'Mujahideen continues attacks through Winter', *The Canberra Times*, 16 January 1985, p.7.

60. See André Brigot and Olivier Roy, *The War in Afghanistan* (London: Harvester-Wheatsheaf, 1988) p.82.

5

Soviet Options

There is no doubt that by the mid-1980s Soviet forces were bogged down in Afghanistan. The military strategy which had been set in place by the Brezhnev leadership had failed to secure the central political objective of consolidating the PDPA's rule. The regime headed by Babrak Karmal had no greater claim to legitimacy than when first it was established and remained rent by factional antagonisms. Its territorial writ remained negligible. The presence of Soviet forces in Afghanistan continued to be an embarrassment—albeit on a diminishing scale—in international forums of which the USSR was a member and needlessly complicated the Soviet Union's international relations. And within the USSR itself the war was the focus of thinly veiled hostility from a significant range of social actors. Nonetheless, as long as the upper echelons of the leadership remained under the sway of Brezhnev associates who were directly inculpated in the invasion, the prospects for any rational reconsideration of the USSR's Afghanistan policy were minimal.

This changed to some extent following Brezhnev's death in November 1982 but a serious reassessment of Soviet policy came about only when Mikhail S. Gorbachev succeeded Konstantin Chernenko as general secretary of the Communist Party of the Soviet Union in February 1985. Gorbachev's accession inaugurated a remarkable period of change in Soviet politics.[1] It coincided with a rapid and substantial turnover of personnel within the Soviet elite. Brezhnev, on replacing N.S. Khrushchev in October 1964, had inaugurated a policy of 'stability of cadres', designed to comfort party *apparatchiki* who had been disturbed by Khrushchev's penchant for substantial reorganisations. Brezhnev's policy produced a stable but steadily ageing elite which by the earlier 1980s was notable for its antiquity and was on the point of dying out *en masse*.[2] Those poised to replace these figures were younger, in general markedly better educated, and on the whole likely to be sympathetic to new policy directions. With the accession of Gorbachev, a multitude of problems which had accumulated during the 'period of stagnation'—in other words, the years of Brezhnev's dominance—were finally addressed. Of these, the Afghanistan problem was one of the most important.

Soviet Options

Against the backdrop of Brezhnev's failure in Afghanistan, the new Soviet leadership had three broad options at its disposal. One was a massive escalation of the war. A second was to end its involvement by immediately and unconditionally withdrawing all its troops and letting the Afghans determine their own future—an option which was demanded by the Afghan resistance and the international community. Its final option was to seek a compromise political solution which would permit it to pull out its troops without altogether sacrificing its protégé regime and foregoing future influence in Afghan politics. From late 1985 signs began to appear that the new Soviet leadership deemed it in its best interests to pursue the third option. The reasons why it chose this third option are not difficult to fathom.

First of all, the option of massive escalation was beset with risks. There was every chance that such an option would exact even higher costs from the Soviets than had thitherto been the case. Given the determination and the human resources of the Afghan resistance, and the unfavourable regional and global circumstances, for the Soviet Union to implement this option it would have needed to increase its troop deployment from the prevailing level of about 120,000 to at least half a million. Furthermore, it would have needed to be ready to expand the war into neighbouring states, especially Pakistan, in order not only to seal off Afghanistan's borders—a task of immense difficulty—but also to penalise Pakistan as heavily as necessary to curtail its support for the Afghan resistance. Soviet human and material losses would certainly have rocketed, as more Soviet troops would have become the targets of the *Mujahideen*. There would also have been a real danger of renewed international agitation over Afghanistan and therefore deterioration of Soviet regional and global relations, for neither regional states nor the Soviets' global adversaries would have found the escalation tolerable. There could have been a larger domestic backlash, for the Soviet public were unlikely to remain as passive in the face of greater losses as they had been in the past. There was also no guarantee that at the end such an escalation would have met with success. On the contrary, there would have been every possibility of Afghanistan's becoming much more than just a 'bleeding wound', a term Gorbachev used to describe it at the 27th Congress of the Soviet Communist Party in March 1986.[3] Consequently, escalation was not an option which the Kremlin was disposed to adopt.

From the leadership's perspective, the option of unconditional withdrawal was also problematic. After many years of deepening involvement and mounting losses it would have meant the total frustration of the very objective for which the Soviets invaded Afghanistan in the first place. First, an unconditional pullout of Soviet troops would have put Karmal's regime at immediate grave risk of falling in favour of a *Mujahideen*-led Islamic government. In such a case, not only would the new government have been unsympathetic to the Soviets and the PDPA surrogates, but also there would have been a possibility of Afghanistan's being plunged into a period of serious domestic power struggles, causing it to become vulnerable to interferences by Soviet adversaries. Second, the fall of a protégé regime would have been a profound humiliation for a new general secretary still in the process of consolidating his power.[4] It would have undermined the Soviet Union's prestige and credibility with its allies, and its status as a world power. It would also have provided concrete proof of the fallibility of Soviet power, from which subject populations, particularly in the Muslim republics of Soviet Central Asia, would undoubtedly have taken heart. Third, a blatant Afghan *débâcle* could have sparked a crisis within the Soviet system itself, playing into the hands of those remaining Brezhnev-generation figures with whom the new leadership was still obliged to deal. Thus, unconditional troop withdrawal was also an option that the Gorbachev leadership manoeuvred to avoid.

As a result, the Soviet leadership found it expedient to promote the third option as the best way to break through the Afghan stalemate and disentangle the USSR from its involvement, while at the same time escalating its commitment of equipment to the conflict—something reflected in the higher level of Afghan civilian casualties in the aftermath of Gorbachev's accession.[5] This third option appeared to rest on the belief that some balance could be struck between what the Soviet Union as a world power would accept in Afghanistan and what would be tolerable to the international community, especially if Western resolve over Afghanistan could be weakened by Soviet diplomatic initiatives addressing other issues of international concern. Thus, the Soviet Union sought to promote a solution which could satisfy both these sides to some extent and enable the Soviets, over a shorter period of time than originally envisaged, to *afghanise* the war.

Early signs of such a 'solution' actually emerged in the second half of 1985, when Moscow shortly before the November superpower summit in Geneva stepped up its publicity about a more serious willingness to negotiate a political settlement of the Afghan crisis. In an unprecedentedly frank editorial in its issue of 21 December, *Pravda*, while upholding the sanctity of the PDPA regime, for the first time admitted that the PDPA rule was not as popular, secure and faultless as Moscow had hitherto described it and called for a more level-headed approach to a resolution of the Afghan problem. It stated: 'By no means everyone in Afghanistan, even among the working people, has accepted the April revolution' and the PDPA policies. Describing the size of the opposition as 'considerable', it continued: 'There have been negative repercussions from the mistakes made during the first stage of the revolution', as 'social reforms' were accelerated 'without due regard for the real situation and the country's specific social and national features'. Further, it said that 'it is necessary to create the atmosphere for a positive dialogue between public and political forces, including those that still hold views that are hostile to the revolution', and that such 'reconciliation presupposes certain compromises'. The editorial ended its expositions by calling on the international supporters of the Afghan resistance, most notably Pakistan and the United States, to respond constructively to the problem and terminate their aid to the *Mujahideen*. It also stressed that 'it is necessary to create the atmosphere for a positive dialogue between public and political forces, including those that still hold views that are hostile to the revolution', and that such 'reconciliation presupposes certain compromises'.[6]

However, a clearer expression of the drift of Soviet thinking came in a major speech which Gorbachev delivered in Vladivostok on 28 July 1986. This wide-ranging address, which canvassed many issues pertinent to the security of the Asia-Pacific region,[7] conveyed three main points upon which a solution of the Afghan problem and a Soviet troop withdrawal were dependent. First, Gorbachev implied that the leading role of the PDPA was not negotiable. He described the April 1978 coup as a 'national-democratic revolution' and emphasised its irreversibility under PDPA leadership, against which all armed hostilities had to stop. He warned that '... if intervention against Democratic Afghanistan continues the Soviet Union will not leave its neighbour in the lurch. Our internationalist solidarity with the Afghan people, as well as the security interests of the Soviet Union rule that out absolutely'. Second, he stressed that at the same time the PDPA's rule had to be strengthened and its power base needed to be expanded through a policy of 'national reconciliation', 'up to the point of creating a government with the participation' of those opposition forces prepared not to question the legitimacy of 'the April revolution' (and therefore the PDPA's leading role) but to 'participate sincerely in the nationwide process of constructing a new Afghanistan'. Third, he intimated that only in conjunction with these two elements, and when a 'political settlement' was finally worked out, primarily with Pakistan, would the Soviet Union pull out all of its troops. Even then it would be 'stage-by-stage', according to timetables which had 'been agreed with the Afghan leadership'. To demonstrate the sincerity of his call for a political settlement he also proposed to pull out six Soviet regiments—one tank, two motorised infantry and three anti-aircraft regiments (about 6,000-7,000 troops in total) before the end of the year.[8]

The Soviet leader's proposals signalled not so much a change in Soviet objectives as in the means chosen to further them. On the one hand, he accepted his predecessors' basic objective: to ensure the long-term survival of the PDPA regime and for that matter Soviet influence in Afghan politics. On the other, he judged very unproductive his predecessors' strategy of long-term, low-cost military pacification and uncompromising reliance on the PDPA as the sole ruling body, and proposed a modification of it by stressing one qualitative difference. That difference was to put stress on *political* means—with certain marginal concessions—rather than on largely *military* means.

The New Approach Takes Effect

Consequently, from 1986 the Soviets pursued a two-dimensional strategy in keeping with the policy lines set out in Gorbachev's Vladivostok remarks. One object of the strategy was to strengthen the PDPA's rule, partly through an internal overhaul of the regime and partly through the development of organic, structural ties between Soviet governmental agencies, and instrumentalities of the Kabul regime and its sympathisers. The other was to seek to create certain conditions conducive to the political settlement desired by the USSR.

In respect of the first objective, while intensifying their military operations against the *Mujahideen* to an unprecedented level throughout the country, with special stress on the provinces bordering Pakistan, the Soviets launched a vigorous campaign to overhaul the PDPA by securing a more effective leadership for it. Babrak Karmal had proved a failure from virtually every perspective. Known colloquially as 'Karmalov', he was despised as the 'Soviet-installed leader of the PDPA' by both the general public and members of the *Khalq*. His 'leadership' was ineffectual and for some years he had been unable to venture outside the Kabul conurbation. As a result, he was incapable of either containing factionalism within the PDPA or expanding its power base. Moscow finally decided in late 1985 to replace him with someone who could prove to be more effective, especially in view of Gorbachev's pending initiatives.[9]

The choice of replacement was particularly difficult, given the fact that there were only a few PDPA leaders whom the Soviets could really trust (in a party which did not appear to command many committed members at all, although it had officially claimed 120,000-140,000[10]). Ultimately, the Soviet Union decided to promote the chief of KHAD, Dr Najibullah, a *Parchami* activist loyal to Moscow since the late 1960s. He was favoured for several reasons. First, he had an impeccable record of loyalty to successive Soviet leaderships. He had been intimately involved in transforming KHAD into the most efficient force bolstering PDPA rule and Soviet control in urban areas where the regime had a presence. Second, at the age of 39 he had gained a reputation as the PDPA's shrewdest tactician, capable of executing the kind of political manoeuvres needed to complement Gorbachev's initiatives. Third, unlike most of the *Parchamis*, including Karmal, he was a full Ghilzai Pushtun, which gave him a greater claim than Karmal to affinity with Afghanistan's largest ethnic group. Indeed, the claim that he was a 'revolutionary patriotic Pushtun' figured prominently in the reasons given to justify his advancement.

Openly criticising the party leadership, the Soviets promoted Najibullah to the secretariat of the PDPA on 21 November 1985. This mirrored a similar move in 1982 by Iu.V. Andropov, who succeeded Brezhnev shortly thereafter. On 4 May 1986, during a three day plenum of the party's Central Committee—held in Kabul amid unprecedentedly tight Soviet security and attended by the Soviet ambassador—he was finally chosen to head the party. Karmal was initially left with the ceremonial position of president of the Revolutionary Council, formally the supreme legislative body of the state, but subsequently in November he was stripped of all his party positions and thus joined the ranks of the Soviet Union's other forgotten Afghan comrades, Nur Mohammad Taraki and Hafizullah Amin. Shortly thereafter, he was flown to Moscow for 'medical treatment' and has not been seen since. Najibullah set out to consolidate his own leadership and launched a campaign to make the PDPA a more effective ruling body, and to purge *Parcham* of Karmal supporters. This caused the *Parcham* faction to split into two parts, essentially consisting of Najibullah's and Karmal's supporters. Warfare between the two sides in early 1987 cost many lives, and was even mentioned on Moscow television by Aleksandr Bovin, who referred to 'dissensions, feuds and bloody clashes within the ruling party itself'.[11] Even after Karmal's removal from all official positions, his supporters continued to undermine

Najibullah's leadership from inside and outside the PDPA structure. Contrary to the Soviets' original expectations, Najibullah's promotion, at least in the short run, *created* rather than solved problems. In addition to causing a serious division within the *Parcham*, it outraged the opposition, which held Najibullah responsible for the loss of thousands of innocent lives during his tenure as chief of KHAD.

Taking his lead from the emerging practice of *glasnost'* (candour) in the Soviet Union following the April 1986 Chernobyl nuclear accident, Najibullah started his job with unprecedented candour about the shortcomings of PDPA. Over the following two months he criticised the party's failure to expunge factionalism and corruption (which had indeed reached epidemic proportions); to expand its territorial control beyond one third of the country; to bolster the depleted Afghan Army, which had dwindled to less than two thirds of its pre-invasion strength of 60,000 due to desertions and refusal to fight; and to win mass support. He even declared: 'We are weak in the tactical and practical sphere. Most of the grand thoughts and plans get drowned in mere words and remain on paper'.[12] Somewhat anomalously, however, he further proclaimed that 'all our work will be based on the continued strengthening and development of friendship with the great Soviet Union , the party of the great Lenin and the heroic and generous Soviet people'.[13] These statements were accompanied by the removal of 'undesirable elements' and their replacement by Najibullah's supporters. Most notable among these were Abdul Wakil and Mohammed Rafi, who by the end of the year assumed the foreign affairs and defence portfolios. Najibullah also instituted a vigorous drive to tighten the conscription laws to ensure the ready recruitment into the army of all males of ages 18-50 from at least the limited areas under the Soviet-PDPA control. KHAD was given even wider powers in order to allow it formally to implement this measure.

Concurrently, the Soviets moved with greater urgency than ever before to cement the organic-institutional ties between the PDPA and the Soviet Union. Soviet measures in this respect included an acceleration of efforts by thousands of Soviet civil and KGB-military *apparatchiki* to give some substance to the PDPA administration, based on KHAD as its central operative mechanism, and to train its members at the Soviet-built Social

Science Institute of the PDPA's Central Committee, which was opened in June 1986 in Kabul.[14] Moreover, the Soviets accepted more Afghans for training in the Soviet Union. For example, in addition to 7,500 mature-age Afghans[15] a large number of Afghan children were forcibly despatched to the USSR.[16] All these pointed to a long-term desire on the Soviet Union's part to change Afghan society through the development of a *janissary* class which could be deployed to bolster the PDPA rule and to protect Soviet interests.

Efforts in these areas were accompanied by greater steps to build the Soviets' and the regime's defence capability in Afghanistan. For instance, the Soviet Union continued not only to strengthen its two large bases in Bagram (outside Kabul) and Shindand (near Herat in the west), but also pushed for the expansion of the third one in Kandahar (in the south) and construction of new but smaller ones in other parts of the country.[17] It was from these bases that Soviet airpower was deployed against the resistance and that the USSR carried out long-range reconnaissance flights over Pakistan and Iran as well as right across the Persian Gulf coastline. There were also reports of Soviet moves to construct signals intelligence sites in Afghanistan additional to the four major ones which had already been developed at strategic locations on the Afghan borders with China, Pakistan and Iran, essentially to intercept signals and monitor military movements in those countries.[18]

Economically, the PDPA regime was heavily dependent on the Soviet Union[19]—hardly surprising given that the regime exercised dominion over a large number of urban dwellers, but possessed few of the agricultural resources needed to feed them. To highlight the degree of the regime's economic integration with the USSR, in late April 1986, in a joint communiqué following an official visit to Moscow by the regime's Prime Minister Sultan Ali Kishtmand, the two sides praised the level of 'Soviet-Afghan economic cooperation' and 'noted that in recent years it has been filled with new content and has become solid and stable.' 'They expressed mutual interest in the development and strengthening of cooperation on a long-term … basis' in both economic and social spheres. The Soviets also expressed readiness to provide further assistance in all fields of the regime's activities in the future. The two sides pledged 'to continue to devote constant attention to Soviet-Afghan ties in the fields of culture, education, public health and sports' and '... to promote the expansion of contacts between Soviet and Afghan organisations and institutions with a view to more thorough familiarisation with the life, labour, experience and achievements of the two countries' peoples'.[20]

The Kremlin put a great deal of effort into depicting the PDPA regime as one acceptable to the Afghan people and the outside world, stressing in the process the vocabulary of 'national reconciliation'. The Soviets started putting this process to test even before Gorbachev's Vladivostok initiatives. For example, in January 1986 the regime announced an expansion of its Revolutionary Council by 79 members in order to give greater representation in the government to 'all social forces', including the 'clergy', and described several new members as 'non-party', although the past association of many of them with the PDPA was unquestionable.[21] This was followed by the regime's staging of a *Jirgah* of 'Free Pushtun Tribes' and several smaller *jirgahs*, to suggest that tribal, particularly Pushtun, support was increasing for it. It did not admit that half of the people attending the *jirgahs* were party members and that the remaining were for the most part paid citizens whose economic destitution under the regime's rule was acute. In the period after July 1986 there was a flurry of such initiatives. The more important ones included a declaration by Najibullah that the party's Central Committee would be expanded from 79 to 147 to provide for larger representation from the provinces. In September 1986, he foreshadowed the establishment of a 'National Reconciliation Commission' to 'normalise' the situation in Afghanistan and thwart 'imperialist counter-revolutionary intervention and fratricide'. Moreover, the regime claimed in October that the first stage of 'local elections' had been 'concluded successfully in all provinces', although few experienced observers were disposed to take the claim seriously.

These measures were backed by a concerted Soviet campaign to gain maximum regional and international support for a prompt political settlement of the Afghan problem. As part of this campaign and in fulfilment of Gorbachev's Vladivostok promise of a partial troop withdrawal, the Soviet Union began pulling out six regiments shortly before the superpower summit at

Reykjavik in October—a 'withdrawal' which was completed by the end of the month. Although the Kabul regime and Moscow hailed it as a significant 'good-will step', the *Mujahideen* and their international supporters were inclined to dismiss it as a propaganda ploy, for two main reasons. First, several of the regiments—notably those concerned with air defence—had proved superfluous given the *Mujahideen*'s total lack of airpower. Second, the withdrawal amounted to no marked reduction in overall Soviet troop strength. Indeed, the US Administration claimed that Moscow had already increased its troops to make up for the withdrawal.[22]

The Weaknesses of the New Approach

Even before the end of 1986 it was clear that neither Moscow's promotion of Najibullah nor its 'reconciliation' efforts nor its partial troop withdrawal had improved either the situation of the PDPA regime or the prospects for a settlement. To the Afghan public, the soothing rhetoric of the regime was utterly hollow, a regurgitation of familiar deceptive devices. The regime's claims of success looked equally absurd in the face of its own admissions that it had accomplished little in implementing the plans that it had on paper; that it had failed in the objective of gaining 'mass support'; and that it had not controlled much more than one third of the country.

Consequently, the Soviets were obliged to move somewhat beyond Gorbachev's Vladivostok pronouncements. During and after a three week visit to Moscow in December 1986, Najibullah detailed what appeared to be a Soviet-designed plan, stressing three points. First, while claiming 'deep respect' for the religion of Islam and emphasising that his team was different from that of his communist predecessors, he declared his readiness for the creation of a 'coalition government of national unity'. He called on the surviving officials of former Afghan regimes living abroad, and the *Mujahideen* leaders, to cease their anti-regime activities and enter dialogue with the PDPA leadership to formulate a new constitution (in which Islam would be enshrined as the religion of the state), elect a national assembly, and participate in the governmental process. Second, he proclaimed a 'general amnesty' for the opposition forces. Third, he promised an 'attractive' timetable for the withdrawal of Soviet troops. To facilitate the implementation of this peace plan he also proclaimed a unilateral 'ceasefire' to be observed by the PDPA-Soviet forces for six months from mid-January 1987, although the start of the ceasefire coincided with the period of the normal winter lull in *Mujahideen* activities. Thus, for the first time, the PDPA and Moscow implicitly dropped their past labelling of the *Mujahideen* as 'imperialist-backed bandits' and recognised them as elements of a popular resistance, whose consent would be crucial to the success of any settlement. However, in echoing Gorbachev's Vladivostok stance, Najibullah preconditioned the implementation of all this on the 'irreversibility of the April revolution' and therefore the continuation of the PDPA leadership; on the 'strengthening' of Afghan-Soviet ties'; and on the 'response' of the opposition and its international supporters.[23]

In early January 1987, during a rare visit to Kabul by a top-level Soviet delegation, the Soviet foreign minister, Eduard Shevardnadze and the Soviet Communist Party Central Committee's senior foreign policy adviser, Anatolii Dobrynin, not only gave official Soviet approval to this settlement plan but also reassured Najibullah of continued Soviet support for the preconditions that he had laid down. The Kremlin once again apparently renewed such an assurance in late July during a second visit to Moscow by Najibullah.[24] After official discussions with Gorbachev, Najibullah declared that while his regime was prepared to share power with the opposition forces, including Zahir Shah (to whom Gorbachev had obliquely referred in May 1987 as someone who could play an important role in the promotion of a political settlement[25]), it would not do so at the cost of the PDPA relinquishing the leadership of Afghanistan. He stressed in mid-July that the PDPA would continue to control the key ministries of Defence, Internal Affairs and KHAD, which had been upgraded to ministry level in early 1986.[26]

Despite these moves, fighting intensified on the battlefield, with the *Mujahideen* sustaining their successes. This was mainly because the compromise solution that the Gorbachev leadership sought was not an option that the resistance could adopt. The *Mujahideen* promptly and predictably rejected the whole settlement plan, including the 'ceasefire', as a 'fraud' and totally unacceptable. The preconditions were exactly those which were anathema to the Afghan resistance and no possibility of conciliation existed between the PDPA and resistance forces after nine years of deep ideological animosity, bloodshed and distrust. No credible figure of the past Afghan regimes, including King Zahir Shah, broke ranks with the *Mujahideen* and chose to share power with the PDPA.[27] Such figures knew that they could do this only at the cost of immense personal risk and of deadly opposition by the resistance forces. The *Mujahideen* viewed Soviet activity as part of a well calculated ploy which sought to use political means, against the background of military failure, to confuse and divide the Afghan people and to undermine international support for the resistance. Hence the aim was to fulfil the basic Soviet objective, irrespective of the Afghan people's demand for the total and unconditional withdrawal of Soviet troops and for self-determination. If anything, the concessions offered to them under the plan further weakened the Soviet position and made the resistance continue their struggle. From their perspective, the best option open to them was to carry on the fight, for they could only gain; they had little more to lose.

The Geneva Process

This determination on the part of the resistance ultimately bore 'fruit' in a different sphere—namely in negotiations which had been pursued fitfully in Geneva by the USSR, the Kabul regime, Pakistan, and the United States. As we have not so far discussed these in any great detail, it is useful to say a few words about how these discussions came about and how they sprang into life in 1987-88.

Almost immediately after the Soviet invasion in December 1979, an Emergency Special Session of the United Nations General Assembly was convened under the Uniting for Peace resolution, to consider the Afghanistan situation. The General Assembly adopted a resolution calling for 'the immediate, unconditional and total withdrawal of the foreign troops from Afghanistan'. Nonetheless, the UN reaction from the start was marked by a degree of ambivalence. The General Assembly accepted the credentials of the delegation of the Soviet-installed regime in Kabul, which duly voted against the resolution. This was a most unfortunate error which gave the regime a standing no puppet regime had been granted since the UN's establishment, and it seriously skewed the course of subsequent negotiations over Afghanistan. Perhaps sensing that this ambivalence weakened the force of the General Assembly's condemnation, the Soviet Union ignored the resolution; but on 14 May 1980 the Karmal regime issued a statement which contained a program for a 'political solution' to the 'tension that has come about in this region'. The Karmal regime proposed 'to the Government of Pakistan that talks should be held to prepare a bilateral agreement on normalizing relations between Afghanistan and Pakistan', containing 'acceptable provisions regarding mutual respect for national sovereignty and a readiness to develop relations based on the principles of good-neighbourliness and non-interference in each other's internal affairs, as well as an undertaking of fundamental responsibility in the area not to permit armed activities or other hostile acts from the territory of one against the other'. It also stated that 'necessary political guarantees by certain governments that may be acceptable to Afghanistan and other parties to the bilateral agreements should be regarded as an inalienable part of the political solution ... So far as the USA is concerned, such guarantees must include a clearly expressed commitment to ban subversive activities against Afghanistan including those being launched from the territory of other countries'. It finally declared 'that the question of the withdrawal of the limited military contingents of the Soviet Union from Afghanistan must be resolved within the context of the political solution'.[28]

It was this programme, rather than the General Assembly's resolution, around which discussions about the future of Afghanistan came to be structured at the international level. This was because it identified the agenda of matters about which the *Soviet Union* was prepared to embark on discussions. Brezhnev made this perfectly clear in his remarks about the 'limited contingent' to the 26th Congress of the Communist Party of the Soviet Union: '... we will be ready to withdraw it with the agreement of the Afghan government. For this, the infiltration of counter-revolutionary bands into Afghanistan must be completely stopped. This must be secured in understandings between Afghanistan and its neighbours. Reliable guarantees are needed that there will be no new intervention. Such is the fundamental position of the Soviet Union and we will keep to it firmly'.[29]

In April 1981 a series of conversations on the Afghan question were inaugurated on behalf of the UN secretary-general by Señor Javier Pérez de Cuéllar, and in 1982, when Pérez de Cuéllar became secretary-general himself, the management of the discussions was taken over by his personal representative, Señor Diego Cordovez. Initially, the UN envoy travelled between capitals in order to conduct the discussions, but from August 1984 the discussions took the form of 'proximity talks', with Cordovez shuttling between delegations from Kabul and Islamabad housed in separate rooms of the *Palais des Nations* in Geneva. No representatives of the *Mujahideen* were present at the talks and Iran refused to participate on the grounds that the *Mujahideen* alone had the right to negotiate on behalf of the Afghan people. This suited both the UN, which had no taste for dealing with non-state actors, and the Soviet Union, which saw its May 1980 agenda clearly reflected in the structure of the talks.

A remarkable amount was sown up in a short space of time, but without any of the key issues being addressed. Agreement was reached on anodyne principles of 'non-interference' in the internal affairs of sovereign states, and on the principles to govern the voluntary repatriation of refugees. However, the issue of free self-determination for the Afghan people, highlighted in UN General Assembly resolutions, did not figure on the agenda and the illegitimacy of the PDPA regime was never discussed. Most importantly of all, the question of a timetable for the withdrawal of Soviet troops was not addressed in terms which had the slightest chance of satisfying the delegation of Pakistan. Initially Kabul proposed that following a cessation of any outside assistance to the *Mujahideen* the Soviet Union be allowed four years to withdraw its forces. This could hardly have been a serious proposal and it drew attention to the fact that the Kremlin was at this stage interested in sustaining the negotiating *process* rather than bringing it to fruition.[30] The negotiations staggered on, although effectively stalled by Soviet intransigence over the withdrawal timetable, until well after Gorbachev's accession to high office.

The stalemate was broken by the supply to the *Mujahideen* of US 'Stinger' missiles from September 1986—a move which dramatically increased the cost of the war for the USSR, especially in terms of expensive equipment. A subsequent detailed study by the US Army identified the Stinger as 'the war's decisive weapon'.[31] However, had it not been for leadership changes within the USSR itself, the Stingers might not have had the impact they produced. Soviet figures of the Brezhnev era, possibly involved in the 1979 intervention decision, could hardly countenance a retreat from Afghanistan, as it would have reflected devastatingly on their lack of judgment at the time of the invasion. But by early 1988 most of those who had been voting members of the Politburo at the time of the invasion had either died (L.I. Brezhnev, A.N. Kosygin, M.A. Suslov, Iu.V Andropov, K.U. Chernenko, A.Ia. Pel'she and D.F. Ustinov), or been retired (A.P. Kirilenko, G.V. Romanov, N.A. Tikhonov, V.V. Grishin, and D.A. Kunaev). Only A.A. Gromyko and V.V. Shcherbitskii remained in office. This leadership change prepared the ground—as Jerry F. Hough anticipated in 1980—for 'a more activist and innovative foreign policy'.[32] Younger figures, remote from the heart of the 1979 decision-making process, were much better placed to undertake a cool-headed assessment of whether the costs of continued combat involvement were worth carrying.

The Soviet Union reappraised its Afghan policy not only through new eyes, but in a changed *policy* context. Gorbachev and a number of his close associates were patently appalled by the stagnant state of the Soviet economy in the wake of Brezhnev's rule, and foresaw domestic political dangers if radical reforms were not undertaken to rectify the gross inefficiencies of the command economy and thereby to improve the supply to Soviet citizens of basic consumer goods. This programme, known as *perestroika* (restructuring), left very little room for costly foreign policy adventures with few obvious political returns. The burden which Afghanistan had come to impose in economic terms was expressly mentioned by Gorbachev in an address to the Moscow City Party Conference in January 1989, when he identified Afghanistan, along with Chernobyl, as one of 'our old sins'.[33]

The reasons for an acceleration of the Geneva process were

therefore compelling. While the option of *afghanisation* of the war was clearly in the minds of key Soviet leaders by the time of the Vladivostok speech, the heightened costs of the war from late 1986 onwards made its pursuit almost a certainty. However, it took nearly two years more before dramatic steps could be taken to terminate the Soviet troop commitment. Gorbachev was obliged to move carefully in order not to overstep the bounds of his own authority, to market the idea of a withdrawal to potentially hostile circles within the Soviet Union, and to allow the PDPA regime some notice that it would shortly be required to survive much more heavily on its own human resources than ever before. It was thus not until 1988 that the decisive breakthrough in Soviet attitudes finally came.

Notes

1. For some discussion of the Gorbachev period, see Moshe Lewin, *The Gorbachev Phenomenon: A Historical Interpretation* (Berkeley: University of California Press, 1988), Boris Meissner, *Die Sowjetunion im Umbruch* (Stuttgart: Deutsche Verlags-Anstalt GmbH, 1988), Jerry F. Hough, *Russia and the West: Gorbachev and the Politics of Reform* (New York: Simon and Schuster, 1990), Stephen White, *Gorbachev in Power* (Cambridge: Cambridge University Press, 1990), Abraham Brumberg (ed.), *Chronicle of a Revolution: A Western-Soviet Inquiry into Perestroika* (New York: Pantheon Books, 1990), and Chandran Kukathas, David W. Lovell and William Maley (eds.), *The Transition from Socialism: State and Civil Society in the USSR* (Melbourne: Longman Cheshire, 1991).

2. Archie Brown, 'Power and Policy in a Time of Leadership Transition, 1982-1988', in Archie Brown (ed.), *Political Leadership in the Soviet Union* (London: Macmillan, 1989) pp.163-217.

3. *Materialy XXVII s"ezda Kommunisticheskoi partii Sovetskogo Soiuza* (Moscow: Politizdat, 1986) p.69.

4. See Archie Brown, 'The Power of the General Secretary of the CPSU', in T.H. Rigby, Archie Brown and Peter Reddaway (eds.), *Authority, Power and Policy in the USSR* (London: Macmillan, 1980) pp.135-157.

5. Marek Sliwinski, *Afghanistan 1978-87: War, Demography and Society* (London: Central Asian Survey Incidental Paper no.6, 1988) p.5.

6. 'Za rasshirenie sotsial'noi bazy afganskoi revoliutsii', *Pravda*, 21 December 1985, p.4.

7. For a range of commentaries on this speech, see Ramesh Thakur and Carlyle A. Thayer (eds.), *The Soviet Union as an Asian Pacific Power:*

Implications of Gorbachev's 1986 Vladivostok Initiative (Boulder: Westview Press, 1987).

8. For the text of the speech, see BBC *Summary of World Broadcasts*, SU/8324/C/1-17, 30 July 1986. This version is preferable to that published in the Soviet press, from which Gorbachev departed at a number of points.

9. For specific indicators of Soviet disaffection see *Soviet Policy on Afghanistan: Signs of Change and Controversy* (Washington D.C.: Foreign Broadcast Information Service, FB 86-100 10, 19 March 1986).

10. See Richard F Staar, 'Checklist of Communist Parties in 1986', *Problems of Communism*, vol.36, no.2, March-April 1987, pp.40-56.

11. BBC *Summary of World Broadcasts*, SU/8494/A3/3, 17 February 1987.

12. BBC *Summary of World Broadcasts*, FE/8260/C/1-2, 16 May 1986.

13. 'Zadacha—ukreplenie edinstva', *Pravda*, 6 May 1986, p.4.

14. 'Torzhestvennoe sobranie v Kabule', *Pravda*, 25 June 1986, p.5.

15. See B. Tret'iachenko, 'Na kanikuly—v Afganistan', *Pravda*, 3 July 1987, p.5.

16. Jeri Laber, 'Afghanistan's Other War', *The New York Review of Books*, vol.33, no.20, 18 December 1986, pp.3, 6-7.

17. Amin Saikal, 'Soviet Policy Toward Southwest Asia', *The Annals of the American Academy of Political and Social Science*, vol.481, September 1985, p.112.

18. Desmond Ball, 'Soviet Signals Intelligence', *The International Countermeasures Handbook* (Palo Alto: E.W. Communications Inc., 1987) p.85.

19. For discussion of the economic situation in Afghanistan following the Soviet invasion, see M.S. Noorzoy, 'Long-Term Economic Relations Between Afghanistan and the Soviet Union: An Interpretive Study', *International Journal of Middle East Studies*, vol.17, 1985, pp.151-173; and A. Ghanie Ghaussy, 'The Economic Effects of the Soviet War in Afghanistan', *Internationales Asienforum*, vol.20, nos.1-2, 1989, pp.117-136.

20. 'Sovmestnoe sovetsko-afganskoe kommiunike', *Pravda*, 25 April 1986, p.4.

21. See William Maley, 'Political Legitimation in Contemporary Afghanistan', *Asian Survey*, vol.27, no.6, June 1987, pp.705-725, at p.722.

22. Craig Karp, *Afghanistan: Seven Years of Soviet Occupation* (Special Report no.155, Bureau of Public Affairs, United States Department of State, Washington D.C., December 1986) pp.10-11.

23. See BBC *Summary of World Broadcasts*, FE/8457/C/1-8, 5 January 1987.

24. See *Far Eastern Economic Review*, 6 August 1987, p.14.

25. See 'Otvety M.S. Gorbacheva na voprosy redaktsii gazety "Unita"' *Pravda*, 20 May 1987, pp.1, 3-4, at p.3.

26. See Najibullah's speech of 14 July 1987, in BBC *Summary of World Broadcasts*, FE/8622/C/1-8, 17 July 1987.

27. For Zahir Shah's rejection of power sharing with the PDPA, see *Far Eastern Economic Review*, 6 August 1987, p.14.

28. BBC *Summary of World Broadcasts* FE/6421C/1-3, 16 May 1980.

29. *XXVI s"ezd Kommunisticheskoi partii Sovetskogo Soiuza: stenograficheskii otchet* (Moscow: Politizdat, 1981) vol.I, p.30.

30. See Amin Saikal, 'The Afghanistan crisis: a negotiated settlement?', *The World Today*, vol.40, no.11, November 1984, pp.481-489.

31. David B. Ottaway, 'Stingers Were Key Weapon in Afghan War, Army Finds', *The Washington Post*, 5 July 1989, p.2.

32. Jerry F. Hough, *Soviet Leadership in Transition* (Washington D.C.: The Brookings Institution, 1980) p.166.

33. BBC *Summary of World Broadcasts*, SU/0365/C1/4, 23 January 1989.

6

The Geneva Débâcle

On 8 February 1988, Gorbachev appeared on Soviet television to make a statement about Afghanistan. It inaugurated a decisive phase of the Kremlin's strategy to maintain its client regime in Kabul. He at last proposed a specific date, 15 May 1988, for the commencement of a Soviet troop withdrawal, as well as a ten-month period for its completion.[1] This heralded to many people a long-awaited breakthrough and created much hope, particularly in the more optimistic of Western circles, that a political settlement of the Afghanistan problem was at hand. Gorbachev shrewdly conveyed the impression that his statement created a fleeting chance for such a settlement and this disposed the United States and Pakistan to sign on 15 April 1988 a set of agreements which became known as the Geneva Accords. In their haste to secure a Soviet troop withdrawal, they embraced terms far more favourable to the USSR than need have been the case and thus set the scene not for a *viable* settlement but for further turmoil and bloodshed. For the Afghan people, the Geneva Accords were in no sense a deliverance. On the contrary, the Accords marked the loss of a unique opportunity for transition to a legitimate Afghan regime and instead sanctioned the continuation of communist rule and massive Soviet non-combat involvement in the country.

There is no doubt that Gorbachev's statement provided the impetus needed to reinvigorate the moribund Geneva process. It addressed one issue—namely the timetable for a troop withdrawal—which up to that point had stalled the negotiations. Gorbachev garnished this concession with the declaration that it was a matter neither for the Soviet Union nor for any other outsider to determine the future form of the Afghan government, but for the Afghan people themselves. This distracted attention from the fact that the issue of the demand for self-determination for the Afghan people had been rigorously excluded from the agenda of the negotiations since their inception.

The Positions of the Resistance's Supporters

Gorbachev's statement created a dilemma for the international supporters of the *Mujahideen*. The positions of leadership circles in Pakistan and the United States were, however, somewhat different. Pakistan's reaction to Gorbachev's moves was complicated by a blurring of lines of authority within the Pakistan government. President Zia ul-Haq in 1986 had presided over a return to civilian rule in Pakistan and in 1988 the Government of Pakistan was headed by Prime Minister Mohammad Khan Junejo, who—contrary to Zia's initial expectations—had come over time to be rather more than simply a puppet of the president. A primary interest shared by Zia and Junejo was to be rid of the 'burden' imposed by the presence on Pakistan's territory of millions of Afghan refugees, and of the headquarters of *Mujahideen* parties. This concern had been repeatedly emphasised by Pakistan's centre-left and left opposition parties and figured prominently in the statements of leading figures in the Pakistan People's Party. Yet while Zia appeared to see a solution of this problem only in a settlement which would put a popular government in place in Kabul, under the auspices of which the refugees would return, Junejo was prepared to settle for somewhat less in the hope that a satisfactory outcome might eventually result. Furthermore, Junejo did not share to the same extent President Zia's desire to see Afghanistan under the control of a leadership dominated by Hekmatyar's *Hezb-i Islami*, firmly committed to friendship with Pakistan and hostile to Pakistan's most important regional adversary, India.

By contrast, except amongst a group of congressional and bureaucratic actors (notably in the Congressional Task Force on Afghanistan and the Defense Department) who remained staunch in their support for the *Mujahideen* and the Afghan people, the dominant US interest, reflected in the attitudes of a number of

State Department and CIA officers, was simply to see the Soviet Union withdraw from Afghanistan.[2] This reflected the fact that the concern of important policymakers—including Secretary of State George Shultz—was principally with the global superpower balance and only in *relation* to this with the regions to which superpower conflict had been exported. The notion that Afghanistan was a launching pad for further Soviet adventures 'in the direction of the Persian Gulf' had waned as the USSR became increasingly bogged down and State Department interest in Afghanistan waned with it. In December 1985, apparently without notifying President Reagan, the State Department had committed the US to ending military aid to the *Mujahideen* at the beginning of a Soviet troop withdrawal.[3] This pointed to a degree of disarray in the process by which US Afghan policy was formulated and created opportunities for the USSR to exploit. While the president remained publicly committed to the cause of the resistance, his position was being quietly undermined by factional politics within his administration.

The US administration was caught somewhat unawares by the 8 February statement. The December 1985 commitment exposed the *Mujahideen* to the threat of concentrated Soviet attack during a troop withdrawal period, to which they would be able to respond only with weapons stockpiled in the past. It was therefore necessary that the United States take some diplomatic steps to deal with this problem. However, because the primary US objective was to facilitate a Soviet withdrawal rather than to procure a viable settlement of the Afghan crisis, the steps that it took to deal with the problem were self-serving, and remarkably ineffective as a source of protection for the Afghan opposition.

President Zia had made it clear in response to the Soviet statement that he regarded the formation of a *Mujahideen* coalition government as necessary before Pakistan would sign any peace accords.[4] He was of the view that even if insistence on this point caused the negotiations to collapse, it would not be too long before the Soviets in their own interest would revive them and a satisfactory settlement would be reached. The US administration, however, appeared to have formed the view that the Kabul regime would rapidly collapse once Soviet troops were withdrawn. In its judgment this made it foolish, in order simply to provide for what in their view was certain to happen anyway, to put at risk the possibility of an agreement *requiring* the USSR to withdraw its troops. The US administration therefore put enormous pressure on Pakistan to drop its demand, and President Zia, faced with opposition from Prime Minister Junejo, was forced to give in.[5] Indeed, Junejo's differences with Zia on this point were an important factor in Zia's subsequent decision to remove him from office.

Forced to concede on the question of a transitional government, Pakistan's other proposal, specifically directed at eliminating the transitional vulnerability of the Afghan resistance, was for 'negative symmetry'—that is, that as US arms supplies to the resistance were cut the USSR should be obliged concomitantly to reduce its support for the Kabul regime. The US administration was initially prepared to support this position, despite the December 1985 commitment, but it met with strenuous opposition from the Soviet leadership.[6] Reportedly, Pakistan then proposed 'positive symmetry'—that as long as the USSR continued to aid the Kabul regime, US aid to the resistance should be permitted to continue.[7] On this there was *no* formal compromise between the US and the USSR, but rather what Washington took to be a tacit understanding with Moscow. Shultz proposed to the Soviet Union that US support for the resistance should be allowed for as long as Soviet support for the regime was maintained. A response was received in a letter from Soviet Foreign Minister Shevardnadze. According to Michael Gordon, after 'some debate within the Administration, it was decided that the letter and oral presentations by Soviet diplomats constituted a positive response to the American plan and Mr Shultz recommended accepting the deal'.[8] On 15 April 1988, the four Geneva Accords on Afghanistan were signed.

The Terms of the Accords

The First Geneva Accord was entitled *Bilateral Agreement Between the Republic of Afghanistan and the Islamic Republic of Pakistan on the Principles of Mutual Relations, in particular on Non-Interference and Non-Intervention*. It set out thirteen separate obligations undertaken by each High Contracting Party. Five were especially noteworthy. Article II(4) obliged each party 'to ensure that its territory is not used in any manner which would violate the sovereignty, political independence, territorial integrity and national unity or disrupt the political, economic and social stability of the other High Contracting Party'. Article II(7) imposed the obligation 'to refrain from the promotion, encouragement or support, direct or indirect, of rebellious or secessionist activities against the other High Contracting Party, under any pretext whatsoever, or from any other action which seeks to disrupt the unity or to undermine or subvert the political order of the other High Contracting Party'. The obligation in Article II(8) was 'to prevent within its territory the training, equipping, financing and recruitment of mercenaries from whatever origin for the purpose of hostile activities against the other High Contracting Party, or the sending of such mercenaries into the territory of the other High Contracting Party and accordingly to deny facilities, including financing for the training, equipping and transit of such mercenaries'. Article II(11) required each party 'to prevent any assistance to or use of or tolerance of terrorist groups, saboteurs or subversive agents against the other High Contracting Party.' Most importantly, Article II(12) outlined the obligation 'to prevent within its territory the presence, harbouring, in camps and bases or otherwise, organising, training, financing, equipping and arming of individuals and political, ethnic and any other groups for the purpose of creating subversion, disorder or unrest in the territory of the other High Contracting Party and accordingly also to prevent the use of mass media and the transportation of arms, ammunition and equipment by such individuals and groups'.

The Second Geneva Accord was entitled *Declaration on International Guarantees*, and its signatories were the USSR and the USA. The signatories undertook 'to invariably refrain from any form of interference and intervention in the internal affairs of the Republic of Afghanistan and the Islamic Republic of Pakistan and to respect the commitments contained in the bilateral Agreement between the Republic of Afghanistan and the Islamic Republic of Pakistan on the Principles of Mutual Relations, in particular on Non-Interference and Non-Intervention.'

The Third Geneva Accord was entitled *Bilateral Agreement between the Republic of Afghanistan and the Islamic Republic of Pakistan on the Voluntary Return of Refugees.* It provided that all

Afghan refugees 'temporarily present in the territory of the Islamic Republic of Pakistan shall be given the opportunity to return voluntarily to their homeland in accordance with the arrangements and conditions set out in the present agreement'. Those arrangements and conditions were set out in some detail.

The Fourth Geneva Accord was entitled *Agreement on the Interrelationships for the Settlement of the Situation relating to Afghanistan*. It was signed by the representatives of the Kabul regime and the government of Pakistan and, in witness, the representatives of the States-Guarantors, the USSR and USA, affixed their signatures. It stated that all Accords would enter into force on 15 May 1988. Its key provision was contained in Paragraph 5: 'In accordance with the timeframe agreed upon between the Union of Soviet Socialist Republics and the Republic of Afghanistan there will be a phased withdrawal of the foreign troops which will start on the date of entry into force mentioned above. One half of the troops will be withdrawn by 15 August 1988 and the withdrawal of all troops will be completed within nine months'. An annexed *Memorandum of Understanding* dealt with the 'modalities and logistical arrangements' for the work of a representative of the secretary-general, and personnel under his authority, who 'shall investigate any possible violations of any of the provisions of the instruments and prepare a report thereon'.

To coincide with the signing of the Accords, the US secretary of state transmitted to the secretary-general an official Statement. The key paragraph read: 'The obligations undertaken by the guarantors are symmetrical. In this regard, the United States has advised the Soviet Union that the U.S. retains the right, consistent with its obligations as guarantor, to provide military assistance to parties in Afghanistan. Should the Soviet Union exercise restraint in providing military assistance to parties in Afghanistan, the U.S. similarly will exercise restraint'.[9]

The Weaknesses of the Accords

The most notable feature of the Accords was that they matched what the Soviet Union had all along demanded and paid no heed to the political interests of the popular opposition. While both the USA and Pakistan explicitly stated that their signing of the

Accords could not be taken to signify recognition of the PDPA regime, the very act of signing gave the Kabul regime a status in the eyes of the international community which otherwise it would have lacked. Furthermore, the Accords left the opposition vulnerable in many respects. No one reading the Accords in ignorance of the recent history of Afghanistan would have realised that it was the *USSR* which had invaded Afghanistan; the First Accord, on the contrary, appeared to legitimate the Soviet claim that the fundamental problem to be confronted in any settlement was 'outside interference' *against* the PDPA regime. By requiring Pakistan even 'to prevent the use of mass media' by groups opposed to the Kabul regime, the First Accord imposed restraints which an advocate of the right to free speech might find difficult to defend. More seriously, it set out a sequence of measures, legally binding on Pakistan, which, if applied effectively, would predictably have had the effect of crippling the Afghan resistance, the most important provision being that in Article II(12).

The stringent provisions in Article II (12) may be usefully contrasted with the requirements placed on the USSR by the Fourth Accord. This Accord failed to identify in any precise manner the Soviet personnel to be embraced by its provisions; the vague expression 'the foreign troops' created almost infinite opportunities for disputation. No attempt was made to determine the *extent* of the 'foreign 'troop' presence in Afghanistan; this rendered the provisions for the *phasing* of the withdrawal quite meaningless. Western countries were left in the invidious position of having to accept the subsequent Soviet claim that there were only 103,000 troops in Afghanistan, as no viable mechanism was established by which such a claim could be tested. The wording of the Fourth Accord also left it unclear whether military advisers, civilian advisers, non-combat personnel with combat potential, and paramilitary, security, and police forces were covered. This was no trivial flaw, as a great deal of the work of regime maintenance had been carried out by such forces. Furthermore, the Accord did not explicitly oblige the Soviet Union to withdraw its five main advanced air-military bases and four major signals intelligence (SIGINT) sites, all strategically located in different parts of Afghanistan. The air bases—most importantly the Bagram base near Kabul, the Shindand base near Herat, and the

Kandahar base—were important links in the chain by which Soviet logistic support for the Kabul regime was maintained.

The matter of Soviet 'non-combat' support was raised at a press conference given by Najibullah after the Accords were signed. He remarked: 'As is known, co-operation between Afghanistan and the USSR in the military sphere began 23 years before the April revolution. It has always played an important role in strengthening the defence capability of our state. We have no intention of renouncing the USSR's help in this sphere, at least as long as the situation on the borders of our homeland obliges us to show concern for the interests of our security.'[10]

The weaknesses of the much-vaunted tacit understanding on 'positive symmetry' were equally apparent. The proponents of this approach seemed to have taken no account of the possibility that once Soviet troops were withdrawn, Soviet staying-power in support of the Kabul regime would exceed US staying-power in support of the resistance. Yet given that there had always been circles in both the CIA and the State Department which had been unenthusiastic about arming the *Mujahideen*, the odds of this happening were quite high.

Finally, and most importantly, the Accords made no provision for self-determination by the Afghan people. The statement by UN Secretary-General Pérez de Cuéllar on 14 April 1988 that the Accords 'lay the basis for the exercise by all Afghans of their right to self-determination, a principle enshrined in the Charter'[11] was extremely disingenuous: this was precisely what the Accords did *not* do. Some provision for self-determination at this point was important not simply as an abstract good but as a key element in war termination—for as Robert Randle has noted, a 'political settlement will be inadequate if the peace negotiators have not reached all the issues and leave unresolved some of the disputes that were the basis for the war'.[12] Cordovez's maladroit diplomacy had shaped a 'peace' settlement which was defective in exactly this way.

Soviet Exploitation of the Accords

In the period between the signing of the Geneva Accords and the formal completion of the Soviet troop withdrawal in mid-

February 1989, the Soviet Union adopted a multidimensional strategy to further its interests in Afghanistan. This strategy had four main elements, pursued simultaneously and with great dexterity. The first was the bolstering of the political cohesion and military capacity of the PDPA regime under Najibullah's leadership. The second was the weakening of Pakistan as the key state supporting the *Mujahideen*. The third was the use of propaganda to create the impression that the USSR and the Kabul regime were abiding strictly by the terms of the Geneva Accords whereas the USA and Pakistan were not, and that Soviet intentions towards Afghanistan had become entirely benign. The fourth was the use of diplomatic devices to exacerbate instability amongst the *Mujahideen* as the Kabul regime approached what the Soviets saw as its moment of truth.

The Soviets were more aware than most that the regime had little chance of surviving unless a vigorous last attempt was made to smother the chronic hostilities between *Khalqis* and *Parchamis* which had debilitated the regime for the best part of a decade.[13] Having sought for quite some time, and with limited success, to *reconcile* the warring groups within the PDPA leadership, the Soviets moved during the withdrawal phase to decapitate the *Khalq* faction. The single most important such step, prompted by an October 1988 coup attempt,[14] was the forced posting as ambassador to the USSR of the most prominent surviving *Khalqi*, Interior Minister Sayid Mohammad Gulabzoi. Up to that point, Gulabzoi had been able to develop the security police of the Interior ministry (*Sarandoy*) as a *Khalqi* outpost to counterbalance the power of the *Parcham*-dominated KHAD.[15] Gulabzoi's travel was followed by the removal to Soviet territory of a number of important *Khalqi* officers, who were not permitted to return to Afghanistan until well after the completion of the withdrawal. This was reinforced by the enlargement of the special Presidential Guard so that it could not only protect Najibullah but also provide him with a personal force which could be deployed both in regular military operations and against internal party rivals. This provided an *overt* source of coercive power in Najibullah's hands to complement the *covert* power which he possessed through control of the secret police.

In order to make the elimination of *Khalqi* influence a somewhat less blatant exercise, the USSR prompted a number of other regime changes which were marketed as elements of 'national reconciliation'. The most striking such move was the replacement on 26 May 1988 of the *Parchami* (and Hazara) prime minister, Sultan Ali Kishtmand, by Dr Mohammad Hasan Sharq, a 'non-party' figure. Sharq's independence was largely illusory, as he had served as the regime's ambassador to India for a number of years, but his appointment blurred the impression of dyadic factional conflict.

In coping with the problem of regime factionalism, the Soviets were, however, also assisted by two distinct factors. The first was that the apparent desperation of the regime's position created overwhelming *prudential* motives for thitherto antagonistic factions to cooperate. The statements of the *Mujahideen* suggested that communists of any faction faced a grim future in the event of the regime's overthrow. Both *Khalqis* and *Parchamis* had a motive to work together lest they be liquidated by a common enemy. The other factor was that one of the considerations which had markedly reduced the chances of the PDPA's getting its own act together and marketing itself to the Afghan people as a credible force had been the presence of the Soviet troops. On the one hand, this factor had been among those prompting the party's members and supporters to engage in intense rivalry in the expectation that the Soviet forces would provide the necessary cushion against the opposition. On the other, it continually underscored the position of the party as nothing more than a delinquent puppet, controlled and run entirely by the Soviets—a fact which led most of the Afghans under the regime's control to detest it and refrain from serving it with any sense of loyalty and commitment.

On the military front, the regime benefited from a number of distinct Soviet moves. Security belts around the major cities were markedly strengthened, as well as pushed further than ever before from the city centres. Furthermore, the Soviet not only left behind vast weapons stocks as they departed—Lieutenant General Boris Gromov stated on 14 May 1988 that the Soviets intended to leave $1 billion worth[16]—but introduced new weapons systems. These included, most importantly, MiG-27 fighter aircraft and an undisclosed number of SCUD 'A' and 'B' guided missiles, turning the regime's airforce and rocketry regiments into some of the best equipped in the region. In addition, Soviet forces, especially in the weeks immediately preceding the completion of the troop withdrawal, undertook a round-the-clock bombardment of a number of regions in which the *Mujahideen* were well-entrenched, confirming fears which had been voiced by a number of critics of the Geneva Accords. The most notable of these operations was against the forces of Ahmad Shah Massoud in the vicinity of the Salang Tunnel; on 23 January 1989 Soviet bombing of villages caused massive civilian casualties, prompting the US administration to accuse the Soviets of carrying out a 'scorched-earth policy'. The purpose of these operations was generally to cause as much damage as possible to the resistance forces best placed to attack Kabul, but particularly to protect the main land route along which Soviet troops were withdrawn and by which supplies were despatched to Kabul.

These moves were directly complementary to the second main strand of the Soviet strategy, namely the weakening of Pakistan's support for the *Mujahideen*. It should of course be noted that well before the signing of the Accords Pakistan had been subjected to a sustained terrorist campaign,[17] involving both incursions into Pakistani airspace by Afghan airforce MiGs which proceeded to dump their payloads on border villages in the Northwest Frontier Province, and the detonation of KHAD bombs in Pakistani cities—most notably Peshawar, which in 1986 was declared a Category I Danger Zone for UN employees. The objectives of this campaign were to increase antagonism from local Pakistanis against both the *Mujahideen* (whose offices were from time to time targets) and against the refugees, as Pakistanis usually figured among the casualties when blasts proved fatal. This campaign was maintained during the Soviet troop withdrawal. In particular, two major incidents in 1988 not only bore the hallmarks of Soviet-instigated sabotage but directly impacted on the military and political developments up to and following the completion of the withdrawal.

On 10 April 1988, only five days before the Geneva Accords were signed, a massive blast ripped through an ammunition dump at the Ojheri army base near Rawalpindi. Heavy explosives rained on Islamabad and extensive civilian casualties resulted. The dump had contained very substantial stocks of armaments destined for the *Mujahideen* and their destruction markedly impacted on the correlation of forces in Afghanistan in the following months; a congressional source in Washington labelled the blast a 'major logistical setback'.[18]

A more dramatic event took place on 17 August 1988. President Zia ul-Haq had travelled by Air Force C-130 Hercules transport plane to Bahawalpur in the south of the country, accompanied by US Ambassador Arnold Raphel and a number of the most senior Pakistani military figures. About ten minutes after the plane took off to return to the north it crashed, killing all aboard. While political considerations apparently hindered a thorough US investigation of the crash, the Pakistan Board of Inquiry, assisted by US Air Force specialists, concluded that the crash was caused by the deliberate sabotage of the plane's main and backup hydraulic systems.[19] The death of Zia created an important leadership vacuum and an immediate political crisis. As we noted earlier, Zia had removed Junejo from the position of prime minister; and had called elections for mid-November. When Zia was killed, the position of president was assumed by Ghulam Ishaq Khan, president of the Senate, and a former Finance minister. However, despite considerable political skill, he was not a serious candidate to fill Zia's shoes. Zia's death in effect opened the way for the Pakistan People's Party under Benazir Bhutto to contest the November elections on reasonably fair terms.

However, this was not all it did. The deaths of Zia's military colleagues in the same crash destabilised the military, reducing the prospects of a concerted military move to abort the march towards the scheduled National Assembly elections. The accident also left Pakistan without a clear and unambiguous Afghan policy, as Zia had tried as far as possible to arrogate policymaking in this area to himself and his close military colleagues. And ultimately, it permitted Benazir Bhutto, hardly famous up to that moment for her sympathy for the Afghan resistance, to become prime minister of Pakistan before the completion of the Soviet troop withdrawal—even though she was constrained to moderate her position on Afghanistan in the run-up to the elections, something which made Pakistan's policy appear even more confused. All this occurred at the very time when any incoherence or irresolution would be ruthlessly exploited by the USSR.

The Soviet Union was also able to extract considerable propaganda mileage from US and Pakistani violations of the Geneva Accords. Once the Accords were in place and the Soviets began their troop withdrawal, Moscow and the Kabul regime rapidly escalated their war of propaganda against Pakistan and the United States for violating the terms of the Accords by continuing their support for the *Mujahideen*. As there was no doubt that Pakistan and the US were doing just that, the Kremlin and the regime were able for the first time since the Soviet invasion to seize the propaganda initiative in a credible way. This seemed to catch the US almost unawares; its responses to the USSR's charges suggested that important US policymakers had genuinely believed that the Soviets shared the State Department's view that the Accords were no more than a meaningless veil for the Soviet withdrawal. The USSR indeed refrained for some time from criticising the USA by name, initially directing its charges against Pakistan. Nonetheless the charges, when they were made, hit home—and their effect was to weaken the firm support of the international community for Western backing for the *Mujahideen*, as the continuation of such support seemed to conflict with the principle, dear to a large number of states, that treaty arrangements should be observed. It was little wonder that the UN General Assembly in 1988 dealt with Afghanistan only in an anodyne consensus resolution.

The Soviets cleverly reinforced this propaganda by deliberately sowing doubt about whether the withdrawal would be completed on time. On 6 November Soviet Deputy Foreign Minister Aleksandr Bessmertnykh announced that the Soviet Union had ceased withdrawing troops from Afghanistan and warned that Soviet adherence to the withdrawal timetable 'depended on other parties complying with the agreement'.[20] The same tactic was used at the beginning January 1989, when Soviet deputy foreign minister and ambassador to Kabul, Iulii Vorontsov, raised the possibility that the 15 February deadline might not be met.[21] It is doubtful whether these threats had any substance; it seems more likely that they were designed to keep the resistance and its international supporters in suspense and off balance. In this they proved quite effective, as the *Mujahideen* and their supporters could not be sure exactly what kind of military and political situation they would face as the scheduled date for the completion of the withdrawal approached.

The End Game

Finally, as the Soviet withdrawal gained momentum, Moscow launched a vigorous diplomatic campaign to bring to bear as much pressure as possible on the *Mujahideen* and their international supporters to abide by the terms of the Geneva Accords. As part of this, the USSR even went to the length of opening direct talks with the Afghan opposition forces. On 27 November a meeting was held in Islamabad between two officials of the Soviet Embassy and two officials of resistance parties.The immediate question was the return to the Soviet Union of prisoners of war in the hands of the resistance. This had become something of an issue in May 1988 when General Aleksei Lizichev, head of the Central Political Directorate of the Soviet Armed Forces, announced at a press conference that 311 Soviet soldiers were missing in action.[22] There followed a flood of letters to the newspaper *Literaturnaia gazeta* on this topic, the effect of which was to create some expectation that no effort would be spared to secure the return of those missing. The *Mujahideen* used this issue in order to bypass the Kabul regime and open a line of direct communications with the Soviet authorities, with a view to broadening the agenda of discussion. Once contact was made the agenda broadened, but *not* to the resistance's advantage. Vorontsov held two meetings—one in early December in Taif (Saudi Arabia) and another a month later in Islamabad—with a delegation of Pakistan-based leaders of the seven main Sunni *Mujahideen* groups. However, to bring pressure on these groups and their regional supporters Vorontsov held separate talks in Rome with the former Afghan King Zahir Shah, and in Teheran with the leadership of eight Iran-based Shiite minority *Mujahideen* groups. He also met with Saudi, Pakistani and Iranian leaders.

However, as could have been expected, the negotiations soon reached a dead end. Vorontsov's unbending support for the claim of the PDPA to play a pivotal role in a settlement, and insistence that the Soviet Union would continue to support the PDPA even after its troop withdrawal, finally prompted both the Sunni and Shia *Mujahideen* leaders to perceive the discussions as nothing but a divisive ploy to enable the Soviet Union to achieve politically what it had failed to accomplish militarily. While all along opposed to any deal with the PDPA as inimical to their struggle, both the Sunni and Shia *Mujahideen* leaders, in an unprecedented display of unity at the Islamabad round of talks, rejected any further discussion with the Soviets until all their troops had withdrawn from Afghanistan and the PDPA regime had been overthrown. The Soviet diplomacy equally cut little ice with either Zahir Shah, or any other credible figures of past Afghan regimes, or the *Mujahideen*'s regional supporters. They could not consent to a coalition settlement with the PDPA.[23]

The Soviet diplomacy, nonetheless, exacerbated two pre-existing schisms within the Afghan resistance. It not only intensified divisions in the resistance along leadership and traditional ethno-tribal and linguistic lines, but also aggravated the sectarian Sunni-Shia split, which can easily be manipulated by elements from inside and outside Afghanistan for self-serving purposes. Furthermore, it brought to the fore the rival and conflicting interests of the regional supporters of the *Mujahideen*. Whereas Pakistan and Saudi Arabia had backed the Sunni *Mujahideen* groups and even then on a preferential basis, Iran's support had been mainly for the Shia groups.[24] To complicate the situation further, the United States, a close friend of Pakistan and Saudi Arabia and adversary of Iran, had had its own regional and international interests in providing support for the Pakistan-based *Mujahideen* groups. Indeed, the Soviets had never failed to exacerbate and exploit these factors to their favour and that of the PDPA.

Nonetheless, if Vorontsov had hoped that the resistance would join a 'coalition' government which the PDPA could dominate, his objectives were frustrated. The continued diplomatic activities of Señor Cordovez proved no more successful in procuring a viable settlement of the Afghanistan problem. In order to legitimate the complete exclusion of the *Mujahideen* from the Geneva process, Cordovez had always maintained that agreements of the kind which were signed in April 1988 would be only the first stage of a two-stage process for procuring a settlement.[25] Whether Cordovez ever seriously entertained the belief that a second stage would eventuate is difficult to say, but in the event it (predictably) did not. The reason for this was quite simple. The Geneva Accords had given the Soviet Union all that it was really interested in procuring from negotiations on Afghanistan. Soviet Foreign Minister Shevardnadze suggested this in October 1989 when he remarked gratefully that without the UN 'it would have been difficult to hope for the conclusion of the Geneva agreements on Afghanistan, which permitted our soldiers to return home in dignity, without losses or loss of face'.[26] As Francis Bacon once observed, it 'is better dealing with men in appetite, than with those that are where they would be',[27] and once the Geneva Accords came into force, they left the USSR satiated. As his efforts failed to bear fruit Cordovez became increasingly shrill and even made the impertinent claim that he spoke for the 'silent majority of Afghans'. He issued various calls for ceasefires, all of which were ignored,[28] and finally took up the position of Foreign Minister of Ecuador,[29] substantially disengaging himself from the chaos he had helped to perpetuate. In October 1990, Ecuador was reported to have established diplomatic ties at ambassadorial level with the Kabul regime.[30]

Thus, by February 1989, as a result of the Geneva Accords—and Soviet exploitation of their weaknesses, as well as deft political manoeuvring—Afghanistan faced a grim and uncertain future. The opportunity to force the Soviets to abandon the PDPA regime—in exchange for a veil to hide the ignominy of their military failure in Afghanistan—had been missed. As a result, the Soviet Union was allowed to withdraw on its own terms rather than on terms which resolute negotiating behaviour might have procured. These terms were virtually indistinguishable from those which the Soviet leadership had outlined shortly after the original invasion. The Soviet Union in the end was not required to abandon the regime altogether; it was simply obliged to alter the mix of policies at its disposal to keep the regime in power. In this context, given that military force had patently failed to guarantee long-term Soviet influence in Afghanistan, the withdrawal could hardly be seen as grossly detrimental to Soviet interests.

The completion of the Soviet withdrawal was not therefore a new dawn for the Afghan people. Mid-February 1989 saw Afghanistan still afflicted with an illegitimate government, almost entirely dependent upon Soviet military aid and *materiel* for its survival. The difference was that there was no longer any obvious way to secure its *peaceful* displacement. Transition to a political order in which Afghan micro-societies were sufficiently integrated in decisionmaking to ensure a degree of stability had been made more remote than ever. The Geneva débâcle simply remitted the matter to the battlefield.

Notes

1. 'Zaiavlenie General'nogo sekretaria TsK KPSS M.S. Gorbacheva po Afganistanu', *Komsomol'skaia pravda*, 9 February 1988, p.1.

2. For differing perspectives on the positions of US actors, see Selig S. Harrison, 'Afghanistan: Soviet Intervention, Afghan Resistance, and the American Role', in Michael T. Klare and Peter Kornbluh (eds.), *Low Intensity Warfare: Counterinsurgency, Proinsurgency, and Antiterrorism in the Eighties* (New York: Pantheon Books, 1988) pp.183-206; and the remarks of Senator Gordon J. Humphrey, 'An Expose of the State Department's Policy on Afghanistan', *Free Afghanistan Report*, January-February 1988, pp.8-10.

3. David K. Shipler, 'Reagan Didn't Know of Afghan Deal', *The New York Times*, 11 February 1988, p.3.

4. Paul Lewis, 'New Kabul Offer in Afghan Parley', *The New York Times*, 4 March 1988, p.11.

5. See Selig S. Harrison, 'Inside The Afghan Talks', *Foreign Policy*, no.72, Fall 1988, pp.31-60, at p.56.

6. Gary Lee, 'Soviets Upset By Terms for Afghan Pact', *The Washington Post*, 15 March 1988, p.1.

7. Zalmay Khalilzad, 'Afghanistan: Anatomy of a Soviet Failure', *The National Interest*, no.12, Summer 1988, pp.101-108, at p.105.

8. Michael R. Gordon, 'U.S. and Moscow Agree on Pullout from Afghanistan', *The New York Times*, 12 April 1988, p.1.

9. *Department of State Bulletin*, vol.88, no.2135, June 1988, p.55.

10. BBC *Summary of World Broadcasts* FE/0141/C/1, 3 May 1988.

11. See *Agreements on Settlement of Situation Relating to Afghanistan Signed at Geneva* (Geneva: United Nations Information Service, Press Release Afghanistan/9, 14 April 1988) p.1.

12. Robert F. Randle, *The Origins of Peace: A Study of Peacemaking and the Structure of Peace Settlements* (New York: The Free Press, 1973) p.487.

13. See the remarks of Major-General K.M. Tsagolov, 'Afganistan—predvaritel'nye itogi', *Ogonek*, no.30, 1988, pp.25-26.

14. See BBC *Summary of World Broadcasts* FE/0292/C/5, 26 October 1988.

15. This was clearly demonstrated in 1986 when during the Central Committee Plenum which replaced Karmal with Najibullah, Soviet tanks were stationed around the Interior Ministry building in Kabul to prevent any attempts to derail the leadership changes which the USSR had decided to make. See *Defense & Foreign Affairs Weekly*, vol.12, no.17, 12-18 May 1986, p.2.

16. See *The Middle East Journal*, vol.42, no.4, Autumn 1988, p.656.

17. See Tom Rogers, 'Afghan refugees and the stability of Pakistan', *Survival*, vol.29, no.5, October 1987, pp.416-429, at pp.423-424.

18. 'Pakistani President Asserts Blast Was Act of Sabotage', *The Washington Post*, 15 April 1988, p.27.

19. See Robert D. Kaplan, 'How Zia's Death Helped the U.S.', *The New York Times*, 23 August 1989, p.21.

20. 'Moscow suspends troop withdrawal from Afghanistan', *Australian Financial Review*, 7 November 1988.

21. Michael Dobbs, 'Soviet Aide Questions Afghan Withdrawal Date', *The Washington Post*, 11 January 1989, p.17.

22. 'Strogo sobliudat' obiazatel'stva', *Pravda*, 26 May 1988, p.5.

23. On these talks, see Amin Saikal, 'Afghanistan: the end-game', *The World Today*, vol.45, no.3, March 1989, pp.37-39.

24. See Ahmed Rashid, 'Islamic Powers Vie over Afghanistan', *The Independent*, 2 February 1989, p.12.

25. See Harrison, 'Inside The Afghan Talks', p.38.

26. BBC *Summary of World Broadcasts* SU/0596/C/8, 25 October 1989.

27. Sir Francis Bacon, 'Of Negotiating', in *Bacon's Essays* (New York: Carlton House, n.d.) pp.259-261, at p.260.

28. For a damning critique of Cordovez's post-April efforts, see Louis Dupree, 'Post-Withdrawal Afghanistan: Light at the End of the Tunnel', in Amin Saikal and William Maley (eds.), *The Soviet Withdrawal from Afghanistan* (Cambridge: Cambridge University Press, 1989) pp.29-51 at pp.46-47.

29. Cordovez did not opt for total silence. When Gorbachev was awarded the Nobel Peace Prize, Cordovez sang his praises in a newspaper article: Diego Cordovez, 'Afghans Should Approve Gorbachev's Peace Prize', *International Herald Tribune*, 1 November 1990. This won him a stinging rebuke from the *Mujahideen*: see Mohammad Es'haq, 'Peace prize for Gorbachev makes Afghans angry', *AFGHANews*, vol.6, no.22, 15 November 1990, pp.1-4.

30. BBC *Summary of World Broadcasts* FE/0898/B/1, 18 October 1990.

7

The Aftermath of the Withdrawal

On 15 February 1989 the last member of the Soviet combat contingent, Lieutenant-General B.V. Gromov, crossed the land frontier between Afghanistan and the Soviet Union, bringing to an apparent end the USSR's longest and most painful military adventure beyond its frontiers. As the date for the completion of the withdrawal had approached, tension rose in Kabul. A large number of Western countries, anticipating that the city might be sacked under circumstances reminiscent of those when *Bacha-i-Saqao* entered Kabul in 1929, withdrew their diplomatic staffs, creating a brooding sense of foreboding. This was accentuated by severe food and fuel shortages which aggravated the strain imposed by an unusually bitter winter. To many observers, the collapse of the regime—as a result either of *Mujahideen* assault or disintegration from within—appeared imminent.

Yet this did not eventuate. As months went by, the regime proved unexpectedly resilient and the *Mujahideen*, while continuing to control the bulk of the countryside, failed to make the inroads on the regime's urban strongholds which had been widely anticipated. As a result, a grim stalemate developed. The explanation for this development lay in a number of factors. Some were external, but others reflected the diversity of Afghan society which we have been at pains to emphasise. The first was the extent of the Soviet commitment to maintain the leading role of the PDPA in Afghan politics in the post-withdrawal period. The second was the inability of Western supporters of the *Mujahideen* to adapt effectively to the requirements of the new situation which the withdrawal of Soviet combat forces had created. The third was the negative effect upon resistance cohesion of attempts by outside powers, most notably Pakistan, Saudi Arabia, and Iran, to boost the position of particular elements in the resistance which they deemed sympathetic to their objectives. And the fourth was the failure of the *Mujahideen* to resist these pressures effectively, and to respond swiftly, and more importantly, *concertedly*, to the new military and political situation with which they were confronted.

The Post-Withdrawal Soviet Commitment

The first manifestation of the USSR's continued commitment to the regime came in the form of a massive operation to relieve the shortages by which Kabul was afflicted. To this day, it is unclear quite how these shortages came about. They may simply have been a consequence of the heavy snows which cloaked the capital, but it is quite possible that they were deliberately contrived by the regime and the USSR in order, on the one hand, to legitimate Soviet dealings with the regime in the post-withdrawal phase by according them an ostensibly 'humanitarian' dimension and, on the other, to allow the regime to buy support by presenting itself as benefactor of an urban population ground down by an alleged resistance blockade of the city. This operation continued apace in the months following the withdrawal. Cities do not feed themselves, particularly when they have no income from productive activity with which to purchase staple commodities, and Kabul required food supply of approximately 700 tonnes per day. This the Soviet Union supplied, in an operation unprecedented in scale since the days of the Berlin blockade.[1]

The 'humanitarian' flights were also the perfect mask for a massive operation to resupply the regime with military equipment. In the first six months of 1989 the USSR reportedly supplied the regime with about $1.4 billion worth of arms.[2] Furthermore, and contrary to popular belief, the Soviets did not leave the military domain entirely to the regime. Senior and middle-rank Soviet officers continued to participate in the planning and direction of all major military operations. The presence of Soviet advisers in Afghanistan was actually admitted by General Valentin Varennikov, commander-in-chief of Soviet Land Forces. Varennikov sought to downplay the importance of the commitment;[3] however, a subsequent confidential US government report stated 'that "all functions connected with the security, transportation, storage and launch of Scud missiles are handled by Soviet advisers" wearing Afghan uniforms'.[4] The weaponry which the USSR sent into Afghanistan was not simply used for deterrent or defensive purposes. On the contrary, the regime made maximum use of its firepower in order to injure the resistance and the civilian populations on whose support the *Mujahideen* in part depended.

In this respect, it is important to note that the USSR's military aid was very carefully directed. The weakness of the Afghan Army had long been a matter openly discussed in both Western and Soviet sources. The USSR therefore supplied equipment mainly for use by the Air Force and Tank Brigade, those elements of the armed forces which had traditionally been trained and equipped by the USSR and which depended to the *least* extent on the loyalty of reluctant conscripts. The superior loyalty of these elements of the armed forces had been pointed out even before the completion of the withdrawal but seemed to have been discounted.[5] In order to augment the position of these elements, and more generally to boost the PDPA's manpower, the USSR also rushed back to Kabul thousands of young Afghans who had been taken to the USSR in previous years to be trained as future janissaries. Because many of these had been shifted to the Soviet Union at young ages and from dislocated or deprived backgrounds, they had been shielded from characteristic Afghan processes of socialisation and instead had been thoroughly indoctrinated by the Soviets to kill and die for the PDPA's cause. By no means all students sent to the USSR proved reliable,[6] but enough did to accord the regime some assistance.

The return of these students coincided with an intensified regime propaganda campaign to capitalise on the fact of the Soviet withdrawal to polish the PDPA's image and present it not as the vanguard socialist force which the platform of the mid-1960s claimed, but rather as a reformist-nationalist force, respectful of Islam and Afghan traditions. Although the regime, apparently at the behest of the USSR, had in its rhetoric deemphasised revolutionary and socialist themes for several years, this had no prospect of carrying any weight as long as Soviet forces were in Afghanistan; even after the withdrawal, it did not appear to win the PDPA any generalised normative support from the broader populace. It managed to make some dent among the highly urbanised, secularised Kabulis, some of whom had grown very nervous about the consequences of an opposition victory and the prospects of life under a *Mujahideen*-led Islamic government. Nonetheless, as this campaign of agitation and propaganda coincided with moves to strengthen the position of the PDPA—notably through the replacement of Prime Minister Sharq by former *Parcham* Prime Minister Sultan Ali Kishtmand, and of other 'non-party' ministers by party members—its message was somewhat blunted.

US and Pakistani Reactions

While the Soviet Union was employing these various devices to improve the position of the regime, the reaction of Western powers was notably flat-footed. In part this was due to the persistence of the power vacuum in Washington associated with transition to a new president. The 'lame duck' period between the presidential election of 8 November 1988 and President Bush's inauguration on 20 January 1989 was to be expected; but the long delay in fully constituting the administration after 20 January was not. The Defense Department lacked a secretary, as the president's nominee, John Tower, ran into ratification difficulties with the US Senate; and this prolonged the ineffectiveness of an agency which had resolutely supported the cause of the *Mujahideen* in US bureaucratic politics. This problem was accentuated by the appointment of an official inexperienced in running an arms supply operation to head the CIA's Afghanistan Task Force, under the auspices of which arms were to be supplied to the *Mujahideen*. Thus, at the very time when the Soviets were cranking up their arms supply operation to top gear, the US operation fell victim to glitches. Furthermore, despite the US reservation, at the time the Geneva Accords were signed, of the right to supply the resistance as long as Soviet supplies to the regime continued, there were also some indications in the first half of 1989, of a diminution in the US administration's commitment. The most striking example of this was the fall in the supply of Stinger missiles to the *Mujahideen*, creating a shortage which was acutely felt as the resistance undertook operations against urban centres which the regime sought to defend with air strikes.[7]

Various circles in Pakistan recognised that the completion of the Soviet withdrawal would create a novel situation in Afghanistan, but the tactics which they employed in order to cope with this situation miscarried spectacularly, as anyone familiar with Afghan society would have expected. The point of departure for the Pakistani approach was the proposition that the Afghan resistance was not unified. This was blatantly obvious and had long been remarked by outside observers. From this point, they reasoned that it was necessary that a unified leadership be secured, and for this purpose they devised the idea of a *Shura* (council) which would meet to legitimate a new leadership of this kind. (Interestingly, the term *Loya Jirga* was avoided, probably so that non-Pushtun groups would not be offended.) The suppressed premiss in this argument was that the disunity in the ranks of the resistance was *capable* of being overcome through the use of such devices—and yet this was an assumption of breathtaking audacity given the diverse social structure from which the resistance had sprung. The upshot was that the prospects for anything useful resulting from the *Shura* were never especially strong.

The Events of the Shura

The *Shura* was eventually held from 10-24 February, coinciding with the completion of the Soviet troop withdrawal. Getting it off the ground proved, however, to be a mammoth task, largely because of disputation about how it should be composed. The most noted flaw in its composition came from the absence of Iran-based Shiite *Mujahideen* groups. This was not for want of trying by some of the more level-headed *Mujahideen* figures. Professor Sibghatullah Mojadiddi, at that time spokesman of the Pakistan-based Islamic Alliance of Afghan Mujahideen, travelled to Teheran to negotiate with the leaders of these groups, and in good faith reached an agreement under which Shiite representatives would secure 100 out of 519 *Shura* seats. This agreement, however, was repudiated by the Council of the Alliance on Mojadiddi's return, and the Shia *Mujahideen* were offered only 70 seats, which they declined to take. Thus, while independent Shiite groups such as the *Shura-i Ettefaq* were given seats, the bulk of the Shiite parties were not. Despite frantic attempts at mediation by Iranian officials, the spokesman of the Iran-based groups, Mohammad Karim Khalili, left in disgust.[8]

The exclusion of the bulk of proposed Shiite representation was by no means the only blemish in the composition of the *Shura*. There was no sense in which it could be described as 'representative'. Mojadiddi admitted as much at a press conference during the *Shura* when he said that it represented at maximum 'one third' of the Afghan population;[9] and former Afghan Justice Minister Shamsuddin Majrooh, in a powerful address to the *Shura* itself, made much the same point. Each of the seven parties in the Islamic Alliance of Afghan Mujahideen was given 60 seats, even though the support which the different parties could command within Afghanistan varied enormously. The bulk of the 'delegates' to the *Shura* came from the Eastern provinces of Afghanistan, and were Pushtuns; the northern provinces were under-represented, as were the Tajiks and other ethnic groups concentrated in the north. At least one *Jamiat* commander from the north, who was a delegate to the *Shura*, actually admitted to boycotting its sessions in protest at the under-representation of his region.[10] The net effect of this was that very few major *Mujahideen* commanders were present at the *Shura*. This clearly undermined its credibility, as there was no obvious reason why determined commanders such as Abdul Haq and Ahmad Shah Massoud, with established power bases of their own within Afghanistan, would subordinate their plans to the *Shura*'s dictates. Massoud subsequently pointed out that he had received an invitation to send representatives to the *Shura* only two days before it started.[11]

Furthermore, the *Shura* was sabotaged above all by self-interested manipulation from the Pakistan Inter-Services Intelligence Directorate, backed by Saudi Arabian paymasters. Each of these groups had a client. The Pakistanis' client was Gulbuddin Hekmatyar, whose longstanding, integral links with

Pakistani military intelligence we have already noted. He had been Zia's personal favourite and was amenable to Zia's suggestions. The Saudis' principal client was Professor Abdul Rasul Sayyaf, although the Saudis were by no means ill-disposed to Hekmatyar either. The Pakistanis and Saudis could not but have been aware, however, that each of these figures had only a narrow appeal within Afghanistan itself, although Hekmatyar's group was (through Pakistani assistance) probably the best supplied with US arms. It was therefore imperative that the status of each be boosted, and the first step in this strategy was to ensure that they were in a position to dominate the united leadership which the *Shura* was designed to legitimate. This consideration, above all, determined Saudi and Pakistani tactics during the *Shura*'s sessions.

First, Hekmatyar and Sayyaf were the figures behind the repudiation of Mojadiddi's agreement with the Teheran-based Shiite groups. Saudi Arabia in particular appeared determined to exclude Iran as a significant actor in the Afghan situation. On the first day of the *Shura*, Sayyaf criticised what he labelled the over-representation of the Shia. He was supported by Hekmatyar, whose dislike of the Shia and hostility to Iran subsequently became clear in a television interview. The crisis over Shia representation immediately paralysed the *Shura*, and was only resolved after several days of secret negotiations. The resolution was a Pyrrhic victory, however, for while it left Sayyaf and Hekmatyar well satisfied, it markedly lessened the *Shura*'s credibility.

Second, Sayyaf and Hekmatyar moved to have the *Shura* support an interim government under their domination. Each was too shrewd to seek personally to head it; their tactic, therefore, was to secure the *Shura*'s endorsement of the previous 'interim government' which had been headed by Sayyaf's complacent deputy, Ahmad Shah. At the same time, they moved for the appointment of Mawlawi Mohammad Nabi Mohammadi as head of state, apparently reasoning that the notoriously quiescent Mohammadi would prove no obstacle to the pursuit of their objectives. Even one of Mohammadi's delegates to the *Shura* was moved to describe this particular manoeuvre as 'a coup d'état',[12] and different groups mobilised to oppose the radicals' strategy. The result was that a committee was appointed under one of the few significant commanders at the *Shura*, Mawlawi Jalaluddin Haqqani, to identify a mechanism for shaping an interim government. It recommended, quite possibly under ISI Directorate pressure, that offices be grouped into seven clusters, which would be controlled by the different party leaders according to the votes they could secure from the *Shura*. When the voting took place, Mojadiddi emerged with the highest total, followed in turn by Sayyaf, Mohammadi, Hekmatyar, Khalis, Rabbani, and Gailani. These results illustrated no more than the unrepresentative character of the *Shura*. After all, Rabbani in the eyes of all specialists enjoyed the most substantial support within Afghanistan, while Mojadiddi had the narrowest power base. As a result of the balloting, Mojadiddi was named head of state, with Sayyaf as prime minister, Mohammadi as Defence minister, Hekmatyar as foreign minister, Khalis as Interior minister, Rabbani as minister for Reconstruction, and Gailani as chief justice. While things had not worked out quite as Hekmatyar and Sayyaf had wanted, they had every reason to be well pleased with the result. Rabbani bore a measure of responsibility for this sorry outcome. Had he been prepared to join forcefully with Mojadiddi to endorse the Teheran agreement on Shiite representation, it is possible that the results of the *Shura* would have been far less palatable to Hekmatyar, Sayyaf, and their backers. While the composition of the *Mujahideen* Interim Government was satisfactory to the ISI Directorate and the Saudis (as well as the United States, which shared the widespread view of Mojadiddi as a Western-inclined moderate), it not only alienated the Shiite *Mujahideen* and the Iranian government, but also left many Sunni *Mujahideen* field commanders and their supporters thoroughly disenchanted with the petulance of *emigré* politics. This played straight into the hands of the Kabul regime and its Soviet backers.

The Jalalabad Campaign

The next step in the strategy of Pakistan's military establishment was to attempt to boost the credibility of the interim government, and particularly its own clients, by securing a city within Afghanistan from which the interim government could operate, and consequently gain international recognition. (Pakistan itself, like the US, had *not* accorded the interim government diplomatic recognition, partly because of the difficulties associated with hosting a government-in-exile, and partly because the Foreign Ministry of Pakistan was not dominated by supporters of Zia's policy to the same extent as was the ISI Directorate.[13]) The result was the disastrous Jalalabad campaign of March-April 1989.

The campaign began on a high note. *Mujahideen* succeeded in capturing the outlying strategic garrison of Samarkhel, well-stocked with equipment and ideally located for a campaign of harrassment against regime positions closer to Jalalabad itself. However, from that point onwards, the *Mujahideen* campaign progressively unravelled. There were a number of reasons why this was the case. First, insufficient attention had been paid to the need to coordinate *Mujahideen* activities, both nationwide and in the Jalalabad region. Ahmad Shah Massoud was later to remark that he learned of the Jalalabad campaign only from the BBC.[14] Simultaneous attacks were not launched on other regime assets around the country, and this permitted the regime to concentrate its forces for the defence of Jalalabad. The *Mujahideen* in the Jalalabad region lacked unified command and operational capacity for set-piece as opposed to guerilla battles. Different groups deployed forces on an *ad hoc* basis, protecting preexisting territorial interests. Second, it is doubtful whether the *Mujahideen* ever deployed enough forces to accomplish their objectives, and there is little doubt that the attackers were hampered by both a shortage of arms and problems in the regular supply of ammunition. Third, the supply route from Kabul to Jalalabad was not closed prior to the commencement of the campaign, and its subsequent surveillance was rotated between different *Mujahideen* groups, not all of which proved equally effective in maintaining a sustained blockade. Fourth, the regime made maximum use of its efficient air force, ruthlessly strafing the *Mujahideen*, who by virtue of their concentration in the one area were vulnerable to such attack in a way which had never previously been the case. It backed this up with the firing from Kabul, under Soviet supervision, of highly destructive SCUD missiles.[15] Fifth, the *Mujahideen* were not helped by defections from regime troops and personnel to anything like the extent which had been anticipated. This was partly due to the success of the regime in trapping people within the city through the placing of minefields in surrounding areas, but also due to massacres of surrendering regime troops by Arab volunteers, a number of them adherents of Wahhabism. The regime immediately publicised these incidents in order to deter further defections.[16]

The negative effects of the Jalalabad shambles can hardly be overstated. The effects on the *Mujahideen* were complex. The failure of the operation was of course immensely dispiriting for those combat *Mujahideen* who bore the brunt of the regime's ferocious counterattack. It was also a humiliating setback for Hekmatyar, Sayyaf, and their backers. For other *Mujahideen* leaders and field commanders, however, the Jalalabad failure was not altogether without benefit, given their desire to minimise the influence of those forces which had flourished mainly as a result of outside patronage rather than support on the ground. The problem, of course, was that these commanders could not insulate themselves from the broader negative effects of the débâcle. The adverse international publicity which the Jalalabad failure attracted, and the drop in international interest in the *Mujahideen* cause which the operation produced, damaged not only those who had orchestrated the operation but the *Mujahideen* as a whole. On the other side of the equation, it enabled the regime to project greater confidence, increased its image of viability as a distinct force (even though in fact it continued to function very much on the strength of Soviet support), and reduced the chance that the USSR would bargain away the PDPA regime in the near future as part of a wider Afghan settlement. This was particularly noticeable in its relations with India: Najibullah had paid an official visit to New Delhi in 1988, and throughout 1989 a steady stream of Indian officials showed up in Kabul to provide assistance for his regime.

The Jalalabad campaign had its casualties in Pakistan as well. The most prominent was the head of the ISI Directorate, Lieutenant-General Hamid Gul, who lost his position in late May 1989.[17] In April, there appeared a report in the Western press, obviously sourced from the ISI, which sought to shift the blame for the Jalalabad campaign away from the Directorate and on to a close aide to Prime Minister Bhutto, Major-General Nasirullah Babar.[18] This alone would have provided a pretext for

Ms Bhutto to remove Hamid Gul, but his days were probably numbered in any case as a result of the failures on the ground.

Internecine Conflicts amongst the Mujahideen

Inevitably, the Jalalabad episode considerably exacerbated the already smouldering tensions which had historically afflicted the resistance, and which had been obvious at the *Shura*. Hekmatyar in particular sought to shift the blame for Jalalabad onto those commanders who had not launched simultaneous attacks on other regime outposts around the country. The main target of his criticism was Ahmad Shah Massoud, whom he had long regarded as an obstacle to the achievement of his political objectives; but he was also outspoken in his criticism of the Shiite groups, whom he denounced in venomous terms. This in many ways reflected the sense of insecurity which had dogged Hekmatyar ever since the death of his main patron, General Zia. With the removal of Hamid Gul, Hekmatyar had no obvious substantial backer to which to turn apart from Saudi Arabia; and criticism of Shiite Islam was an effective tactic to ingratiate him and the *Hezb-i Islami* in Saudi circles. In a press conference he denounced the Iranian leadership, particularly in the light of links between Moscow and Iranian *Majlis* Speaker Rafsanjani; in a subsequent interview with the BBC 'Panorama' programme, he explicitly asserted that followers of Shiite Islam were 'not good Muslims'.

Things came to a head in early July. Massoud had held a major meeting of the Supervisory Council of the North. If there was any resistance organisation capable of serving as a viable alternative to the Kabul regime, this was it. On 9 July, at the Farkhar pass, a *Hezb-i Islami* commander, Sayed Jamal, slaughtered thirty of Massoud's colleagues who were returning from the meeting with detailed instructions for their subordinates on how the next and decisive phase of action against the Kabul regime should be undertaken. As the victims had traversed the pass five days earlier with no problems, it was clear that the cause of the massacre was not a local feud, as *Hezb-i Islami* sources later alleged, but rather orders from above.[19]

While the massacre was a serious setback for Massoud's plans, it did Hekmatyar enormous harm. It made sense only as a desperate attempt by an ambitious leader to cripple a perceived rival, and it came on top of a number of other alleged *Hezb-i Islami* killings, including the murders of the British photographer Andy Skrzypkowiak and the French aid worker Thierry Niquet.[20] These had already led Western European governments to distance themselves from Hekmatyar. The Farkhar massacre was not the first attack on fellow *Mujahideen* for which Hekmatyar's *Hezb* had been blamed, but the presence in the vicinity of Western visitors, including the writer Craig Weintraub, meant that this particular episode was rapidly and credibly reported, and could not plausibly be denied by *Hezb* spokesmen.[21] For once, the other *Mujahideen* groups, whose patience had been sorely tested by Hekmatyar over many years, were in a strong position to move against him, as even his most loyal backers found themselves in an impossible position. Rabbani and Mojadiddi united to denounce Hekmatyar at a public meeting in Peshawar and moved for his suspension from the interim government. Realising that he was in danger of expulsion, Hekmatyar himself suspended his participation in the interim government, claiming that only an election in Afghanistan could render it representative. The Farkhar massacre also brought criticisms of Hekmatyar in US circles to a head, culminating in press reports that he was owner of the world's largest heroin factory and in a US request that he withdraw his application for a visa to enter the United States in order to lobby delegates to the 44th Session of the UN General Assembly.[22] Hekmatyar responded to the outrage at the massacre in the only way possible. He intensified his attacks on Iran and allied himself firmly with the Saudis.

Iran's position during the post-withdrawal period was precarious. On the one hand, it was generally supportive of the *Mujahideen*'s objectives; but on the other, with the withdrawal of Soviet ground forces, its concern became increasingly to boost the position of Shiite elements in any new political arrangements. Three factors shaped the Iranian position. First, the effective snub to the Afghan Shia which the February *Shura* entailed led the Iranian government to adopt what was in effect an anti-Saudi position. Second, the growing deradicalisation of the

Iranian regime, initially manifested through the July 1988 ceasefire in the Iran-Iraq war and assisted by the death of Ayatollah Khomeini in June 1989, prompted the Iranian government to improve its relations with the Soviet Union.[23] Third, Iran remained profoundly hostile to US involvement in support of the Sunni *Mujahideen*. This prompted a participant in a seminar on Afghanistan organised by the Iranian Foreign Ministry to remark that some other participants, closely linked to the Iranian government, 'went so far in emphasizing the danger of American involvement in Afghanistan that they rarely mentioned the atrocities committed by the Soviet Union in ten years of occupation'.[24] Despite Iran's concern at the Soviet action on 19 January 1990 to put down the nationalist movement in Soviet Azerbaijan, there was no doubt that some Iranian officials at least could see their way to cooperating with the Soviets to procure some sort of political settlement of the Afghanistan problem, even if it involved leaving Najibullah in place.

The Position of the Regime

All these developments broadly favoured the Kabul regime. A year after the completion of the Soviet troop withdrawal it found itself in much the same position as before the withdrawal. This meant that it (a) had control of the major urban centres—Kabul, Kandahar, Herat, Jalalabad, Kunduz and Mazar-i-Sharif; (b) controlled some but not all of the roads between these centres, although the main road link with the USSR, through the Salang Pass, came under intermittent attack; (c) had little or no presence in rural areas, where the bulk of the internal population remained. The regime had no notable success in establishing control over areas in which the *Mujahideen* had long been dominant but given the expectations of imminent regime collapse which had accompanied the Soviet withdrawal, it managed to look successful simply by hanging on to its existing territories. These expectations had been generated not so much by the more prominent *Mujahideen* commanders and leaders but by outside observers—both Soviet and Western. (Even Najibullah's brother had predicted his fall.[25]) Only Hekmatyar among the leaders of the seven-party alliance had spoken explicitly in these terms, and the failure of a *series* of predictions he made in 1989 about the regime's imminent collapse contributed in part to his declining credibility. The US chargé d'affaires, on quitting Kabul in January, had confidently predicted the regime's collapse by the middle of the year, a belief shared by a number of other Western diplomats. This belief in part explained why the US administration was so ill-prepared to cope with the regime's survival.[26] In April 1989 it appointed a career diplomat, Peter Tomsen, as special envoy to the *Mujahideen*, but the most obvious result was enhanced conflict in US bureaucratic circles, mirroring the conflicts amongst the *Mujahideen*.[27]

The appearance of regime unity proved, however, to be misleading. As the immediate fears which had prompted prudential cooperation between the *Khalqis* and *Parchamis* dissipated, the longstanding and irreconcilable rivalry between *Khalq* and *Parcham* resurfaced. With Sayid Mohammad Gulabzoi isolated in the Afghan Embassy in Moscow, the *Khalqi* Defence minister, Shahnawaz Tanai, rapidly assumed a dominating position amongst those *Khalqis* who had originally given their loyalty to Hafizullah Amin. Tanai had participated in the 1978 coup, but came to prominence through his effective command of the 37th Commando Brigade during operations in the Panjshir Valley. This led to his promotion first to the position of chief of the general staff, and then, in August 1988, to the position of minister of Defence. While this gave effect to Najibullah's stated aim of promoting party unity, the longer-term consequences proved negative. Within a matter of a few months of the withdrawal of Soviet forces, Tanai had begun to plot against Najibullah. He attempted a coup in July 1989, and another four months later. Amazingly, neither cost him his government position, fuelling suspicions that he was being protected by the Soviets. Finally, on 6 March 1990 he moved decisively against Najibullah in a major coup attempt which led to extensive loss of life and material damage in the Kabul area. The plotters were unable to muster sufficient coercive capacity to overwhelm the forces which remained loyal to Najibullah. While Gulbuddin Hekmatyar immediately supported Tanai's move, he found himself alone, as other *Mujahideen* leaders declined, even in the face of Pakistani pressure, to strike so obviously opportunistic an alliance with a hard-line communist. The defeat of the coup attempt resulted in Tanai's fleeing Kabul and in an extensive purge at the top of the PDPA. On 18 March twenty four members of the Central Committee were expelled. Included in this number were such prominent *Khalqis* as Tanai, Gulabzoi, Asadullah Sarwari, Saleh Mohammad Zeary, and Dastagir Panjsheri. In the aftermath of the coup attempt, in May, Najibullah made a further attempt to improve the image of the regime by removing Kishtmand as prime minister and replacing him with Fazel Haq Khaleqiar, a 'non-party member' who only months before had been wounded in a spectacular *Mujahideen* operation in Herat. And later still, in a further cosmetic move, the name of the PDPA was changed to the 'Homeland Party' (*Hezb-i Watan*).

Initially, the survival of the regime had helped it and its Soviet backers to exude a degree of confidence and to become more active on the international level, most importantly at the 44th Session of the UN General Assembly which passed a muted consensus resolution acceptable to the Kabul and Soviet delegations.[28] Its supporters, most notably the Soviet Union and India, were assiduous in arguing that it was a more significant force in Afghan politics than any *Mujahideen*-led alternative. Nevertheless, the regime's survival remained entirely dependent upon the USSR's willingness to supply both food and arms; it was in effect a Soviet appendix, an island in a hostile sea of micro-societies unreconciled to its position. It had survived on account of a Soviet-supplied life-support system, and of the lack of cohesion between the micro-societies which opposed it. Yet while the prospects of *Mujahideen* unity seemed poor, the continued regime fragility which the March coup attempt exposed, together with the crises which began to engulf the Soviet Union itself, made long-term Soviet support for the PDPA regime appear increasingly problematical.

Notes

1. See John F. Burns, 'In Kabul, Soviet Airlift Brings Bread and Guns', *The New York Times*, 24 May 1989, p.12. For some details from a Soviet source, see *Krasnaia zvezda*, 26 April 1989.
2. Steve Coll, 'U.S. and Pakistan Shift Afghan Tactics', *International Herald Tribune*, 4 September 1989, pp.1,6.

3. 'The Russians Return to Afghanistan?', *Moscow News*, 20 August 1989, p.1.

4. Robert Pear, 'U.S. Asserts Soviet Advisers Are Fighting in Afghanistan', *The New York Times*, 10 October 1989, p.1.

5. See Rosanne Klass, 'Afghanistan: The Accords', *Foreign Affairs*, vol.66, no.5, Summer 1988, pp.922-945, at p.939.

6. See *Report on the USSR*, vol.1, no.2, 13 January 1989, p.30.

7. David B. Ottaway, 'CIA Removes Afghan Rebel Aid Director', *The Washington Post*, 2 September 1989, p.1.

8. For a detailed discussion of these unfortunate circumstances, see Afghan Information Centre *Monthly Bulletin*, no.95, February 1989, pp.7-8. There is little doubt that the effective exclusion of the Iranian-based Shia was largely due to pressure on the Pakistan-based *Mujahideen* from Saudi Arabian interests.

9. At a press conference in Islamabad attended by one of the authors, 18 February 1989.

10. In conversation in Peshawar with one of the authors, 21 February 1989.

11. See *AFGHANews*, vol.5, no.10, 15 May 1989, p.7.

12. In conversation in Islamabad with one of the authors, 18 February 1989.

13. See Olivier Roy, 'Un consensus régional est-il possible?', *Les Nouvelles d'Afghanistan*, no.45, December 1989-January 1990, pp.14-15, at p.14.

14. For the full text of Massoud's interview, see *AFGHANews*, vol.5, nos.18-19, 1 October 1989, pp.6-7.

15. See David B. Ottaway, 'Kabul Forces Gain Combat Edge: Guerrillas Reeling under Scud Missiles, High-Altitude Bombing', *The Washington Post*, 27 June 1989, p.11.

16. For some discussion of Arab volunteers in Afghanistan, see Sandy Gall, *Afghanistan: Agony of a Nation* (London: The Bodley Head, 1988) pp.48-51; and 'Uneasy Partners', *Asiaweek*, 28 April 1989, p.33. On Arab massacres, see Barnett R. Rubin, 'The Fragmentation of Afghanistan', *Foreign Affairs*, vol.68, no.5, Winter 1989-90, pp.150-168, p.155.

17. John Kifner, 'Bhutto, in Fateful Move, Ousts a Top General', *The New York Times*, 1 June 1989, p.5.

18. Henry Kamm, 'Pakistanis Report Ordering Attack by Afghan Rebels', *The New York Times*, 23 April 1989, p.1.

19. For a *Jamiat* account of this event, see *A'lamiah-i Jamiat-i Islami Afghanistan* (Peshawar: Jamiat-i Islami Afghanistan, 1989).

20. On the Skrzypkowiak case, see *Afghanistan: a quarterly magazine*, no.8, 1988, p.24; on the Niquet case, see Gilles Rossignol, 'La mort de Thierry Niquet', *Les Nouvelles d'Afghanistan*, no.37, March 1988, pp.24-25.

21. See Craig Weintraub, 'Ferkhar Massacre of Jami'at commanders

gives a sad air to Eid celebrations', *AFGHANews*, vol.5, no.15, 1 August 1989, pp.6-7.

22. See Hazhir Teimourian, 'Drugs baron in the border hills', *The Times*, 25 September 1989, p.15.

23. See Amin Saikal, 'Iran: A turn to pragmatism?', *Pacific Defence Reporter*, vol.16, nos.6-7, December 1989-January 1990, pp.61-64.

24. 'Second Seminar on Afghanistan studies ways of achieving peace', *AFGHANews*, vol.5, no.20, 15 October 1989, p.8.

25. Mark Fineman, 'Brother Calls Najibullah "Weak Puppet" Who Will Fall', *The Los Angeles Times*, 16 August 1988, Part I, p.16.

26. See David B. Ottaway, 'U.S. Misread Gorbachev, Official Says—Afghanistan Airlift Has Sustained Kabul', *The Washington Post*, 10 September 1989, p.1.

27. See Steve Coll, 'U.S. Envoy Reassigned In Afghan Policy Clash', *The Washington Post*, 10 August 1989, p.27.

28. See United Nations General Assembly *Resolution* 44/15 15 November 1989.

8

The Destructuring of Afghanistan

No matter what regime rules in Kabul from now on, the future of Afghanistan appears bleak. The course of Afghan social development will be substantially if not overwhelmingly shaped by the legacy of long term structural damage to the population, society, economy and political system which the Soviet Union bequeathed as part of its attempt to impose on the Afghans a regime which lacked popular legitimacy. This will be the case even if Afghan communism is in due course consigned to the ruin which has overtaken fraternal communist parties in all the Soviet Union's Eastern European satellites. To appreciate the force of this point, it is necessary that one examine in some detail the precise character of this damage.

The extent of mortality as a result of the Afghan war is staggering, even in a century not noted for low casualty rates in battle. The late Andrei Sakharov, in a speech to the Congress of People's Deputies in Moscow in June 1989, put it very bluntly: 'A war of annihilation was waged against a whole people. A million people perished.'[1] In an earlier publication he had estimated that 60 per cent of this total was the result of 'the war of the villages', with the remainder due to hunger and epidemics.[2] A study carried out for the French charity *Médecins Sans Frontières*, based on detailed research conducted in refugee camps in Pakistan between August and December 1987, concluded that some 9 per cent of the Afghan population had perished through war-related conditions since the April 1978 coup. This the author assessed to represent 1.24 million deaths, although uncertainty about the exact size of the pre-coup population meant that the error associated with this figure was ± 15 per cent.[3] A more conservative study, based on component population projection, arrives at a figure of 876,825 war deaths between 1978 and 1987.[4] If one accepts the official estimate of the number of Soviet deaths, namely 13,833,[5] it appears that over 60 Afghans may have perished for every one Soviet death during the war. The Afghan dead were drawn disproportionately from the male part of the population: the *Médecins Sans Frontières* study concludes that the mortality rate was 13.4 per cent amongst men, as opposed to 3.8 per cent amongst women. Furthermore, the mortality rate was highest amongst men in the 31-40 age group, at 22.4 per cent.[6] The potential effects of mortality in this particular cohort are enormous, as it is men of this age who have traditionally performed some of the most important roles in production and exchange in rural Afghanistan. Even survivors from this age group may be poorly placed to resume their previous occupations: for the number of Afghans wounded there are virtually no reliable figures but any visitor to the city of Peshawar cannot but be struck by the large number of handicapped refugees whom one encounters in the streets.

The massive refugee movements which we noted in Chapter Four have enormous implications for Afghanistan's future. Of the refugees in Pakistan, 59.5 per cent are under the age of 20.[7] Denied both access to traditional institutions of training for productive activity, and hope for the future, they run the risk of drifting into patterns of anomic or nihilistic behaviour which will compound the damage done to the fabric of Afghanistan's micro-societies. In almost as parlous a position are the estimated 2 million internal refugees driven by the war from the countryside into the larger cities, especially Kabul. As well as being traumatised by their experiences, these unfortunates have come to constitute a deprived underclass within urban areas, forced to take on the menial and hazardous occupations which previously were often left for the Hazaras.[8] The Afghan diaspora has also changed the composition of the surviving internal population of Afghanistan. The refugee population in Pakistan has been disproportionately composed of Pushtuns, 84.6 per cent according to one study.[9] The combined effect of the spatial distribution of battle zones—which were heavily located in areas with predominantly Pushtun populations—and of the pattern of exodus was to reduce the percentage of Pushtuns remaining within the country[10] from prewar figures which put the Pushtuns at between 40 and 50 per cent (although these figures may well have been inflated to strengthen Afghanistan's case in the Pushtunistan dispute). The changed pattern of ethnic composition within the internal population has enormous implications for the future distribution of power within Afghanistan, as well as for the prospects of a viable political settlement providing the degree of internal order needed to permit an effective process of postwar reconstruction to be commenced.

These demographic changes have been accompanied by massive economic dislocation. It is worth noting first of all that labour is an important factor of production. For this reason, the death or displacement of a large proportion of the labour force has enormous economic effects, especially in the labour-intensive agricultural sector. More palpable, however, has been the physical damage to Afghanistan's economic infrastructure. One recent study assesses material losses at more than US$12 billion,[11] in a country which was very poor even before the war began. While the pattern of destruction is not uniform throughout the country, the magnitude of damage in the worst-affected areas is difficult to overstate. Following a UN-sponsored visit to Herat, one observer remarked that 'visiting western Herat is like a visit to Verdun in 1919: for 20 kilometres there is nothing but ruins; the roads and fields are overgrown with weeds. In a landscape churned up by shells and bombs, people frequently uncover the remains of peasants buried in their houses. The hulls of tanks lie rusting on the verges. Unexploded 500 kilogram bombs lie stuck in the ground like beetroots.'[12] Another observer, visiting the once fertile countryside, remarked that it was as if a bomb had gone off in the Garden of Eden.[13]

The effects of this destruction on agriculture have been profound. Before the communist coup, Afghanistan was largely self-sufficient in food production: as Brigot and Roy concluded, it was 'a poor country but not a country of hunger'.[14] This is no longer the case. The transport networks which permitted the efficient delivery of produce to rural markets, and from one region to another, have been severely disrupted. But more seriously, the overall level of output has dropped dramatically[15] as a result of the killing or exodus of members of the labour force,

damage to farmlands and irrigation systems, and the destruction
of animal stocks. This was clear within a few years of the start of
the war, as the threat of famine emerged in various regions,[16]
and by 1987 agricultural output was only one third of what it had
been in 1978. Yields from the land which remained under
cultivation had fallen by up to a half, largely as a result of the
scarcity of inputs, and 40 per cent of draught oxen had been
killed.[17] This was not simply an *unintended* offshoot of conflict. As
a number of scholars have noted, the destruction of the rural
economy was an integral part of Soviet strategy for denying the
resistance access to the food resources on which the continuation
of their struggle depended. Incendiary devices were specially
deployed to set fire to crops; irrigation systems were deliberately
blown up; and orchards were razed.[18]

As well as suffering direct damage, the Afghan economy has
been weakened by Soviet exploitation of Afghanistan's natural
resources.[19] Natural gas exports to the Soviet Union were
metered on the Soviet side of the frontier and even then
'purchased' at prices well below those prevailing in the world
market.[20] In 1980, as Shroder and Assifi have reported, the Soviet
Union 'took the uniquely obscene step of crediting its imports of
Afghan natural gas against the cost of maintaining the "friendly,
fraternal assistance" of its "limited military contingent" in
Afghanistan', thus forcing the Afghans 'to pay with their natural
resources for the brutal invasion and occupation of their own
country and the destruction of their own people'.[21] Furthermore,
the USSR embarked on the secret mining of uranium in the
mountains near Kabul, the Khakriz area of Kandahar, and Mir
Daoud Koh between Herat and Shindand.[22] All these acts of
exploitation had the effect of depleting the resources upon which
Afghans could draw in attempting the task of postwar
reconstruction.

These demographic and economic changes are intimately
related to changes in social structure. Ten years of war have
inevitably affected the pattern of social relationships in both
urban and rural areas. These effects have been apparent within
both families and wider social groups. In urban centres,
relationships between members of many families have been
strained or shattered as individual family members, for a variety
of reasons, prudential and ideological, adopted different stances

towards the Soviet presence, the regime, and the resistance. This essentially split many families which had traditionally been a source of considerable social stability in urban centres, particularly Kabul. This was much less the case in rural areas, where people's dependence upon governmental goodwill for their day-to-day livelihoods was minimal and the prudential reasons for political accommodation far less compelling. Rural micro-societies were also subjected to centripetal forces, but of a different kind. Those individuals who had achieved prominence in rural societies through the dispensing of patronage or the exercise of negotiating skills frequently witnessed the erosion of their influence. Because of the war, the resources required for the dispensing of patronage became increasingly scarce, and those clientelist ties which were not firmly reinforced by affective loyalties began to break down. Military skills and access to arms, rather than the ability to dispense patronage or negotiate, acquired new salience as an element of political leadership. This somewhat undermined the position not only of the *khans* but also of the consensual bodies with which they had historically dealt.

These effects were accentuated, amongst those who quit the country, by the environment of the refugee camp. The agencies administering the refugee camps were obliged, in order to perform even the most menial tasks, to work in concert with particular individuals. These were by no means always the traditional *khans*. Their position was undermined by the altered context within which they were functioning. They were no longer on their own territory, using time-honoured methods to block the intrusion of the state into their bailiwicks. On the contrary, their status as refugees had substantially deprived them of self-sufficiency, putting them in the position of supplicant in their interactions with the host authorities. The mediatory roles which they had previously performed increasingly fell to younger, literate Afghans, often associated with *Mujahideen* parties.[23]

A further consequence of the communist takeover was the obliteration of much of the (in-any-case small) educated elite. This was begun with a vengeance by Taraki and Amin, under the eyes of Soviet advisers, and was continued by Karmal and Najibullah. By the time of the Soviet withdrawal, virtually all of Afghanistan's most distinguished intellectual and public figures were either dead or in exile. Afghanistan's higher educational institutions, most importantly Kabul University, had been wrecked by the flight of most of the skilled staff[24] and by the debauching of the curriculum through the introduction of compulsory classes in Marxist-Leninist 'theory'. Diplomas were awarded for political loyalty rather than scholastic attainment and the graduates were distinguished by their alienation from their traditional roots, which, while making them heavily dependent on the regime for sustenance and employment, hardly equipped them to deal with the complex problems facing the country.

In sum, the decade of war in Afghanistan has changed the structure of Afghan society in complex ways. Most obviously, the war drastically altered the networks of social and political relationships which had traditionally provided for order. The *khans* who flourished by maintaining a symbiotic relationship between the periphery and the state are no longer in a position to do so. Local religious dignitaries who previously derived authority from religious standing have been subordinated to younger Islamic activists, often from secular backgrounds. In the context of war, the power entailed by the possession of arms has frequently counterbalanced or outweighed the authority derived from traditional sources. The need for rapid decisions in the context of war also strengthened the position of resistance commanders at the expense of local *jirgahs* and *shuras*. The cost in terms of political order has been considerable. The new powerholders have little familiarity with the practice of negotiating with a central state, and have every reason to concentrate on the protection of their own independence. Prudential considerations may lead them to make compromises from time to time with other powerholders; but the legitimacy of the state which had increasingly constrained the leaderships of micro-societies in the 1950s and 1960s has been thoroughly dissipated. Power and authority are presently in an extreme state of flux in Afghanistan, and the reestablishment of some kind of political order constitutes an almost insurmountable problem.

The specific character of micro-societies has been affected at a number of distinct levels. The sharply-altered numerical strengths of different ethnic groups within Afghanistan is pregnant with implications for future power relations in the country.[25] This has already been apparent in the divisive politics of the resistance, especially in respect of the position of the Shiite Hazaras, but its ramifications are much wider. On the one hand, the Pushtuns are no longer in a position to demand as large a share of political power as they did up to the communist coup.· However, this needs to be qualified by the observation that while the Durrani Pushtuns, who dominated the top civil and military leaderships before 1978, are very poorly represented within the Ghilzai-dominated *Mujahideen* leadership, the Durrani communities in the south and southwest of the country have been less severely affected by the conflict than the Ghilzai Pushtun communities in the east. On the other hand, the Tajiks, Turkomans, Uzbeks, and Hazaras in particular are well placed to demand an increased share of power.

Apart from these Durrani-Ghilzai distinctions, the Pushtuns have also been weakened by tribal divisions, which have the potential to resurface with a vengeance in the wake of the Soviet troop withdrawal and the inability of the Kabul regime to extend its influence beyond urban areas. While there has been a considerable leadership turnover at the tribal level, the newly prominent figures may feel as bound as their predecessors—or perhaps to an even greater extent, given the erosion of obligations to the state—by a commitment to the tribal micro-society as the primary focus of loyalty. However, the *character* of this commitment may well have changed, as a number of the newly-prominent figures, as well as other members of the various micro-societies, have undergone experiences of political socialisation of a totally different kind to their elders. This has been less of a problem for the more homogeneous Tajiks, whose non-tribal structure of social organisation has permitted a more effective degree of cooperation between different—usually village-based— micro-societies.

These changes raise major doubts about the possibility of reestablishing the kind of political equilibrium, based on norms of reciprocity and clientelist ties, which previously connected micro-societies to specific elements of the central state mechanism. Political, military, and bureaucratic-administrative leaderships may in the future no longer be dominated by particular groups to the same extent as in the past; furthermore, there is no certainty that such leaderships will be either in a *position* to, or *disposed* to, develop comparable ties with particular groups. This may inhibit the reemergence of stable relationships between the state and the micro-societies, and therefore the reemergence of political stability. Failing a new equilibrium of this kind, it seems likely that the traditional pattern of a weak state and strong society will resurface, but in far sharper and more perilous form. A robust state-society equilibrium will be unobtainable in the short run, and is at best problematical even in the medium to longer term. The internal conflicts which have visibly rent the *Mujahideen* since the Soviet troop withdrawal reflect in part these broader complexities.

The Positions of Political Actors

The fragmentation of the *Mujahideen* since February 1989 has serious implications for the restoration of political order within Afghanistan. Yet it is well to remember that the radical *Mujahideen* parties in particular are not *direct* products of Afghan society, but have arisen from the combining of certain cultural attributes with ideological positions which themselves have only shallow roots within Afghan micro-societies. As the experience of the 'Constitutional Experiment' showed, there has been no tradition in Afghanistan of individuals subordinating their particular desires to the broader programme of a political party so that they can achieve some of their broader objectives. Parties have never been a significant channel for interest articulation. As a consequence, there has been no tradition of party *organisation* in Afghanistan, let alone of orderly coalitions between parties. The conflicts between *Parchamis* and *Khalqis* and between different *Mujahideen* parties in the Afghan Interim Government have therefore been very much what one would naturally expect. The 'parties' which have functioned over the last decade owe a great deal to the emulation, by small collections of individuals, of organisational structures entirely foreign to the Afghan political experience—whether these be Leninist 'vanguard' parties, on the one hand, or radical Middle Eastern groups such as the Muslim Brotherhood, on the other.

Despite their lack of historical analogues in Afghan politics, the *Mujahideen* parties were able to survive because they proved to be convenient mechanisms for outside backers of the resistance to use to channel support to combatants in the field. This in itself attracted a considerable amount of funding which sustained the parties' operations and boosted the status of the individual leaders. The leaders who attracted the most support were—as one might have expected—those who most willingly allied themselves to external patrons, although skill in convincing these patrons of the party's military and political significance undoubtedly played a role in the *initial* securing of funding. While this helped secure an international profile for the parties and their leaders, at the same time it severely constrained their freedom of action. What this meant, furthermore, was that the leaders of the parties acquired a direct interest in the survival of parties as dominant organisations, no matter what obstacle this might pose to the reestablishment of political order in Afghanistan. The February 1989 *Shura* failed in large part because the party leaders were determined to maintain the principle that *party* was the basic unit of representation, even though this was utterly alien to the political culture of micro-societies. Traditionally, Afghan *jirgas* have worked as institutions for the development and sanctioning of consensus: the entanglement of antagonistic parties in the *Shura* virtually guaranteed that no consensus could be obtained. There are good reasons to suspect that with the same pattern of parties, the same impasse may prevail at future *Shuras*.

While the *Khalqis* and *Parchamis* survived on the strength of Soviet patronage, the *Mujahideen* parties could not easily have continued to secure outside funding in the absence of integral relations with Afghan micro-societies. Yet while such ties undoubtedly developed in a way that was fruitful for both partners, none of the *Mujahideen* parties succeeded in building a broad base of support from a *wide* range of micro-societies. The loyalties of the different Ghilzai Pushtun micro-societies were spread between a number of the Peshawar-based parties, creating on the ground a kaleidoscopic pattern of loyalties, with affiliates of one party rubbing shoulders with associates of another. In addition, while some Durrani Pushtuns became attached to Pir Gailani's party, a large number remained somewhat aloof from Peshawar politics, as the territories in which they were concentrated were less the targets of attack than were centres of Ghilzai concentration. Only the *Jamiat-i Islami* came close to securing the loyalty of an entire *ethnie*, complementing its appeal to other minorities such as the Uzbeks and Turkomans. This was a major reason why the Supervisory Council of the North came to be an effective force. However, the *Jamiat* was also inhibited by its general lack of appeal to Ghilzai Pushtuns.

Furthermore, relations between the *Mujahideen* parties and micro-societies have been conditional rather than absolute. In the wake of the Soviet withdrawal the Kabul regime concentrated on protecting its urban strongholds and more or less abandoned the Soviet strategy of periodically attempting the massive projection of power into the countryside. This to some extent weakened the prudential basis for leaderships of various micro-societies to maintain links with the Pakistan-based parties—especially after the Jalalabad campaign exposed the logistical incapacities of the parties which had pushed for it. This weakening was especially marked amongst the Pushtuns, and created the potential for the defection of these micro-societies to some other focus of loyalty. The Kabul regime was an improbable candidate to be such a focus—given all the bloodshed of the war, dealings between the regime and these micro-societies, dealings which the regime almost continuously claimed were taking place, could never be more than prudential.

The regime, drawing the bulk of its limited support from urbanised and as a rule detribalised circles originating from a range of micro-societies, ultimately faces difficulties of a different character but just as great an order, as do the *Mujahideen* parties. It has virtually no prospect of securing generalised *normative* support, and relies for its survival on mechanisms of *non-legitimate* domination which are far costlier than survival on the basis of legitimacy. Prudential alliances with certain important elements of micro-societies, while of some benefit to the regime in terms of public relations, would constitute an increased drain on the regime's resources while providing no guarantee of normative support in the longer term. In other words, the regime can secure its survival only through massive dependence on a patron power—in the present case the Soviet Union, and to some extent India. Given developments in the USSR and the international arena since the Soviet troop withdrawal, this is a far from comfortable position.

Changes in the International Environment

As former US President Nixon recently remarked, 'The Red Army's withdrawal from Afghanistan in February 1989 became the opening round in the collapse of much of the Kremlin's empire'.[26] Elites in a number of East European countries—Poland, Hungary, the German Democratic Republic, Czechoslovakia and to a lesser extent Bulgaria—had long been sustained in the face of very low mass popularity by the implicit threat that any moves to interfere with the leading role of the ruling party would be contained by Soviet intervention, as in Hungary in 1956 and Czechoslovakia in 1968. This was given ideological grounding in the so-called 'Brezhnev Doctrine', which asserted that a threat to any one component of the 'Socialist Commonwealth' was a threat to socialism in its entirety.[27] However, the failures of the Soviet Army in the Afghan theatre made it increasingly unlikely that any remotely similar operation would be attempted by the Soviet leadership for quite some time; this in turn reduced the credibility of the Soviet guarantee of the positions of the Soviet-backed East European elites. Combined with local factors which fuelled antagonisms towards these elites—related in particular to their inexpert policy choices and corrupt lifestyles—and with explicit changes in the Soviet Union's assessment of the importance of maintaining by force a glacis of states between itself and Western Europe,[28] this was enough to unleash a series of pre-revolutionary agitations which led to the collapse of one-party 'real socialism' in the Eastern Bloc.

The Soviet Union's acceptance of moves towards pluralism in Eastern Europe made the position of Najibullah's regime increasingly anomalous. In a major address in October 1989 Soviet Foreign Minister Shevardnadze admitted that with the invasion of Afghanistan, the Soviets had set themselves against the world community, 'violated the norms of conduct and moved against interests common to all mankind'. Nonetheless, in a totally inconsistent fashion, he went on to state that 'however difficult it might be for us, we do not have the moral right to refuse the Afghan people our support'.[29] In the context of the massive arms shipments to Kabul going on even as he was speaking, 'Afghan people' of course meant 'PDPA regime'. In a manner reminiscent of the Kremlin's tortuous approach to the position of the Baltic states, the USSR thus showed itself keen to retain the *fruits* of aggression even while denouncing the aggression itself. Such an approach to Afghanistan contrasted starkly with the substance of Soviet 'new thinking'[30] about international relations. This was not a point to which the US administration, or for that matter many other Western observers, paid much attention at the time. The tumult of the sensational events in Eastern Europe, from the destruction of the Berlin Wall to the Romanian revolution to major Soviet concessions on troop numbers in the European theatre, proved more than sufficient to drown out the sound of Soviet missiles and MiGs in Afghanistan. This was even more the case after the Iraqi invasion of Kuwait on 2 August 1990. The US desire to prevent a Soviet veto of UN Security Council resolutions condemning Iraq, and—most importantly of all—authorising the use of force to secure an Iraqi withdrawal, dictated almost complete silence on the continuing Afghanistan issue.

Nonetheless, the inconsistency in the Soviet position was one which had the potential to cause difficulties for the Soviet leadership in its relations with parts of the wider world, with Muslim peoples within the USSR, and with other Soviet citizens who viewed continued aid for the Kabul regime as an unnecessary drain in times of economic stringency, and as an obstacle to the return of Soviet prisoners of war in the hands of the *Mujahideen*.[31] Such citizens included not only Major-General Kim Tsagolov,[32] but also Boris El'tsin, Chairman of the Supreme Soviet of the Russian Republic.[33] It was furthermore an inconsistency which few beyond the leading circles of the Soviet Communist Party would be likely to be keen to defend. In this respect, the decision of a Central Committee Plenum in Moscow in early February 1990 to accept the removal of the constitutional guarantee of the leading role of the party in the USSR itself could not but have unsettled Najibullah and his associates.

Future Directions

While the damage inflicted upon Afghanistan will shape the broad course of Afghanistan's development, the specific character of the regime in Kabul may well be affected by attempts to procure a 'settlement' of the current impasse between the *Mujahideen* and the regime of Dr Najibullah. There are several possible directions that the situation in Afghanistan may take. Six possible paths in particular are worthy of attention, although we would be the last to deny that the situation in Afghanistan is radically uncertain and that political outcomes quite different from those that we canvass may eventuate.

The first possibility is a continuation of stalemate—with the PDPA regime in control of Kabul, other major cities, and important strategic points, while the countryside remains in the hands of the *Mujahideen*. The duration of such a stalemate would primarily depend on a number of factors. The first is the commitment of the USSR to continue sustaining the Kabul regime through costly shipments of arms and food. The second is the access of the *Mujahideen* to outside support in sufficient quantities to prevent the regime from forcibly extending its territorial writ. The third is the extent to which the *Mujahideen* continue to be crippled by disunity and the extent to which the regime manages to prevent the resurfacing of disunity. The fourth is disposition of the superpowers in concert with regional actors to attempt to impose on Afghanistan a settlement of their own devising as was attempted unsuccessfully through the Geneva Accords. A continued stalemate would be very costly for the Afghan population, adding salt to the wounds which a decade of war has already inflicted. A low-grade war of attrition between not only the *Mujahideen* and PDPA forces but possibly between different *Mujahideen* groups could become the order of the day. This would exacerbate the already debilitated state of the Afghan economy, and could well lead to renewed pre-famine conditions in particular parts of the country, and population movements adding to the numbers of both external and internal refugees. It would also delay the commencement of large-scale reconstruction activities and could well deter potential donors from contributing to relief programmes. Finally, it would help sustain the instability of the South Asia region, afflicted by a number of destabilising regional disputes notwithstanding the recent dramatic improvement in superpower relations. However, this scenario would also involve continuing heavy costs for the PDPA's Soviet patron, and this may militate against its durability.

The second possibility is the slow dissipation of popular resistance to the regime, allowing it to consolidate its position. This could occur in a number of different circumstances: if prudential considerations prompted a sufficiently large number of micro-societies to reach compromises with the regime; or if outside support for the resistance fronts were either substantially or completely severed, literally starving them of the capacity to continue their struggle, as a result either of a superpower agreement or a unilateral cut in external arms supplies; or if the major resistance forces obliterated each other through a process of sustained internecine conflict. The first of these circumstances does not appear very likely. The millions of Afghan refugees in Pakistan and Iran are heavily linked to the resistance forces and cannot readily be suborned; in any case, they are largely inaccessible to the agents of the Kabul regime. Furthermore, as we have noted earlier, prudential ties unreinforced by normative commitment would be very costly for the regime to sustain. Thus, field commanders and the people under their influence within Afghanistan itself would also be difficult to suborn on the scale required, although some commanders undoubtedly will strike such compromises. The second of these circumstances is by no means beyond the bounds of possibility. We have more to say below about the possibility of an arms cut-off in the context of some broader superpower agreement; nonetheless, it is important to recognise that the arms flow could also be cut by factors such as growing disillusionment in the US Congress with the resistance's performance. This would not necessarily bring war in Afghanistan to a halt, although it would have the perverse effect of strengthening the relative position of resistance groups backed by Saudi money. After all, the resistance managed before the Soviet invasion to procure arms for use against the Kabul regime, partly by capturing regime arsenals and partly by purchasing from the international arms market. The third of these circumstances is the worst possible contingency which the resistance could face and it would be enormously costly for the wider civilian population as well. We have already noted the way in which internecine conflict erupted in July 1989 between Hekmatyar's *Hezb* and the *Jamiat*, at significant cost to the resistance's immediate operational capacity. The risk of a recurrence of such conflict is appreciable. Nonetheless, the combat *Mujahideen* within Afghanistan are not as politicised and locked into serious struggle for power as the party leaders in Peshawar. The physical geography of Afghanistan in many areas places barriers between different micro-societies and helps limit friction between them. Furthermore, as mentioned earlier, it is impossible for the party leaders in Peshawar to exercise day-to-day control over *Mujahideen* operations, and it is therefore very difficult for antagonistic party leaders simply to export their conflicts into Afghanistan at the stroke of a pen. Indeed, in October 1990, a major gathering of *Mujahideen* commanders was held in Shah Salim, attended by Ahmad Shah Massoud, Amin Wardak, Abdul Haq, Jalaluddin Haqqani, and a large number of less widely-known figures. The participants agreed on the importance of coordination, and following the meeting, Massoud visited Pakistan for the first time since the April 1978 coup, and held high-level discussions with a range of individuals.[34] Whether the promised coordination can eventuate is a different question; but it is clear that the popular resistance within Afghanistan is not on the verge of disintegration.

The third possibility is the disintegration of the regime, either through internal disunity, or through a unilateral cessation of Soviet support. As we have noted earlier, such a disintegration was widely expected to occur following the withdrawal of Soviet forces. That it did not was in no small measure due to the extent of Soviet backing, and to the unexpectedly high level of cooperation between *Khalqis* and *Parchamis* which was secured during those difficult days and maintained to some extent in the months which followed. However, the increasing disharmony within the regime throughout 1989, and most spectacularly the March 1990 coup attempt, suggest that this cooperation was grounded in the desperation of the situation in which the members of the two factions found themselves rather than in an effective and durable settlement of the deeper hostilities which divided them. And the increasingly catastrophic food supply

situation in the Soviet Union has the potential to affect the
dependent Kabul regime as well.

The fourth possibility is an increase in the effectiveness of
Mujahideen activities. Given the disunity within the resistance,
this could take a number of different forms. In the light of both
the fractionalisation within the Pushtun-dominated *Mujahideen*
groups, particularly in the east and southeast of Afghanistan, and
the demographic changes which have diluted the presence of
Pushtuns within Afghanistan, a serious military challenge to the
regime seems more likely to come from the north. There is no
doubt that the *Jamiat* forces in northern Afghanistan under
Massoud are the best-organised anywhere in the country, an
attribute grounded in the greater homogeneity of micro-societies
in this area than in other parts of the country. Throughout the
war, Massoud has demonstrated a greater degree of *strategic*
vision than any other commander and has been unique in seeking
to train personnel in a systematic fashion to undertake different
forms of combat operation—resulting in a force of roughly
10,000, the closest the *Mujahideen* have come to developing
anything like a regular army. The northern *Mujahideen* are also
assisted by their fortuitous proximity to the road route between
the USSR and Kabul, which leaves them well-placed to attempt a
blockade of the capital. The hold of the regime on this highway
has always been fragile and vulnerable, and it is costly for the
PDPA regime to keep it open (even though it would be even more
costly for the regime to let it close). Massoud has not so far
demonstrated the capacity to close the highway permanently and
his reported remarks suggest a reluctance to do so, as the costs of
the closure would fall heavily—although not exclusively—on
innocent civilians. However, a change in Massoud's strategy
could see supplies to Kabul seriously disrupted. This could be
either induced or accentuated by disturbances in Soviet Central
Asia of the kind which erupted in Tajikistan in February 1990,[35]
not to mention the emerging possibility of secession by Central
Asian republics. The successful blockade of the Armenian union
republic mounted over a period of many months by nationals of
the Azerbaijan republic would seem to establish this as at least a
possibility. Nonetheless, Massoud faces a number of difficulties.
The first is that the Soviet Union may be exceedingly reluctant to
relinquish influence in the north, and consequently may go to

unusual lengths to protect the regime from a threat from that direction.[36] The second is that Massoud's relative remoteness from either Pakistan or Iran makes it difficult for him to maintain secure supply routes for arms and materiel. The third is that, for the same reason, the north is particularly vulnerable to famine, which may occur either naturally or as a result of the deliberate introduction of agricultural pests by the Soviets or the regime. A serious famine in the north would seriously weaken the fabric of the micro-societies on which Massoud has drawn so effectively for support.

A fifth possibility would be a realignment between different *Mujahideen* forces accompanied by the return of Zahir Shah. The events of 1989—most notably the failure of the Ghilzai Pushtuns in the Jalalabad campaign—and even more the discrediting of Hekmatyar as a result of his rush to associate himself with Tanai at the time of the March 1990 coup, have somewhat increased the likelihood of this possibility. Hekmatyar's ability to exercise any kind of veto over the activities of other *Mujahideen* leaders has substantially disintegrated, just as Najibullah's image of strength has been shattered. In terms of the parties in Peshawar, this scenario would involve the striking of a solid agreement between Rabbani and Zahir Shah's supporters Gailani, Mojadiddi and Mohammadi. Nonetheless, such an an outcome could only eventuate and be sustained if certain conditions were met. The first would be a departure by the *Jamiat* from its longstanding position of hostility to Zahir Shah. From late 1988 the tone of references to Zahir Shah in *Jamiat* publications improved noticeably and in October 1989 a *Jamiat* publication stated that Zahir Shah was 'considered an opponent of the Soviet occupation and the communist regime'.[37] The second would be effective protection for those involved in such a realignment from a decapitating strike launched by Hekmatyar, possibly with outside support. The third would be a favourable attitude towards Zahir Shah from regional actors, particularly the Governments of Pakistan and Iran. The fourth would be securing support for the return of Zahir Shah from Iran-based *Mujahideen* groups which have rather negative feelings towards him on account of the poor social position which Shiite Hazaras enjoyed in Afghanistan when he was on the throne. This would be most likely to occur as a result of a prior shift in position by the

Jamiat, which has attempted to maintain good relations with both the Iranian government and the Persian-speaking Shia. And the fifth would be a decision by Zahir Shah to make a move. In the past, the former monarch has stated that he would return to play whatever role was demanded of him upon the invitation of the Afghan people, but has left it somewhat unclear exactly how the desire of the Afghan people for his return would be assessed. Olivier Roy has argued that if the Tajiks, Durranis and Shia could make agreement between themselves, 'they could overturn the Kabul regime and establish a true multi-ethnic government'.[38] This could prove the best solution to the problem of fragmented authority in Afghanistan, but it remains to be seen whether anything like it will eventuate.

The last of these possibilities would be some kind of superpower agreement over Afghanistan, and the consequent involvement of the United Nations in attempts to facilitate or impose a 'political settlement', possibly involving a *Loya Jirgah*,[39] which also could entail a role for Zahir Shah. In late November 1990, Najibullah flew unexpectedly from Kabul to Geneva and reportedly held talks with General Abdul Wali—Zahir Shah's cousin and son-in-law, and the most significant member of his entourage. There were also reports that Gorbachev had met with Zahir Shah in Rome during a brief visit before the Paris meeting of the Conference on Security and Cooperation in Europe. A UN official heavily involved in negotations over Afghanistan was also present in Geneva during Najibullah's visit. All these developments suggest that a UN-brokered 'settlement' of some sort may indeed be attempted.

By early 1990 the idea of such a 'solution' received support from the UN, from the USA, and from the Soviet Union and the Kabul regime, each for its own reasons. The UN General Assembly in its November 1989 resolution on Afghanistan requested the secretary-general 'to encourage and facilitate the early realization of a comprehensive political settlement in Afghanistan in accordance with the provisions of the Geneva Agreements and of the present resolution'.[40] In the wake of frustration at the disunity between the *Mujahideen* parties and at the lack of progress on the battlefield, the Bush Administration came to favour a negotiated settlement, and was prepared to make significant concessions to promote one: at a press conference in Moscow on 9 February 1990, the US secretary of state, James Baker, announced that 'it would not be a precondition that Mr Najibullah step down in advance of beginning discussions on a political settlement or transitional government, provided that everyone was assured that he would leave at the conclusion of any such negotiation or discussions'.[41]

Perhaps in response, Soviet Foreign Minister Shevardnadze published a long article in *Izvestiia* on 14 February 1990 setting out ten 'stages' on the way to an Afghan settlement.[42] These were: (1) a 'broad dialogue with the participation of all political forces operating in Afghanistan'; (2) the creation of 'appropriate conditions' for an 'Afghan dialogue', most importantly that 'the fighting must stop'; (3) an 'Afghan peace conference' to focus on 'the nuts and bolts of the Afghan settlement'; (4) a 'mechanism for the internal settlement'; (5) the possible 'preservation of the territorial status quo between the factions participating in the dialogue'; (6) announcements from the Afghan negotiating parties that they 'pledge to recognise the results of the general elections and will not try to change them by force', with 'effective international control' of elections, with the UN, the Islamic Conference, and the Non-Aligned Movement all possibly involved (Najibullah in fact pledged this in Kabul on 24 January 1990); (7) a conference of the USSR, USA, Pakistan and Iran to build consensus 'on the main aspects of the political settlement', with the USSR as mediator in recognition of the poor relations between Teheran and Washington; (8) participation in such a conference by the 'warring parties', with the agenda and participants to be determined by 'a working group at expert level'; (9) the complete termination of all arms deliveries to the warring parties in Afghanistan; (10) the consolidation by an international conference of Afghanistan's status as 'neutral and demilitarised'. He also expressed the USSR's readiness to open dialogue with 'field commanders' and 'leaders of Peshawar and other groups', as well as 'Zahir Shah and his associates', and 'all those who would like to help settle the Afghan people'.

This set of proposals doubtless was intended in part to put the USSR in a favourable light, and to purge the Soviet Union of guilt for what it had done in Afghanistan over a period of years. On paper, the proposals appeared impressive and possessed a number of features which ostensibly would help to promote a settlement in Afghanistan. In contrast to the flawed Geneva process, the proposals did not appear to exclude vital *issues* from the agenda, or vital *actors*—most importantly the *Mujahideen*—from the negotiations. They also foreshadowed a constructive role in controlling a settlement for states uncontaminated by previous direct involvement in support of a combatant. However, the proposals left many questions unanswered, relating both to the substance of a workable settlement and the mechanisms for its implementation.

Immediate problems arise from the first two points. A 'broad dialogue' has long figured in the proposals of the regime and the Soviet Union for 'national reconciliation', but has just as regularly been rejected by *Mujahideen* groups, on the basis that Najibullah and the PDPA were not acceptable negotiating partners. Zahir Shah, too, expressed concisely the nature of this problem: 'The Afghans have sacrificed more than one million lives and the country is destroyed. Why did the people offer these sacrifices? The people made these sacrifices in rejection of an imposed regime that renounced their beliefs and ideology. After ten years of war how would it be possible to sit down with this regime and negotiate a distribution of power? At the present time it is impossible to negotiate with this communist regime'.[43] Following the March 1990 coup, he went even further, stating that communists had 'no place, even on a short-term basis, in a possible future national coalition government'.[44] Any hope that fighting could be stopped as a precondition to a broad dialogue is also optimistic, given that most of the important commanders are not subject to day-to-day control from party leaderships. As Dupree points out, 'a ceasefire is only workable when two armies face each other across definable boundaries or zones'; given the radically different situation in Afghanistan, 'to expect a nationwide ceasefire to work would be fantasy'.[45]

The idea of successfully holding free and fair elections in Afghanistan as part of a settlement process also seems optimistic. First, in a cultural milieu where elections have *not* historically been an important device for political legitimation, it is far from clear that a 'pledge to recognise the results of general elections' could be enforced against the losers—even if it could be extracted from relevant participants in the first place. Second, the logistic obstacles to the mounting of free and fair elections in Afghanistan would be formidable. Any such elections would be astronomically expensive to mount and it is unclear who would pick up the bill.

The successful Namibian elections of November 1989, specifically mentioned by Shevardnadze, are a poor precedent for Afghanistan. Namibia had excellent roads and airfields and a reasonable telecommunications system; Afghanistan has nothing comparable. Furthermore, while refugees were able to return to Namibia before the poll, it is extremely unlikely that Afghan refugees in Pakistan and Iran would take the risk of doing so; while polling could probably be organised more easily in refugee camps than in Afghanistan itself, the Kabul regime would be completely unable to campaign safely amongst the refugees— amongst whom the *Mujahideen* and Zahir Shah enjoy widespread support—even if the governments of Pakistan and Iran would let it make the attempt. In Namibia there was a well-entrenched system of political parties which had become major institutions of interest articulation and aggregation. This permitted the use of a 'list' system of proportional representation. In Afghanistan, an assembly with members determined exclusively by the parties contesting an election would almost inevitably exclude important power holders without strong party affiliations, thereby reducing the legitimacy of the assembly. Namibia had a voting population of only 700,000, compared to the millions of Afghans who might be eligible to vote. In Namibia there were relatively few internal actors, and only one major external actor—South Africa—which in any case wanted a fair election in order to put an end to its involvement in Namibia. In Afghanistan, as we have already noted, there is an almost unmanageably large number of internal actors as well as a number of external actors which, on the basis of their own perceived interests, are far from indifferent to the specific outcome of an election. In Namibia, the administering authorities managed to secure a high degree of trust from the participants in the election. In Afghanistan, given *Mujahideen* resentment at their exclusion from the Geneva process, there remains considerable distrust of the UN system which would have to be overcome. In Namibia there were no serious efforts made to disrupt the polling, and the election was won by the only party likely to take up arms in the event that it lost. In Afghanistan the disruption of polling would be ludicrously simple, and there are numerous actors likely to take up arms in the event of a loss. Finally, in Namibia a single party won an absolute majority of the vote. This would be most unlikely in Afghanistan unless Zahir Shah were able to assemble a grand coalition to contest a poll.

The Soviet proposal for the cessation of arms supplies appears blatantly self-serving, given that it had rejected such a proposal at the time of the Geneva Accords so that it could deluge the Kabul regime with massive stockpiles of advanced military equipment. In the light of the relatively smaller supplies of the US to the *Mujahideen* following the Soviet withdrawal, such a proposal for the cessation of arms supply could hardly be expected to build the confidence of the opposition in the integrity of the settlement process. A Soviet offer to withdraw some of the advanced equipment supplied in 1989 would be the kind of confidence-building measure the situation requires.

Finally, the proposal for the demilitarisation of Afghanistan by an international conference implies a definite limitation on the sovereignty of the Afghan state. A demilitarised Afghanistan could be vulnerable to self-serving pressures in the future from its neighbours, accentuated by its landlocked character. Furthermore, demilitarisation by agreement between external powers has historically been imposed on defeated parties to a war; it is far from clear why Afghanistan's sovereignty should be diminished simply as a consequence of its having fallen victim to external aggression.[46]

Whichever of these possibilities might materialise, the problems of war damage will continue to haunt the Afghan people for a long time. The destructuring of Afghanistan which the Soviets and their surrogates have imposed on the country immensely complicates the task of finding a viable solution to the Afghanistan problem but guarantees a long period of misery and uncertainty for those who have survived the the trauma of Soviet occupation. A viable solution will have to restructure not only the Afghan political system but also the social contexts within which politics is played out. The Afghanistan which will emerge from this process will feature a normative order markedly different from that which maintained relative stability from 1929 to 1978. Nonetheless, one can be reasonably sure that the Afghan state will be as weak for the foreseeable future as it was for most of its history, and that micro-societies will continue to play important roles in Afghan social and political affairs. All the Soviets and their protegés managed to do was to increase enormously the suffering of the Afghan people.

Notes

1. BBC *Summary of World Broadcasts*, SU/0480/C/10, 12 June 1989.

2. Andrei Sakharov, 'Neizbezhnost' perestroiki', in Iu.N. Afanas'ev (ed.), *Inogo ne dano* (Moscow: Progress, 1988) pp.122-134, at p.136.

3. Marek Sliwinski, *Afghanistan 1978-1987: War, Demography and Society* (London: Central Asian Survey Incidental Paper no.6, 1988) p.3.

4. Noor Ahmad Khalidi, *Demographic Consequences of War in Afghanistan* (Research Note no.116, International Population Dynamics Program, Department of Demography, Research School of Social Sciences, The Australian National University, 15 November 1990).

5. See BBC *Summary of World Broadcasts*, SU/0545/A3/1, 26 August 1989 This figure is not the only one, however, to have appeared in the Soviet press. On 29 January 1989 the Estonian Komsomol newspaper *Noorte Haal* claimed that 50,000 Soviets had died in Afghanistan: see Valerii Konovalov, 'Legacy of the Afghan War: Some Statistics', *Report on the USSR*, vol.1, no.14, 7 April 1989, pp.1-3 at p.1.

6. Sliwinski, op.cit., p.7.

7. Ibid., p.14.

8. See Office of the United Nations Co-ordinator for Humanitarian and Economic Assistance Programmes Relating to Afghanistan, *First Consolidated Report* (Geneva: UNOCA/1988/1, September 1988) p.1.

9. Sliwinski, op.cit., p.18.

10. Ibid., p.18. Sliwinski estimates that the percentage of Pushtuns fell to 22 per cent, as compared to 34 per cent for the Tajiks. However, there are methodological problems with this estimate, as a result of Sliwinski's assumption that the ethnic composition of the Iranian refugee population mirrored that of the refugee population in Pakistan. See Pierre Centlivres, 'La nouvelle carte ethnique de l'Afghanistan', *Les Nouvelles d'Afghanistan*, no.47, April 1990, pp.4-11, at p.8.

11. A. Ghanie Ghaussy, 'The Economic Effects of the Soviet War in Afghanistan', *Internationales Asienforum*, vol.20, nos.1-2, 1989, pp.117-136, at p.134.

12. Olivier Roy, quoted in Annick Billard, 'Afghanistan: Operation Salam', *Refugees*, no.61, February 1989, pp.11-14, at p.12.

13. Gavin Bell 'Paradise lost in Afghan valley of death', *The Times*, 21 July 1987, p.7.

14. André Brigot and Olivier Roy, *The War in Afghanistan* (London: Harvester Wheatsheaf, 1988) p.10.

15. Grant M. Farr and Azam Gul, 'Afghan Agricultural Production: 1978-1982', *Journal of South Asian and Middle Eastern Studies*, vol.8, no.1, Fall 1984, pp.65-79. See also Mohammad Qasim Yusufi, 'Effects of the War on Agriculture', in Bo Huldt and Erland Jansson (eds.), *The Tragedy of Afghanistan: The Social, Cultural and Political Impact of the Soviet Invasion* (London: Croom Helm, 1988) pp.197-216.

16. Frances D'Souza, *The Threat of Famine in Afghanistan* (London: Afghanaid, 1984).

17. See *The Agricultural Survey of Afghanistan. First Report* (Peshawar: The Swedish Committee for Afghanistan, May 1988) pp.29-31. For further details on the state of agriculture, see *The Agricultural Survey of Afghanistan. Second Report: Farm Power* (Peshawar: The Swedish Committee for Afghanistan, April 1989); *The Agricultural Survey of Afghanistan. Third Report: Crops and Yields* (Peshawar: The Swedish Committee for Afghanistan, August 1989); *The Agricultural Survey of Afghanistan. Fourth Report: Fertiliser* (Peshawar: The Swedish Committee for Afghanistan, February 1990); *The Agricultural Survey of Afghanistan. Fifth Report: Seeds* (Peshawar: The Swedish Committee for Afghanistan, June 1990).

18. See Jeri Laber and Barnett R. Rubin, *"A Nation is Dying": Afghanistan under the Soviets 1979-87* (Evanston: Northwestern University Press, 1988) pp.58-65.

19. For detailed discussion, see Leslie Dienes, 'Central Asia and the Soviet "Midlands": Regional Position and Economic Integration', in Milan Hauner and Robert L. Canfield (eds.), *Afghanistan and the Soviet Union: Collision and Transformation* (Boulder: Westview Press, 1989) pp.61-100; and John F. Shroder, Jnr, 'Afghanistan Resources and Soviet Policy in Central and South Asia', in Milan Hauner and Robert L. Canfield (eds.), *Afghanistan and the Soviet Union: Collision and Transformation* (Boulder: Westview Press, 1989) pp.101-119.

20. M.S. Noorzoy, 'Long-term Economic Relations between Afghanistan and the Soviet Union: An Interpretive Study', *International Journal of Middle East Studies*, vol.17, 1987, pp.151-173, at pp.161-162.

21. John F. Shroder, Jnr. and Abdul Tawab Assifi, 'Afghan Resources and Soviet Exploitation', in Rosanne Klass (ed.), *Afghanistan—The Great Game Revisited* (New York: Freedom House, 1987) pp.97-134, at p.113.

22. See Amin Saikal, 'Soviet Policy toward Southwest Asia', *The Annals of the American Academy of Political and Social Science*, no.481, September 1985, pp.104-116, at p.111.

23. See Pierre Centlivres and Micheline Centlivres-Demont, 'Hommes d'influence et hommes de partis: L'organisation politique dans les villages de réfugiés afghans au Pakistan', in Erwin Grötzbach (ed.), *Neue Beiträge zur Afghanistanforschung* (Liestal: Stiftung Bibliotheca

Afghanica, 1988) pp.29-46, at pp.33-37.

24. See Kacem Fazelly, 'Under a foreign yoke', *Index on Censorship*, vol.10, no.5, October 1981, pp. 5-6; Anthony Hyman, 'Victims of a Wicked Stepmother', *The Times Higher Education Supplement*, 2 November 1984, p.17; and S.M. Yusuf Elmi, 'The Impact of Sovietization on Afghan Education and Culture', in S.B. Majrooh and S.M. Y. Elmi (eds.), *The Sovietization of Afghanistan* (Peshawar: Afghan Information Centre and Afghan Jehad Works Translation Centre, 1986) pp.72-125.

25. For excellent discussions of ethnic factors, see Olivier Roy, 'Afghanistan: back to tribalism or on to Lebanon?', *Third World Quarterly*, vol.11, no.4, October 1989, pp.70-82; and Richard S. Newell, 'Post-Soviet Afghanistan: The Position of the Minorities', *Asian Survey*, vol.29, no.11, November 1989, pp.1090-1108.

26. Richard Nixon, 'Operation Kabul: a call to arms', *The Australian*, 19 February 1990.

27. On the 'Brezhnev Doctrine', see Robert A. Jones, *The Soviet Concept of 'Limited Sovereignty' from Lenin to Gorbachev: The Brezhnev Doctrine* (London: Macmillan, 1990).

28. See Kevin Devlin, 'Brezhnev Doctrine Dead: No More Invasions', *Report on the USSR*, vol.1, no.39, 29 September 1989, pp.14-15.

29. BBC *Summary of World Broadcasts*, SU/0596/C/4-11, 25 October 1989.

30. On Soviet 'new thinking', see Anatolii Gromyko and Vladimir Lomeiko, *Novoe myshlenie v iadernyi vek* (Moscow: Izdatel'stvo 'Mezhdunarodnye otnosheniia', 1984); and Vendulka Kubálková and A.A. Cruickshank, *Thinking New about Soviet 'new thinking'* (Berkeley: Institute of International Studies, University of California, 1989).

31. See Viktor Yasmann, 'Afghanistan Comes Up, *Glasnost*' Goes Down', *Report on the USSR*, vol.1, no.45, 10 November 1989, pp.9-10.

32. See Major-General Kim Tsagolov, 'More Questions Than Answers: Soviets still in Afghanistan two years after withdrawal', *Moscow News*, 25 November-2 December 1990, p.13.

33. See BBC *Summary of World Broadcasts*, SU/0819/i, 18 July 1990.

34. For a report on the Shah Salim meeting, see *AFGHANews*, vol.6, nos.20-21, 1 November 1990, pp.1, 5.

35. See Eden Naby, 'Tajiks Reemphasize Iranian Heritage as Ethnic Pressures Mount in Central Asia', *Report on the USSR*, vol.2, no.7, 16 February 1990, pp.20-22.

36. For arguments about the significance of the north, see Joseph Newman, Jr., 'The Future of Northern Afghanistan', *Asian Survey*, vol.28, no.7, July 1988, pp.729-739.

37. 'US official meets with Zahir Shah', *AFGHANews*, vol.5, nos.18-19, 1 October 1989, p.1.

38. Roy, 'Afghanistan: back to tribalism or on to Lebanon?', p.80.

39. See Diego Cordovez, 'Afghanistan: A Way to Bring Peace ...', *The Washington Post*, 12 April 1990, p.A25. These arguments were repeated in Diego Cordovez, 'Uregulirovanie—delo samikh Afgantsev', *Pravda*, 23 April 1990, p.4.

40. United Nations General Assembly, *Resolution* 44/15, 15 November 1989.

41. See 'Baker: U.S., Soviets "made substantial progress"', *Official Text* (Canberra: United States Information Service, 14 February 1990).

42. Eduard Shevardnadze, 'Afganistan—trudnaia doroga k miru', *Izvestiia*, 14 February 1990, p.5.

43. Afghan Information Centre *Monthly Bulletin*, nos.105-106, December 1989-January 1990, p.19.

44. *The Frontier Post*, 19 March 1990, p.1.

45. Louis Dupree, 'Post-Withdrawal Afghanistan: Light at the End of the Tunnel', in Amin Saikal and William Maley (eds.), *The Soviet Withdrawal from Afghanistan* (Cambridge: Cambridge University Press, 1989) pp.29-51, at p.46.

46. For a useful discussion of related issues, see Cyril E. Black, Richard A. Falk, Klaus Knorr, and Oran R. Young, *Neutralization and World Politics* (Princeton: Princeton University Press, 1968).

9

Conclusion

This is no doubt that the process of state-building in Afghanistan has at all times been a task of great complexity, and the events since 1978 have enormously added to the difficulty of legitimating state action in terms which will resonate amongst Afghanistan's micro-societies. Yet in the long-run the establishment of a legitimate regime in Kabul is a matter of enormous importance. While a respectable argument can be advanced that the instrumentalities of the state have in recent years brought more sorrow than joy for the Afghan people, there are nonetheless reasons for seeking a capable central actor in Afghanistan. Of these, two in particular are important. First, there are numerous tasks of postwar reconstruction which can be carried out, or carried out *efficiently*, only if a legitimate regime is in place. Second—and more ominously—as the war has obliterated the role of the state as a mediating force and altered traditional patterns of authority within Afghan micro-societies it has also had the effect of sharpening tensions between groups on ethnic and linguistic lines. The instrumentalities of a legitimate state may therefore be needed to play a mediatory role in order to keep the members of hostile micro-societies from each others' throats. There is no serious prospect that a *strong* state—one endowed in high order with penetration, regulation, extraction and appropriation capabilities—will soon emerge. The war has weakened both state and micro-societies, but the state has been weakened to a relatively greater extent. Nevertheless, as compromises between micro-societies become more difficult to strike, there may be a constructive role for even a weak state to play, as long as those who control it are committed to consensual decision-making, have mediation skills of a high order, and do not identify themselves exclusively with some narrow and sectional support base. In the previous chapter we noted the ways in which Afghanistan had been damaged by a decade of war. We also identified a number of paths which might result in the emergence of a new regime in Afghanistan. It remains now only to discuss briefly the deeper question of what kind of broader patterns of political organisation would need to emerge in order to ensure that a future Afghan regime would be stable in the medium to long term.

The prospects of such stability emerging, it must be conceded, are not particularly bright. In polities which are not deeply fractionalised, general elections may be the most effective way of procuring a non-autocratic stable government and, more fundamentally, of consolidating a pluralistic politics. In severely divided societies, however, majoritarian democracy is unlikely to provide the basis for a stable and legitimate political order. In recognition of this fact, various analysts have defended the claims of a somewhat different prototype, under the name of *consociational* democracy. The experience in political systems which have employed consociational devices has been far from universally satisfactory, and it is undoubtedly the case that unless consociational devices are reinforced by informal social sanctions, they are prone to come to grief. Nonetheless, they provide some glimmer of hope in what is a fairly gloomy landscape.

The consociational model has four major elements. The first and most important is 'government by a grand coalition of the political leaders of all significant segments of the plural society'. The second is the 'mutual veto' which 'serves as an 'additional protection of vital minority interests'. The third is 'proportionality as the principal standard of political representation, civil service appointments, and allocation of public funds'. The fourth is 'a high degree of autonomy for each segment to run its own affairs'.[1] A number of historical cases have been cited as examples of successful consociationalism, notably Austria, Switzerland, Belgium, The Netherlands, Colombia, and Venezuela.[2] However, it is questionable to what extent consociationalism should receive the credit for the stability which some of these countries have enjoyed;[3] and consociationalism has had some serious failures: Cyprus, Malaysia at one time,[4] and, most spectacularly, Lebanon.[5]

Some of these elements are almost inevitable in Afghanistan. Others, however, are likely to be achievable only in somewhat modified forms. A grand coalition of sorts was what the traditional institution of the *Loya Jirga* involved, as a device of consensus-building and regime legitimation, if not directly of government itself. A realignment of various *Mujahideen forces* accompanied by the return of Zahir Shah, such as we canvassed in the previous chapter, could permit the holding of a successful *Loya Jirgah* or *Shura* and lay the foundation for the emergence of such a coalition. It may be for this reason that UN sources, most noticeably Cordovez, have put emphasis on a consensual *Loya Jirgah* rather than competitive general elections which are as likely to accentuate divisions as eliminate them. (Of course, a *Shura* can easily be hijacked by interested outside powers, as was the case in February 1989, and to avoid this it would best be organised under the auspices of a disinterested outside state such as Sweden, with the full support of the permanent members of the UN Security Council.) An unlimited mutual veto would be unlikely to work in Afghanistan, given the disposition of different groups to use the veto power vexatiously. It would need to be modified so as to allow the state to exercise overriding authority except on matters going to the heart of the distinct identities of the various micro-societies. The third element, proportionality, would have a reasonably good chance of taking root in Afghanistan. In a sense, the pre-communist situation in which the political establishment and armed forces were Pushtun-dominated and the bureaucracy Tajik-dominated represented a crude kind of proportionality of political influence. Furthermore, during the 'Constitutional Period', the King to some extent used proportionality between different ethnic groups as a rule of thumb when making appointments to the seats he was empowered to fill in the Upper House (*Meshrano Jirgah*). Finally, given that the state will be weak in Afghanistan, it is unlikely to stand in the way of a high degree of autonomy for each segment to run its affairs. What is more problematical is whether the individual segments will respect each others' autonomy on the ground.

Beyond its institutional manifestations, consociationalism demands a degree of common commitment from social groups to maintain what is at best a delicate equilibrium, as well as a continuing absolute guarantee of *non-interference by external actors*. The consociational system broke down in Lebanon largely for three reasons. First, the system lacked the flexibility to adjust to changes in the relative demographic strengths of the different segments within the population—and as a consequence it could not satisfy those groups whose political expectations were rising. Second, the system entrenched rather than corrected imbalances between the welfare of different social groups, and the worst-off came to doubt that they had a genuine stake in the maintenance of the system. Third, disgruntled goups could easily secure the support of outside powers to press their objections to the structure of the political system. Some of these obstacles could be avoided in Afghanistan. The UN or its specialised agencies could attempt a detailed analysis of the ethnic and linguistic breakdown of the population in order to establish a 'benchmark' for proportionality, and could offer to do so on a continuing basis to facilitate institutional adjustments necessary to keep the principles of the system intact. Furthermore, the UN would have to protect Afghanistan from the kind of outside interference which so destabilised Lebanon, although the difficulties associated with providing such protection would be immense.

In the end, Afghanistan is a nation in tatters. It is in dire need of international assistance. If the world community turns its back on the Afghan tragedy, the misery of the Afghans can only increase. While a consociational model of institutional design is far from perfect, it holds more promise than most others to provide the kind of stability which is required if Afghanistan's immense long-term problems, with all their regional consequences, are to be addressed. Its prospects for success ultimately go back to the micro-societies whose importance we have emphasised throughout this book. For the foreseeable future, the state will be able to discharge its functions successfully only if it receives sufficient cooperation from these micro-societies to do so. Amongst all the ironies of the last decade of regime change in Afghanistan, perhaps the heaviest is that something like the fundamental structure of power which the self-styled 'revolutionaries' set themselves the task of overthrowing must now be used to repair the ruin which they created.

Notes

1. Arend Lijphart, *Democracy in Plural Societies: A Comparative Exploration* (New Haven: Yale University Press, 1977) p.25.

2. Robert A. Dahl, *Democracy and Its Critics* (New Haven: Yale University Press, 1989) pp.257-258.

3. See Brian Barry, *Democracy, Power and Justice: Essays in Political Theory* (Oxford: Oxford University Press, 1989) pp.100-155.

4. Dahl, op.cit., p.258.

5. John P. Entelis, '"How Could Something So Right Go So Wrong?": The Collapse of Lebanon's Ethnoconfessional Democracy', in Farhad Kazemi and R.D. McChesney (eds.), *A Way Prepared: Essays in Islamic Culture in Honor of Richard Bayly Winder* (New York: New York University Press, 1988) pp.216-240.

Bibliography of Works Cited

Books and Articles

Adamec, Ludwig W., *Afghanistan's Foreign Affairs to the Mid-Twentieth Century: Relations With the USSR, Germany, and Britain* (Tucson: The University of Arizona Press, 1974).

Ahmed, Akbar S., *Millennium and Charisma among Pathans: A Critical Essay in Social Anthropology* (London: Routledge and Kegan Paul, 1976).

Allison, Roy, *The Soviet Union and the Strategy of Non-Alignment in the Third World* (Cambridge: Cambridge University Press, 1988).

Almond, Gabriel A. and Coleman, James S. (eds.), *The Politics of the Developing Areas* (Princeton: Princeton University Press, 1960).

Almond, Gabriel A. and Powell, G. Bingham *Comparative Politics: A Developmental Approach* (Boston: Little, Brown & Co., 1966).

Amnesty International, *Violations of Human Rights and Fundamental Freedoms in the Democratic Republic of Afghanistan* (London: ASA 11/04/79, September 1979).

Amnesty International, *Democratic Republic of Afghanistan: Background Briefing on Amnesty International's Concerns* (London: ASA/11/13/83, October 1983).

Amnesty International, *Afghanistan: Torture of Political Prisoners* (London: ASA/11/04/86, November 1986).

Amnesty International, *Afghanistan—Unlawful Killings and Torture* (London: ASA/11/02/88, May 1988).

Amstutz, J. Bruce, *Afghanistan: The First Five Years of Soviet Occupation* (Washington D.C.: National Defense University Press, 1986).

Anderson, Jon W., 'There are no Khans Anymore: Economic Development and Social Change in Tribal Afghanistan', *The Middle East Journal*, vol.32, no.2, Spring 1978, pp.167-183.

Anwar, Raja, *The Tragedy of Afghanistan: A First-hand Account* (London: Verso, 1988).

Arnold, Anthony, *Afghanistan's Two Party Communism: Parcham and Khalq* (Stanford: Hoover Institution Press, 1983).

Arnold, Anthony, *Afghanistan: The Soviet Invasion in Perspective*

(Stanford: Hoover Institution Press, 1985).

Azmi, Muhammad R., 'Soviet Politico-Military Penetration in Afghanistan, 1955 to 1979', *Armed Forces & Society*, vol.12, no.3, Spring 1986, pp.329-350.

Azoy, G. Whitney, *Buzkashi: Game and Power in Afghanistan* (Philadelphia: University of Pennsylvania Press, 1982).

Bacon, Sir Francis, 'Of Negotiating', in *Bacon's Essays* (New York: Carlton House, n.d.) pp.259-261.

Baldick, Julian, *Mystical Islam: An Introduction to Sufism* (London: I.B. Tauris, 1989).

Ball, Desmond, 'Soviet Signals Intelligence', *The International Countermeasures Handbook* (Palo Alto: E.W. Communications Inc., 1987) pp.73-89.

Banuazizi, Ali and Weiner, Myron (eds.), *The State, Religion, and Ethnic Politics: Afghanistan, Iran, and Pakistan* (Syracuse: Syracuse University Press, 1986).

Barber, Noel, *Seven Days of Freedom: The Hungarian Uprising 1956* (London: Macmillan, 1974).

Barfield, Thomas J., 'Weak Links on a Rusty Chain: Structural Weaknesses in Afghanistan's Provincial Government Administration', in M. Nazif Shahrani and Robert L. Canfield (eds.), *Revolutions & Rebellions in Afghanistan: Anthropological Perspectives* (Berkeley: Institute of International Studies, University of California, 1984) pp.170-183.

Barker, Rodney, *Political Legitimacy and the State* (Oxford: Oxford University Press, 1990).

Barry, Brian, *Democracy, Power and Justice: Essays in Political Theory* (Oxford: Oxford University Press, 1989).

Barry, Michael, *Afghanistan* (Paris: Éditions du Seuil, 1974).

Barry, Michael, 'Répressions et guerre soviétiques', *Les Temps Modernes*, no.408-409, July-August 1980, pp. 171-234.

Barry, Michael, *Le Royaume de L'Insolence: La résistance afghane du Grand Moghol à l'invasion soviétique* (Paris: Flammarion, 1984).

Barry, Michael, Lagerfelt, Johan, and Terrenoire, Marie-Odile, 'International Humanitarian Enquiry Commission on Displaced Persons in Afghanistan', *Central Asian Survey*, vol.5, no.1, 1986, pp.65-99.

Barth, Fredrik, *Political Leadership among Swat Pathans* (London: The Athlone Press, 1959).

Beliaev, Igor' and Gromyko, Anatolii, 'Tak my voshli v Afganistan', *Literaturnaia gazeta*, 20 September 1989, p.14.

Belitsky, Sergei, 'Authors of USSR's Afghan War Policy', *Report on the USSR*, vol.1, no.17, 28 April 1989, pp.11-12.

Bell, Gavin, 'Paradise lost in Afghan valley of death', *The Times*, 21 July 1987, p.7.

Bennigsen, Alexandre, 'The Impact of the Afghan War on Soviet Central Asia', in Rosanne Klass (ed.), *Afghanistan—The Great Game Revisited* (New York: Freedom House, 1987) pp.287-299.

Billard, Annick, 'Afghanistan: Operation Salam', *Refugees*, no.61, February 1989, pp.11-14.

Black, Cyril E., Falk, Richard A., Knorr, Klaus, and Young, Oran R., *Neutralization and World Politics* (Princeton: Princeton University Press, 1968).

Bogomolov, Oleg, 'Kto zhe oshibalsia?', *Literaturnaia gazeta*, 16 March 1988.

Bonner, Arthur, *Among the Afghans* (Durham: Duke University Press, 1987).

Bradsher, Henry S., *Afghanistan and the Soviet Union* (Durham: Duke University Press, 1985).

Bradsher, Henry S., 'Communism in Afghanistan', in Hafeez Malik (ed.), *Soviet-American Relations with Pakistan, Iran and Afghanistan* (London: Macmillan, 1987) pp.333-354.

Brezhnev, L.I., *Izbrannye proizvedeniia* (Moscow: Politizdat, 1981) Vol.III.

Brigot, André, and Roy, Olivier, *The War in Afghanistan* (London: Harvester Wheatsheaf, 1988).

Brown, Archie, 'The Power of the General Secretary of the CPSU', in T.H. Rigby, Archie Brown and Peter Reddaway (eds.), *Authority, Power and Policy in the USSR* (London: Macmillan, 1980) pp.135-157.

Brown, Archie, 'Power and Policy in a Time of Leadership Transition, 1982-1988', in Archie Brown (ed.), *Political Leadership in the Soviet Union* (London: Macmillan, 1989) pp.163-217.

Brumberg, Abraham (ed.), *Chronicle of a Revolution: A Western-Soviet Inquiry into Perestroika* (New York: Pantheon Books, 1990).

Brzezinski, Zbigniew, *Power and Principle: Memoirs of the National Security Adviser 1977-1981* (New York: Farrar, Strauss & Giroux, 1983).

Burns, John F., 'In Kabul, Soviet Airlift Brings Bread and Guns', *The New York Times*, 24 May 1989, p.12.

Canfield, Robert L., 'Western Stakes in the Afghanistan War', *Central Asian Survey*, vol.4, no.1, 1985, pp.121-135.

Canfield, Robert L., 'Ethnic, Regional, and Sectarian Alignments in Afghanistan', in Ali Banuazizi and Myron Weiner (eds.), *The State, Religion, and Ethnic Politics: Afghanistan, Iran, and Pakistan* (Syracuse: Syracuse University Press, 1986) pp.75-103.

Canfield, Robert L., 'Afghanistan: The Trajectory of Internal Alignments', *The Middle East Journal*, vol.43, no.4, Autumn 1989, pp.635-648.

Caroe, Sir Olaf, *The Pathans* (Karachi: Oxford University Press, 1983).

Carter, J.E., *Keeping Faith: Memoirs of a President* (London: Collins, 1982).

Centlivres, Pierre, 'La nouvelle carte ethnique de l'Afghanistan', *Les Nouvelles d'Afghanistan*, no.47, April 1990, pp.4-11.

Centlivres, Pierre and Centlivres-Demont, Micheline, *Et si on parlait de l'Afghanistan?* (Paris: Editions de la Maison des science de l'homme, 1988).

Centlivres, Pierre, and Centlivres-Demont, Micheline, 'Hommes d'influence et hommes de partis: L'organisation politique dans les villages de réfugiés afghans au Pakistan', in Erwin Grötzbach (ed.), *Neue Beiträge zur Afghanistanforschung* (Liestal: Stiftung Bibliotheca Afghanica, 1988) pp.29-46.

Centlivres, Pierre, and Centlivres-Demont, Micheline, 'The Afghan Refugees in Pakistan: A Nation in Exile', *Current Sociology*, vol.36, no.2, Summer 1988, pp.71-92.

Coll, Steve, 'U.S. Envoy Reassigned In Afghan Policy Clash', *The Washington Post*, 10 August 1989, p.27.

Coll, Steve, 'U.S. and Pakistan Shift Afghan Tactics', *International Herald Tribune*, 4 September 1989, pp.1,6.

Collins, Joseph J., *The Soviet Invasion of Afghanistan: A Study in the Use of Force in Soviet Foreign Policy* (Lexington: Lexington Books, 1986).

Cordovez, Diego, 'Afghanistan: A Way to Bring Peace ...', *The Washington Post*, 12 April 1990, p.A25.

Cordovez, Diego, 'Uregulirovanie—delo samikh Afgantsev', *Pravda*, 23 April 1990, p.4.

Cordovez, Diego, 'Afghans Should Approve Gorbachev's Peace Prize', *International Herald Tribune*, 1 November 1990.

Crone, Patricia, 'The Tribe and the State', in John A. Hall (ed.), *States in History* (Oxford: Basil Blackwell, 1986) pp.48-77.

D'Souza, Frances, *The Threat of Famine in Afghanistan* (London: AfghanAid, 1984).

Dahl, Robert A., *Democracy and Its Critics* (New Haven: Yale University Press, 1989).

Danishyar, Abdul Aziz, *The Afghanistan Republic Annual* (Kabul: Government Press, 1974).

Delloye, Isabelle, *Des Femmes d'Afghanistan* (Paris: Éditions Des Femmes, 1980).

Devlin, Kevin, 'Brezhnev Doctrine Dead: No More Invasions', *Report on the USSR*, vol.1, no.39, 29 September 1989, pp.14-15.

Dienes, Leslie, 'Central Asia and the Soviet "Midlands": Regional Position and Economic Integration', in Milan Hauner and Robert L. Canfield (eds.), *Afghanistan and the Soviet Union: Collision and Transformation* (Boulder: Westview Press, 1989) pp.61-100.

Dietl, Wilhelm, *Brückenkopf Afghanistan: Machtpolitik im Mittleren Osten* (Munich: Kindler Verlag, 1984).

Dil, Shaheen F., 'The Cabal in Kabul: Great-Power Interaction in Afghanistan', *American Political Science Review*, vol.71, no.2, June 1977, pp.468-476.

Dobbs, Michael, 'Soviet Aide Questions Afghan Withdrawal Date', *The*

Washington Post, 11 January 1989, p.17.

Doxey, Margaret, 'Sanctions Against the Soviet Union: The Afghan Experience', *The Year Book of World Affairs 1983* (London: Stevens & Sons, 1983) pp.63-80.

Dupaigne, Bernard (ed.), *Les droits de l'homme en Afghanistan* (Paris: AFRANE, 1985).

Dupaigne, Bernard (ed.), *Femmes en Afghanistan* (Paris: Amitié Franco-Afghane, 1986).

Dupree, Louis, 'Afghanistan: Problems of a Peasant-Tribal Society', in Louis Dupree and Linette Albert (eds.), *Afghanistan in the 1970s* (New York: Praeger, 1974) pp.1-12.

Dupree, Louis, *Red Flag Over the Hindu Kush: Part III: Rhetoric and Reforms, or Promises! Promises!* (American Universities Field Staff Reports: No. 23-Asia, 1980).

Dupree, Louis *Afghanistan* (Princeton: Princeton University Press, 1980).

Dupree, Louis, 'Cultural changes among the Mujahidin and Muhajerin', in Bo Huldt and Erland Jansson (eds.), *The Tragedy of Afghanistan: The Social, Cultural and Political Impact of the Soviet Invasion* (London, Croom Helm, 1988) pp.20-37.

Dupree, Louis, 'Post-Withdrawal Afghanistan: Light at the End of the Tunnel', in Amin Saikal and William Maley (eds.), *The Soviet Withdrawal from Afghanistan* (Cambridge: Cambridge University Press, 1989) pp.29-51.

Dupree, Nancy Hatch, 'Revolutionary Rhetoric and Afghan Women', in M. Nazif Shahrani and Robert L. Canfield (eds.), *Revolutions & Rebellions in Afghanistan: Anthropological Perspectives* (Berkeley: Institute of International Studies, University of California, 1984) pp.306-340.

Dupree, Nancy Hatch, 'The Demography of Afghan Refugees in Pakistan', in Hafeez Malik (ed.), *Soviet-American Relations with Pakistan, Iran, and Afghanistan* (London: Macmillan, 1987) pp.366-395.

Dupree, Nancy Hatch, 'Demographic Reporting on Afghan Refugees in Pakistan', *Modern Asian Studies*, vol.22, no.4, October 1988, pp.845-865.

Edwards, David Busby, 'The Evolution of Shi'i Political Dissent in Afghanistan', in Juan R.I. Cole and Nikki R. Keddie (eds.), *Shi'ism and Social Protest* (New Haven: Yale University Press, 1986) pp.201-229.

Edwards, David Busby,'Origins of the Anti-Soviet Jihad', in Grant M. Farr and John G. Merriam (eds.), *Afghan Resistance: The Politics of Survival* (Boulder; Westview Press, 1987) pp.21-50.

Eisenstadt, S.N., *The Political Systems of Empires: The Rise and Fall of the Historical Bureaucratic Societies* (New York: The Free Press, 1969).

Elmi, S.M. Yusuf, 'The Impact of Sovietization on Afghan Education and Culture', in S.B. Majrooh and S.M. Y. Elmi (eds.), *The Sovietization of Afghanistan* (Peshawar: Afghan Information Centre and Afghan Jehad Works Translation Centre, 1986) pp.72-125.

Elster, Jon *The Cement of Society: A study of social order* (Cambridge: Cambridge University Press, 1989).

Emadi, Hafizullah, *State, Revolution, and Superpowers in Afghanistan* (New York: Praeger, 1990).

Entelis, John P., '"How Could Something So Right Go So Wrong?": The Collapse of Lebanon's Ethnoconfessional Democracy', in Farhad Kazemi and R.D. McChesney (eds.), *A Way Prepared: Essays in Islamic Culture in Honor of Richard Bayly Winder* (New York: New York University Press, 1988) pp.216-240.

Es'haq, Mohammad 'Evolution of the Islamic movement in Afghanistan', *AFGHANews*, vol.5, nos.1-4, January-February 1989.

Es'haq, Mohammad 'Peace prize for Gorbachev makes Afghans angry', *AFGHANews*, vol.6, no.22, 15 November 1990, pp.1-4.

Étienne, Gilbert, *L'Afghanistan ou Les Aléas de la Coopération* (Paris: Presses Universitaires de France, 1972).

Étienne, Gilbert, *Rural Development in Asia: Meetings with Peasants* (New Delhi: Sage Publications, 1985).

Evtushenko, Evgenii 'Po moemu mneniiu', *Sovetskaia kul'tura*, 15 April 1986, p.3.

Farr, Grant M., and Gul, Azam, 'Afghan Agricultural Production: 1978-1982', *Journal of South Asian and Middle Eastern Studies*, vol.8, no.1, Fall 1984, pp.65-79.

Farr, Grant M., and Merriam, John G. (eds.), *Afghan Resistance: The Politics of Survival* (Boulder: Westview Press, 1987).

Fazelly, Kacem, 'Under a foreign yoke', *Index on Censorship*, vol.10, no.5, October 1981, pp. 5-6.

Fineman, Mark, 'Brother Calls Najibullah "Weak Puppet" Who Will Fall', *The Los Angeles Times*, 16 August 1988, Part I, p.16.

Franceschi, Patrice, *Guerre en Afghanistan* (Paris: La Table Ronde, 1984).

Fry, Maxwell J., *The Afghan Economy: Money, Finance and the Critical Constraints to Economic Development* (Leiden: E.J. Brill, 1974).

Fullerton, John, *The Soviet Occupation of Afghanistan* (Hong Kong: South China Morning Post, 1983).

Gall, Sandy *Behind Russian Lines: An Afghan Journal* (London: Sidgwick and Jackson, 1983).

Gall, Sandy *Afghanistan: Agony of a Nation* (London: The Bodley Head, 1988).

Garthoff, Raymond L., *Détente and Confrontation: American-Soviet Relations from Nixon to Reagan* (Washington D.C.: The Brookings Institution, 1985).

Gellner, Ernest, 'The Tribal Society and Its Enemies', in Richard Tapper (ed.), *The Conflict of Tribe and State in Iran and Afghanistan* (London: Croom Helm, 1983) pp.436-448.

Ghani, Ashraf, 'Islam and State-Building in a Tribal Society: Afghanistan 1880-1901', *Modern Asian Studies*, vol.12, no.2, 1978, pp.269-284.

Ghani, Ashraf, 'The Afghan State and its Adaptation to the Environment of Central and Southwest Asia', in Hafeez Malik (ed.), *Soviet-American Relations with Pakistan, Iran and Afghanistan* (London: Macmillan, 1987) pp.310-332.

Ghaus, Abdul Samad, *The Fall of Afghanistan: An Insider's Account* (McLean: Pergamon-Brassey's, 1988).

Ghaussy, A. Ghanie, 'The Economic Effects of the Soviet War in Afghanistan', *Internationales Asienforum*, vol.20, nos.1-2, 1989, pp.117-136.

Ghobar, Mir Mohammad Ghulam, *Afghanistan dar masir-i tarikh* (Kabul: n.p., 1967).

Gill, Graeme, 'Personality Cult, Political Culture and Party Structure', *Studies in Comparative Communism*, vol.17, no.2, Summer 1984, pp.111-121.

Gille, Etienne, 'Avec les manifestants d'avril à Kaboul', *Les Nouvelles d'Afghanistan*, no.2, November 1980, pp.18-19.

Gille, Etienne, 'La mort de Maywandwâl', *Les Nouvelles d'Afghanistan*, no.44, October 1989, p.20.

Gille, Etienne, 'L'"appel"', *Les Nouvelles d'Afghanistan*, no.45, December 1989-January 1990, pp.22-24.

Girardet, Edward R., *Afghanistan: The Soviet War* (London: Croom Helm, 1985).

Goodwin, Jan, *Caught in the Crossfire* (London: Macdonald, 1987).

Gordon, Michael R., 'U.S. and Moscow Agree on Pullout from Afghanistan', *The New York Times*, 12 April 1988, p.1.

Gregorian, Vartan, *The Emergence of Modern Afghanistan: Politics of Reform and Modernization 1880-1946* (Stanford: Stanford University Press, 1969).

Gromyko, Anatolii and Lomeiko, Vladimir, *Novoe myshlenie v iadernyi vek* (Moscow: Izdatel'stvo 'Mezhdunarodnye otnosheniia', 1984).

Hammond, Thomas T., *Red Flag Over Afghanistan* (Boulder: Westview Press, 1984).

Haqshenas, S.N., *Dasayis wa junayat-i Rus dar Afghanistan: Az Amir Dost Mohammad Khan ta Babrak* (Teheran: Komiteh-i Farhangi Daftar-e Markazi Jamiat-i Islami Afghanistan, 1984).

Harrison, Selig S., 'The Afghan arms alliance', *South*, no.53, March 1985, pp.16-21.

Harrison, Selig S., 'Afghanistan: Soviet Intervention, Afghan Resistance, and the American Role', in Michael T. Klare and Peter Kornbluh (eds.), *Low Intensity Warfare: Counterinsurgency, Proinsurgency, and Antiterrorism in the Eighties* (New York: Pantheon Books, 1988) pp.183-206.

Harrison, Selig S., 'Inside The Afghan Talks', *Foreign Policy*, no.72, Fall 1988, pp.31-60.

Hauner, Milan and Canfield, Robert L. (eds.), *Afghanistan and the Soviet*

Union: Collision and Transformation (Boulder: Westview Press, 1989).

Heller, Agnes, 'Phases of Legitimation in Soviet-type Societies', in T.H. Rigby and Ferenc Fehér (eds.), *Political Legitimation in Communist States* (London: Macmillan, 1982) pp.45-63.

Hodson, Peregrine, *Under a Sickle Moon: A Journey through Afghanistan* (London: Hutchinson, 1986).

Hough, Jerry F., *Soviet Leadership in Transition* (Washington D.C.: The Brookings Institution, 1980).

Hough, Jerry F., *Russia and the West: Gorbachev and the Politics of Reform* (New York: Simon and Schuster, 1990).

Huldt, Bo and Jansson, Erland (eds.), *The Tragedy of Afghanistan: The Social, Cultural and Political Impact of Soviet Invasion* (London: Croom Helm, 1988).

Humphrey, Senator Gordon J., 'An Expose of the State Department's Policy on Afghanistan', *Free Afghanistan Report*, January-February 1988, pp.8-10.

Hyman, Anthony, 'Afghan intelligentsia 1978-81', *Index on Censorship*, no.2, 1982, pp.8-10, 13.

Hyman, Anthony, 'Victims of a Wicked Stepmother', *The Times Higher Education Supplement*, 2 November 1984, p.17.

Hyman, Anthony, *Afghanistan under Soviet Domination 1964-83* (London: Macmillan, 1984).

Jones, Robert A., *The Soviet Concept of 'Limited Sovereignty' from Lenin to Gorbachev: The Brezhnev Doctrine* (London: Macmillan, 1990).

Kakar, Hasan Kawun, 'The Fall of the Afghan Monarchy in 1973', *International Journal of Middle East Studies*, vol.9, 1978, pp.195-214.

Kakar, Hasan Kawun, *Government and Society in Afghanistan: The Reign of Amir 'Abd al-Rahman Khan* (Austin: The University of Texas Press, 1979).

Kamali, Mohammad Hashem, *Law in Afghanistan: A Study of the Constitutions, Matrimonial Law and the Judiciary* (Leiden: E.J. Brill, 1985).

Kamm, Henry, 'Pakistanis Report Ordering Attack by Afghan Rebels', *The New York Times*, 23 April 1989, p.1.

Kaplan, Robert D., 'How Zia's Death Helped the U.S.', *The New York Times*, 23 August 1989, p.21.

Karklins, Rasma, 'The Dissent/Coercion Nexus in the USSR', *Studies in Comparative Communism*, vol.20, nos.3-4, Autumn-Winter 1987, pp.321-341.

Karp, Craig, *Afghanistan: Seven Years of Soviet Occupation* (Special Report no.155, Bureau of Public Affairs, United States Department of State, Washington D.C., December 1986).

Kautsky, John H., *The Politics of Aristocratic Empires* (Chapel Hill: The University of North Carolina Press, 1982).

Kennan, George F., *The Nuclear Delusion: Soviet-American Relations in the Atomic Age* (London: Hamish Hamilton, 1984).

Kertzer, David I., *Ritual, Politics and Power* (New Haven: Yale University Press, 1988).

Khalidi, Noor Ahmad, *Demographic Profile of Afghanistan* (Research Note no.106, International Population Dynamics Program, Department of Demography, Research School of Social Sciences, The Australian National University, 14 December 1989).

Khalidi, Noor Ahmad, *Demographic Consequences of War in Afghanistan* (Research Note no.116, International Population Dynamics Program, Department of Demography, Research School of Social Sciences, The Australian National University, 15 November 1990).

Khalili, Khalilullah, *'Ayari az Khorasan: Amir Habibullah, Khadim-i Din-i Rasul Allah* (Peshawar: Tarikh-e Ramadan, 1984).

Khalilzad, Zalmay, 'Soviet-Occupied Afghanistan', *Problems of Communism*, vol.29, no.6, November-December 1980, pp.23-40.

Khalilzad, Zalmay, *The Security of Southwest Asia* (New York: St. Martin's Press, 1984).

Khalilzad, Zalmay, 'Intervention in Afghanistan: Implications for the Security of Southwest Asia', in William L. Dowdy and Russell B. Trood (eds.), *The Indian Ocean: Perspectives on a Strategic Arena* (Durham: Duke University Press, 1985) pp.338-351.

Khalilzad, Zalmay 'Afghanistan: Anatomy of a Soviet Failure', *The National Interest*, no.12, Summer 1988, pp.101-108.

Kifner, John, 'Bhutto, in Fateful Move, Ousts a Top General', *The New York Times*, 1 June 1989, p.5.

Klass, Rosanne (ed.), *Afghanistan—The Great Game Revisited* (New York: Freedom House, 1987).

Klass, Rosanne, 'Afghanistan: The Accords', *Foreign Affairs*, vol.66, no.5, Summer 1988, pp.922-945.

Knabe, Erika, 'Afghan Women: Does Their Role Change?', in Louis Dupree and Linette Albert (eds.), *Afghanistan in the 1970s* (New York: Praeger, 1974) pp.144-166.

Konovalov, Valerii, 'Legacy of the Afghan War: Some Statistics', *Report on the USSR*, vol.1, no.14, 7 April 1989, pp.1-3.

Kubálková, Vendulka, and Cruickshank, A.A., *Marxism-Leninism and theory of international relations* (London: Routledge and Kegan Paul, 1980).

Kubálková, Vendulka, and Cruickshank, A.A., *Thinking New about Soviet 'new thinking'* (Berkeley: Institute of International Studies, University of California, 1989).

Kukathas, Chandran, Lovell, David W., and Maley, William (eds.), *The Transition from Socialism: State and Civil Society in the USSR* (Melbourne: Longman Cheshire, 1991).

Kushkaki, Sabahuddin, *Daha-i Qanun Asasi: Ghaflat Zadagi Afghanha wa*

Fursat Talabi Rusha (Peshawar: Shurai-i saqafati Jihad-i Afghanistan, 1986).

Kuzio, Taras, 'Opposition in the USSR to the Occupation of Afghanistan', *Central Asian Survey*, vol.6, no.1, 1987, pp.99-117.

Laber, Jeri, 'Afghanistan's Other War', *The New York Review of Books*, vol.33, no.20, 18 December 1986, pp.3, 6-7.

Laber, Jeri, and Rubin, Barnett R., *"A Nation is Dying": Afghanistan under the Soviets 1979-87* (Evanston: Northwestern University Press, 1988).

Lapidus, Ira M., *A History of Islamic Societies* (Cambridge: Cambridge University Press, 1988).

Latynski, Maya, and Wimbush, S. Enders 'The Mujahideen and the Russian Empire', *The National Interest*, no.11, Spring 1988, pp.30-42.

Lee, Gary, 'Soviets Upset By Terms for Afghan Pact', *The Washington Post*, 15 March 1988, p.1.

Lemercier-Quelquejay, Chantal, 'Muslim National Minorities in Revolution and Civil War', in S. Enders Wimbush (ed.), *Soviet Nationalities in Strategic Perspective* (London: Croom Helm, 1985) pp.36-60.

Lemercier-Quelquejay, Chantal, and Bennigsen, Alexandre, 'Soviet Experience of Muslim Guerilla Warfare and the War in Afghanistan', in Yaacov Ro'i (ed.), *The USSR and the Muslim World* (London: George Allen & Unwin, 1984) pp.206-214.

Lewin, Moshe, *The Gorbachev Phenomenon: A Historical Interpretation* (Berkeley: University of California Press, 1988).

Lewis, Bernard, *The Political Language of Islam* (Chicago: The University of Chicago Press, 1988).

Lewis, Paul, 'New Kabul Offer in Afghan Parley', *The New York Times*, 4 March 1988, p.11.

Lijphart, Arend, *Democracy in Plural Societies: A Comparative Exploration* (New Haven: Yale University Press, 1977).

Machiavelli, Niccolò *The Prince* (Cambridge: Cambridge University Press, 1988).

Magnus, Ralph H., (ed.), *Afghan Alternatives: Issues, Options, and Policies* (New Brunswick: Transaction Books, 1985).

Magnus, Ralph H., 'The Military and Politics in Afghanistan: Before and After the Revolution', in Edward A. Olsen and Stephen Jurika, Jnr. (eds.), *The Armed Forces in Contemporary Asian Societies* (Boulder: Westview Press, 1986) pp.325-344.

Male, Beverley, *Revolutionary Afghanistan* (New York: St Martin's Press, 1982).

Maley, William, 'Political Legitimation in Contemporary Afghanistan', *Asian Survey*, vol.27, no.6, June 1987, pp.705-725.

Maley, William, 'Afghan Refugees: From Diaspora to Repatriation', in Amin Saikal (ed.), *Refugees in the Modern World* (Canberra: Canberra

Studies in World Affairs no.25, Department of International Relations, Research School of Pacific Studies, Australian National University, 1989) pp.17-44.

Maley, William, 'Social Dynamics and the Disutility of Terror: Afghanistan 1978-1989', in V. Shlapentokh, C. Vanderpool, T. Bushnell and J. Sundram (eds.), *State Organized Terror: The Case of Violent Internal Repression* (Boulder: Westview Press, forthcoming).

Malik, Hafeez (ed.), *Soviet-American Relations with Pakistan, Iran and Afghanistan* (London: Macmillan, 1987).

Marx, Karl, *Critique of Hegel's 'Philosophy of Right'* (Cambridge: Cambridge University Press, 1970).

Meissner, Boris, *Die Sowjetunion im Umbruch* (Stuttgart: Deutsche Verlags-Anstalt GmbH, 1988).

Mel'gunov, S.P. *'Krasnyi terror' v Rossii* (Berlin: n.p., 1924).

Migdal, Joel S., *Strong Societies and Weak States: State-Society Relations and State Capabilities in the Third World* (Princeton: Princeton University Press, 1988).

Momen, Moojan, *An Introduction to Shi'i Islam: The History and Doctrines of Twelver Shi'ism* (New Haven: Yale University Press, 1985).

Monks, Alfred L., *The Soviet Intervention in Afghanistan* (Washington DC: American Enterprise Institute for Public Policy Research, 1981).

Naby, Eden, 'The Changing Role of Islam as a Unifying Force in Afghanistan', in Ali Banuazizi and Myron Weiner (eds.), *The State, Religion, and Ethnic Politics: Afghanistan, Iran, and Pakistan* (Syracuse: Syracuse University Press, 1986) pp.124-154.

Naby, Eden, 'The Concept of Jihad in Opposition to Communist Rule: Turkestan and Afghanistan', *Studies in Comparative Communism*, vol.19, nos.3-4, Autumn-Winter 1986, pp.287-300.

Naby, Eden, 'Islam within the Afghan Resistance', *Third World Quarterly*, vol.10, no.2, April 1988, pp.787-805.

Naby, Eden, 'Tajiks Reemphasize Iranian Heritage as Ethnic Pressures Mount in Central Asia', *Report on the USSR*, vol.2, no.7, 16 February 1990, pp.20-22.

Newell, Richard S. *The Politics of Afghanistan* (Ithaca: Cornell University Press, 1972).

Newell, Richard S., 'Post-Soviet Afghanistan: The Position of the Minorities', *Asian Survey*, vol.29, no.11, November 1989, pp.1090-1108.

Newell, Nancy Peabody and Newell, Richard S,, *The Struggle for Afghanistan* (Ithaca: Cornell University Press, 1981).

Newman, Joseph, Jr., 'The Future of Northern Afghanistan', *Asian Survey*, vol.28, no.7, July 1988, pp.729-739.

Nixon, Richard, 'Operation Kabul: a call to arms', *The Australian*, 19 February 1990.

Noorzoy, M.S., 'Long-Term Economic Relations Between Afghanistan and the Soviet Union: An Interpretive Study', *International Journal of Middle East Studies*, vol.17, 1985, pp.151-173.

Noorzoy, M.S., 'Soviet Economic Interests in Afghanistan', *Problems of Communism*, vol.36, no.3, May-June 1987, pp.43-54.

Nossal, Kim Richard, 'Knowing when to fold: Western sanctions against the USSR 1980-1983', *International Journal*, vol.44, no.3, Summer 1989, pp.698-724.

Olcott, Martha Brill, 'The Basmachi or Freemen's Revolt in Turkestan 1918-24', *Soviet Studies*, vol.33, no.3, July 1981, pp.352-369.

Ottaway, David B., 'Kabul Forces Gain Combat Edge: Guerrillas Reeling under Scud Missiles, High-Altitude Bombing', *The Washington Post*, 27 June 1989, p.11.

Ottaway, David B., 'Stingers Were Key Weapon in Afghan War, Army Finds', *The Washington Post*, 5 July 1989, p.2.

Ottaway, David B., 'CIA Removes Afghan Rebel Aid Director', *The Washington Post*, 2 September 1989, p.1.

Ottaway, David B., 'U.S. Misread Gorbachev, Official Says—Afghanistan Airlift Has Sustained Kabul', *The Washington Post*, 10 September 1989, p.1.

Pakulski, Jan, 'Legitimacy and Mass Compliance: Reflections on Max Weber and Soviet-Type Societies, *British Journal of Political Science*, vol.16, Part I, 1986, pp.35-56.

Pakulski, Jan, 'Eastern Europe and "Legitimacy Crisis"', *Australian Journal of Political Science*, vol.25, no.2, November 1990, pp.272-288.

Pear, Robert, 'U.S. Asserts Soviet Advisers Are Fighting in Afghanistan', *The New York Times*, 10 October 1989, p.1.

Penkovskiy, Oleg, *The Penkovskiy Papers* (New York: Doubleday, 1965).

Plato, *The Republic of Plato* (London: Oxford University Press, 1941).

Poggi, Gianfranco *The Development of the Modern State: A Sociological Introduction* (London: Hutchinson, 1978).

Poullada, Leon B., *Reform and Rebellion in Afghanistan, 1919-1929: King Amanullah's Failure to Modernize a Tribal Society* (Ithaca: Cornell University Press, 1973).

Poullada, Leon B., 'Afghanistan and the United States: The Crucial Years', *The Middle East Journal*, vol.35, no.2, Spring 1981, pp.178-190.

Poullada, Leon B., 'The Failure of American Diplomacy in Afghanistan', *World Affairs*, vol.145, no.3, Winter 1982-1983, pp.230-252.

Pye, Lucian W., *Aspects of Political Development* (Boston: Little, Brown & Co., 1966).

Pye, Lucian W., 'The Legitimacy Crisis', in Leonard Binder et.al., *Crises and Sequences in Political Development* (Princeton: Princeton University Press, 1971) pp.135-158.

Quested, R.K.I., *Sino-Russian Relations* (London: George Allen & Unwin, 1984).

Rahimi, Fahima, *Women in Afghanistan* (Liestal: Stiftung Bibliotheca

Afghanica, 1986).

Randle, Robert F., *The Origins of Peace: A Study of Peacemaking and the Structure of Peace Settlements* (New York: The Free Press, 1973).

Rashid, Ahmed, 'Islamic Powers Vie over Afghanistan', *The Independent*, 2 February 1989, p.12.

Ridout, Christine F., 'Authority Patterns and the Afghan Coup of 1973', *The Middle East Journal*, vol.29, no.2, Spring 1975, pp.165-178.

Roberts, Cynthia, *'Glasnost'* in Soviet Foreign Policy: Setting the Record Straight?', *Report on the USSR*, vol.1, no.50, 15 December 1989, pp.4-12.

Rogers, Tom, 'Afghan refugees and the stability of Pakistan', *Survival*, vol.29, no.5, October 1987, pp.416-429.

Rossignol, Gilles, 'La mort de Thierry Niquet', *Les Nouvelles d'Afghanistan*, no.37, March 1988, pp.24-25.

Rousseau, Jean-Jacques, *The Social Contract and Discourses* (London: J.M. Dent, 1973).

Roy, Olivier, 'What is Afghanistan Really Like?', *Dissent*, vol.28, no.1, Winter 1981, pp.47-54.

Roy, Olivier, *L'Afghanistan: Islam et modernité politique* (Paris: Éditions du Seuil, 1985).

Roy, Olivier, 'Nature de la Guerre en Afghanistan', *Les Temps Modernes*, no.503, June 1988, pp.1-37.

Roy, Olivier, 'Afghanistan: back to tribalism or on to Lebanon?', *Third World Quarterly*, vol.11, no.4, October 1989, pp.70-82.

Roy, Olivier, 'Naissance de la Résistance hérati', in Etienne Gille (ed.), *Herat ou l'art meurti* (Paris: Amitié Franco-Afghane, 1989).

Roy, Olivier, 'Un consensus régional est-il possible?', *Les Nouvelles d'Afghanistan*, no.45, December 1989-January 1990, pp.14-15.

Rubin, Barnett R., 'Lineages of the State in Afghanistan', *Asian Survey*, vol.28, no.11, November 1988, pp.1188-1209.

Rubin, Barnett R., 'The Fragmentation of Afghanistan', *Foreign Affairs*, vol.68, no.5, Winter 1989-90, pp.150-168.

Ryan, Nigel, *A Hitch or Two in Afghanistan: A Journey behind Russian Lines* (London: Weidenfeld and Nicolson, 1983).

Saikal, Amin, *The Rise and Fall of the Shah* (Princeton: Princeton University Press, 1980).

Saikal, Amin, 'The Pakistan Disturbances and the Afghanistan Problem', *The World Today*, vol.40, no.3, March 1984, p.102-107.

Saikal, Amin 'The Afghanistan crisis: a negotiated settlement?', *The World Today*, vol.40, no.11, November 1984, pp.481-489.

Saikal, Amin, 'Soviet Policy toward Southwest Asia', *The Annals of the American Academy of Political and Social Science*, no.481, September 1985, pp.104-116.

Saikal, Amin, 'The Conceptual Origins and Interpretations of Islamic Socialism', *Australian Outlook*, vol.40, no.1, April 1986, pp.39-47.

Saikal, Amin, 'Islam: resistance and reassertion', *The World Today*, vol.43, no.11, November 1987, pp.191-194.

Saikal, Amin, 'The Regional Politics of the Afghan Crisis', in Amin Saikal and William Maley (eds.), *The Soviet Withdrawal from Afghanistan* (Cambridge: Cambridge University Press, 1989) pp.52-66.

Saikal, Amin, 'Afghanistan: the end-game', *The World Today*, vol.45, no.3, March 1989, pp.37-39.

Saikal, Amin, 'Iran: A turn to pragmatism?', *Pacific Defence Reporter*, vol.16, nos.6-7, December 1989-January 1990, pp.61-64.

Saikal, Fazel Haq, and Maley, William, *Afghan Refugee Relief in Pakistan: Political Context and Practical Problems* (Canberra: Department of Politics, University College, The University of New South Wales, 1986).

Sakharov, Andrei, 'Neizbezhnost' perestroiki', in Iu.N. Afanas'ev (ed.), *Inogo ne dano* (Moscow: Progress, 1988) pp.122-134.

Segal, Gerald, 'China and Afghanistan', *Asian Survey*, vol.21, no.11, November 1981, pp.1159-1174.

Seymour-Ure, Colin, 'Rumour and Politics', *Politics*, vol.17, no.2, November 1982, pp.1-9.

Shahrani, M. Nazif, and Canfield, Robert L. (eds.), *Revolutions and Rebellions in Afghanistan: Anthropological Perspectives* (Berkeley: Institute of International Studies, University of California, 1984).

Shahrani, M. Nazif, 'State Building and Social Fragmentation in Afghanistan: A Historical Perspective', in Ali Banuazizi and Myron Weiner (eds.), *The State, Religion, and Ethnic Politics: Afghanistan, Iran, and Pakistan* (Syracuse: Syracuse University Press, 1986) pp.23-74.

Shevardnadze, Eduard, 'Afganistan—trudnaia doroga k miru', *Izvestiia*, 14 February 1990, p.5.

Shipler, David K., 'Reagan Didn't Know of Afghan Deal', *The New York Times*, 11 February 1988, p.3.

Shroder, John F., Jnr, and Assifi, Abdul Tawab, 'Afghan Resources and Soviet Exploitation', in Rosanne Klass (ed.), *Afghanistan—The Great Game Revisited* (New York: Freedom House, 1987) pp.97-134.

Shroder, John F., Jnr, 'Afghanistan Resources and Soviet Policy in Central and South Asia', in Milan Hauner and Robert L. Canfield (eds.), *Afghanistan and the Soviet Union: Collision and Transformation* (Boulder: Westview Press, 1989) pp.101-119.

Sikorski, Radek *Dust of the Saints: A Journey to Herat in Time of War* (London: Chatto and Windus, 1989).

Sliwinski, Marek, *Afghanistan 1978-87: War, Demography and Society* (London: Central Asian Survey Incidental Paper no.6, 1988).

Sliwinski, Marek, 'Afghanistan: The Decimation of a People', *Orbis*, vol.33, no.1, Winter 1989, pp.39-56.

Smith, Anthony D., *The Ethnic Origins of Nations* (Oxford: Basil Blackwell, 1986).

Staar, Richard F., 'Checklist of Communist Parties in 1986', *Problems of*

Communism, vol.36, no.2, March-April 1987, pp.40-56.

Strand, Richard F., 'The Evolution of Anti-Communist Resistance in Eastern Nuristan' in M. Nazif Shahrani and Robert L. Canfield (eds.), *Revolutions & Rebellions in Afghanistan: Anthropological Perspectives* (Berkeley: Institute of International Studies, University of California, 1984) pp.77-93.

Swedish Committee for Afghanistan, *The Agricultural Survey of Afghanistan. First Report* (Peshawar: Swedish Committee for Afghanistan, May 1988).

Swedish Committee for Afghanistan, *The Agricultural Survey of Afghanistan. Second Report: Farm Power* (Peshawar: Swedish Committee for Afghanistan, April 1989).

Swedish Committee for Afghanistan, *The Agricultural Survey of Afghanistan. Third Report: Crops and Yields* (Peshawar: Swedish Committee for Afghanistan, August 1989).

Swedish Committee for Afghanistan, *The Agricultural Survey of Afghanistan. Fourth Report: Fertiliser* (Peshawar: Swedish Committee for Afghanistan, February 1990).

Swedish Committee for Afghanistan, *The Agricultural Survey of Afghanistan. Fifth Report: Seeds* (Peshawar: Swedish Committee for Afghanistan, June 1990).

Tabibi, Latif, 'Die afghanische Landreform von 1979: Ihre Vorgeschichte und Konsequenzen', unpublished doctoral dissertation, Freie Universität Berlin, 1981.

Tahir-Kheli, Shirin, *The United States and Pakistan: The Evolution of an Influence Relationship* (New York: Praeger, 1982).

Tapper, Richard (ed.), *The Conflict of Tribe and State in Iran and Afghanistan* (London: Croom Helm, 1983).

Tapper, Richard, 'Introduction' in Richard Tapper (ed.), *The Conflict of Tribe and State in Iran and Afghanistan* (London: Croom Helm, 1983) pp.1-82.

Tapper, Richard, 'Minorities and the problem of the state', *Third World Quarterly*, vol.10, no.2, April 1988, pp.1027-1041.

Tapper, Richard, 'Ethnic Identities and Social Categories in Iran and Afghanistan', in Elizabeth Tonkin, Maryon McDonald and Malcolm Chapman (eds.), *History and Ethnicity* (London: Routledge, 1989) pp.232-246.

Tarzi, Ayesha, *Red Death* (Cambridge: The Islamic Texts Society, 1985).

Tavakolian, Bahram, 'Women and Socioeconomic Change among Sheikhanzai Nomads of Western Afghanistan', *The Middle East Journal*, vol.38 no.3, Summer 1984, pp.433-453.

Teimourian, Hazhir, 'Drugs baron in the border hills', *The Times*, 25 September 1989, p.15.

Thakur, Ramesh, and Thayer, Carlyle A. (eds.), *The Soviet Union as an Asian Pacific Power: Implications of Gorbachev's 1986 Vladivostok*

Initiative (Boulder: Westview Press, 1987).

Trainor, Bernard E., 'Afghan Air War: U.S. Missiles Score', *The New York Times*, 7 July 1987, p.6.

Tret'iachenko, B., 'Na kanikuly—v Afganistan', *Pravda*, 3 July 1987, p.5.

Tsagolov, Major-General K.M., 'Afganistan—predvaritel'nye itogi', *Ogonek*, no.30, 1988, pp.25-26.

Tsagolov, Major-General K.M., 'More Questions Than Answers: Soviets still in Afghanistan two years after withdrawal', *Moscow News*, 25 November-2 December 1990, p.13.

Urban, Mark, *War in Afghanistan* (London: Macmillan, 1990).

Vertzberger, Yaacov Y.I., *China's Southwestern Strategy: Encirclement and Counterencirclement* (New York: Praeger, 1985).

Walker, Christopher, 'Poll reveals most Russians want Afghanistan pull-out', *The Times*, 2 November 1987, p.9.

Weber, Max, 'Politics as a Vocation', in H.H. Gerth and C. Wright Mills (eds.), *From Max Weber: Essays in Sociology* (London: Routledge and Kegan Paul, 1948) pp.77-128.

Weber, Max, *Economy and Society: An Ouline of Interpretive Sociology* (Berkeley and Los Angeles: University of California Press, 1978).

Weintraub, Craig, 'Ferkhar Massacre of Jami'at commanders gives a sad air to Eid celebrations', *AFGHANews*, vol.5, no.15, 1 August 1989, pp.6-7.

White, Stephen, *Gorbachev in Power* (Cambridge: Cambridge University Press, 1990).

Yasmann, Viktor, 'Afghanistan Comes Up, *Glasnost'* Goes Down', *Report on the USSR*, vol.1, no.45, 10 November 1989, pp.9-10.

Yusufi, Mohammad Qasim 'Effects of the War on Agriculture', in Bo Huldt and Erland Jansson (eds.), *The Tragedy of Afghanistan: The Social, Cultural and Political Impact of the Soviet Invasion* (London: Croom Helm, 1988) pp.197-216.

Other

Afghan National Liberation Front, *Brief Biography of Professor Sibghatullah al-Mojaddedi* (Peshawar: n.d.).

Foreign and Commonwealth Office, *Afghanistan Chronology: January-May 1983* (London: August 1983).

Foreign and Commonwealth Office, *Afghanistan: Chronology of Events Since April 1978* (London: September 1980).

Foreign Broadcast Information Service, *Soviet Policy on Afghanistan: Signs of Change and Controversy* (Washington D.C.: FB 86-100 10, 19 March 1986).

Jamiat-i Islami Afghanistan, *A'lamiah-i Jamiat-i Islami Afghanistan* (Peshawar: 1989).

Politizdat, *XXVI s"ezd Kommunisticheskoi partii Sovetskogo Soiuza: stenograficheskii otchet* (Moscow: 1981).

Politizdat, *Materialy XXVII s"ezda Kommunisticheskoi partii Sovetskogo Soiuza* (Moscow: 1986).

Radio Free Europe/Radio Liberty, *The Soviet Public and the War in Afghanistan: Perceptions, Prognoses, Information Sources* (Munich: Soviet Area Audience and Opinion Research, AR 4-85, June 1985).

United Nations General Assembly, *Resolutions* 36/34, 18 November 1981; 37/37, 29 November 1982; 38/29, 23 November 1983; 39/13, 15 November 1984; 40/12, 13 November 1985; 41/33, 5 November 1986; 42/15, 10 November 1987; 44/15, 15 November 1989.

United Nations General Assembly, Sixth Emergency Special Session, *Provisional Verbatim Record of the Third Meeting*, Document (A/ES-6/PV.3, General Assembly, 11 January 1980).

United Nations, *Agreements on Settlement of Situation Relating to Afghanistan Signed at Geneva* (Geneva: United Nations Information Service, Press Release Afghanistan/9, 14 April 1988).

United Nations, Office of the United Nations Co-ordinator for Humanitarian and Economic Assistance Programmes Relating to Afghanistan, *First Consolidated Report* (Geneva: UNOCA/1988/1, September 1988).

United Nations, *Rapport sur la situation des droits de l'homme en Afghanistan* (E/CN.4/1985/21, Human Rights Commission, Economic and Social Council, 19 February 1985).

United Nations, *Report on the Situation of Human Rights in Afghanistan* (A/42/667, General Assembly, 23 October 1987).

United Nations, *Report on the Situation of Human Rights in Afghanistan* (E/CN.4/1986/24, Human Rights Commission, Economic and Social Council, 17 February 1986).

United Nations, *Report on the Situation of Human Rights in Afghanistan* (E/CN.4/1988/25, Human Rights Commission, Economic and Social Council, 26 February 1988).

United Nations, *Report on the Situation of Human Rights in Afghanistan* (E/CN.4/1989/24, Human Rights Commission, Economic and Social Council, 16 February 1989).

United Nations, *Situation of Human Rights in Afghanistan* (A/40/843, General Assembly, 5 November 1985).

United Nations, *Situation of Human Rights in Afghanistan* (A/41/778, General Assembly, 9 January 1987).

United Nations, *Situation of Human Rights in Afghanistan* (A/43/742, General Assembly, 24 October 1988).

United Nations, *Situation of Human Rights in Afghanistan* (A/44/669, General Assembly, 30 October 1989).

United States Department of State, 'USSR: Unofficial Poll on Popular Opposition to Afghan War', *Current Analyses* (Washington D.C.: Bureau of Intelligence and Research, Report 1107-CA, 18 June 1985).

United States Information Service, 'Baker: U.S., Soviets "made substantial progress"', *Official Text* (Canberra: 14 February 1990).

Index